"Coming in hot. Keep your heads down!" the pilot said almost casually as the RTO passed along the reply. The helicopter gunship was roaring in for a rocket and minigun strafing run. Thousands of 7.62 machine-gun rounds from the minigun mounted on the nose of the gunship tore into the jungle in just seconds, and exploding rockets sent up flames and shrapnel in deadly patterns.

Any notion of immediate victory that the Viet Cong might have had was clouded by the gunship's runs as it made passes on target time and again. The cavalry hadn't arrived, but one of its gunships had. Then the small battle began literally to heat up: the small grass fire that had sprung up on the edge of the knee-deep grass of the dry meadow turned into a fast-moving, rising wall of flames. . . .

By Kregg P. J. Jorgenson

ACCEPTABLE LOSS: An Infantry Soldier's Perspective*
BEAUCOUP DINKY DAU
MIA RESCUE: LRRPs in Cambodia*

Published by Ivy Books

Books published by The Ballantine Publishing Group
are available at quantity discounts on bulk purchases
for premium, educational, fund-raising, and special
sales use. For details, please call 1-800-733-3000.

THE GHOSTS
OF THE
HIGHLANDS

1st Cav LRRPs in Vietnam, 1966–67

Kregg P. J. Jorgenson

IVY BOOKS • NEW YORK

An Ivy Book
Published by The Ballantine Publishing Group
Copyright © 1999 by Kregg P. J. Jorgenson

All rights reserved under International and Pan-American Copyright Conventions. Published in the United States by The Ballantine Publishing Group, a division of Random House, Inc., New York, and simultaneously in Canada by Random House of Canada Limited, Toronto.

www.randomhouse.com/BB/

Library of Congress Catalog Card Number: 98-93277

ISBN 0-8041-1597-4

Manufactured in the United States of America

First Edition: January 1999

10 9 8 7 6 5 4 3 2 1

To Harvey Volzer, friend and attorney par excellence; and for those who served as LRRP/Rangers during the Vietnam War and those who risked everything to rescue them when it was necessary

If you cause opponents to be unaware of the place and time of battle, you can always win.

—Sun Tzu

ACKNOWLEDGMENTS

A book of this kind is a collective effort, and for their kind help, comments, and suggestions, I am indebted to the following people: specifically to the Cav's first LRRP/Rangers, Col. James D. James (U.S. Army, Ret), Ron Hall, Jim Ross, Rodolpho "Rudy" Torres, Patrick O'Brien, John Simones, Walter "Spanky" Seymour, Marvin "Doc" Suggs, the collective Joe Klines, and several of the other "Dog Robbers" for their candor and insight.

Thanks also go to some of the Screaming Eagle LRRPs of the 101st Airborne Division, including: Rey Martinez, Kenn Miller, Derby Jones, Gary Linderer, Riley Cox, Pat Kinzer, John Looney, and Jim "Limey" Walker for their suggestions, humor, and occasional white lightning.

I'm grateful to LRRP/Ranger Bob "Moose" McClure for the use of his extensive military library and personal accounts of An Khe, also to retired Special Forces sergeant major John Larsen, who is a former Vietnamese Ranger Adviser and a virtual CD-ROM of military history, and to LRRP/Ranger Danny Pope for the LRRP view from a six-foot-six-inch point man!

For the CIA perspective, I have to thank a trusted "spook" and friend, whose book I hope one day to write. Another "Mr. Smith," at least for now.

Finally, I thank my family—Kap, Kelli, Kristen, Katie, and baby Dave—for their support and for allowing me the time to complete this project; a special tribute must go to my teenage daughters who taught my two-and-a-half-year-old son to refer to me as, "Daddy Who?"

If I have forgotten anyone, I apologize and offer my sincere gratitude and thanks.

AUTHOR'S NOTE

This book is based on the collective accounts and recollections of various key personnel who helped form the 1st Air Cavalry Division's Long-Range Reconnaissance Patrol Detachment in Vietnam in late 1966. These were small units of specially trained army soldiers charged with carrying out five-to-six-man, behind-the-lines patrols in the rugged jungle strongholds of the Viet Cong in the Central Highlands.

This book is the result of eighteen months of research into official documents and records, books, newspaper accounts, as well as formal and informal interviews with some of the surviving combat veterans.

Those gracious enough to weather the interviews and my "Oh, by the way, I only have one or two more questions to ask . . ." Detective Columbo follow-ups, were also kind enough to review working drafts of the manuscript to help guide its direction and tone.

I relied heavily upon personal accounts in this retelling rather than the official histories since I believe they offer a story rather than data, and they provide a view of the "other truths" that are too briefly mentioned or omitted entirely from the unit histories. "History" records that, at the battle of Waterloo in 1815, the French general Cambronne, when called upon to surrender, said to his English, Dutch, German, and Prussian enemies, "The Old Guard dies, but never surrenders!"; personal accounts of French officers who witnessed the exchange say that the general actually replied, "Merde!" which is French for "shit!"

I prefer the more honest, less varnished approach because I believe that it shows us something of the human side that official versions so often omit. Mirrors can do more than flatter, depending upon the stance and perception, and any reflection of the 1st Cav's first LRRPs is based upon how I have held the mirror in place. Any blind spots are my own. Conversations have been reconstructed, and one principle participant, the Dog Robber, is based on several veterans who prefer to remain anonymous but who offered their accounts as "other truths" worth considering.

Having said that, I must add that this book is not meant to be the definitive study or history of the 1st Cav's LRRP detachment but is just one version of the remarkable story of the people and of the unit who, through five and a half years of hard-fought combat service throughout the Republic of South Vietnam, became the highest decorated Ranger unit in American history.

—KREGG P. J. JORGENSON
Seattle, Washington

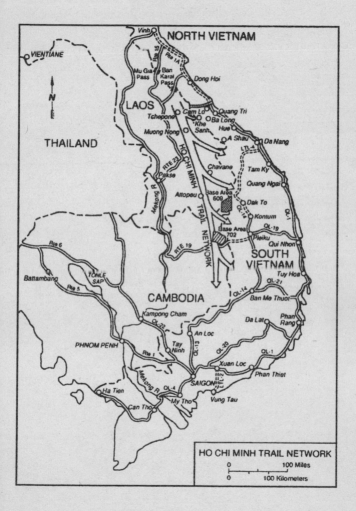

VIENTIANE

NORTH VIETNAM

Vinh

Mu Gia Pass

Ban Karai Pass

Dong Hoi

LAOS

Tchepone

Cam Lo

Quang Tri

Ba Long

Khe Sanh

Hue

Muong Nong

A Shau

Da Nang

LTL-4

THAILAND

RTE 23

Chavane

Tam Ky

Pakse

Quang Ngai

Mekong R.

Attopeu

Base Area 609

Dak To

QL-1

QL-14

Kontum

QL-19

Base Area 702

Pleiku

RTE 19

Qui Nhon

Rte 6

SOUTH VIETNAM

HO CHI MINH TRAIL NETWORK

Tuy Hoa

TONLE SAP

QL-14

QL-21

Battambang

Rte 5

Ban Me Thuot

CAMBODIA

Da Lat

Phan Rang

Kampong Cham

QL-22

An Loc

QL-20

PHNOM PENH

Rte 1

Tay Ninh

QL-13

QL-1

Xuan Loc

Phan Thiet

Mekong R.

QL-4

SAIGON

Ha Tien

My Tho

Vung Tau

Can Tho

| HO CHI MINH TRAIL NETWORK |
| 0   100 Miles |
| 0   100 Kilometers |

PROLOGUE

The An Lao Valley was an emerald green paradise, and it was a son of a bitch to everyone who was cast out or trying hard not to be. The Viet Cong and North Vietnamese Army owned it, which was why the 1st Air Cavalry Division operated landing zones Uplift and English in the area adjacent to the valley and the smaller fire support bases throughout the Bong Son Plains. The Cav wanted to let the Communists know they had their foot in the door and were holding an eviction notice.

The numerous small battles and firefights fought there were vicious and costly for the VC and the NVA as well as for the Cav's helicopter scouts or ground reconnaissance units who worked the valley. Both sides moved like veteran boxers in a jungle ring, looking for openings and hitting hard and furious when they found them. Although finding them was getting more difficult to do.

The Viet Cong had tucked one of their many operational base camps beneath the double canopied jungle that buffered the An Lao Valley on the west to avoid detection from the 1st of the 9th Cav's reconnaissance aircraft that patrolled the territory. The thick branches, vines, and foliage over the base camp combined to form a natural ceiling blocking an aerial view of the jungle floor below. The base camp had avoided detection.

But when a tandem team of the small OH-13 scout helicopters from Bravo Troop, flying a late afternoon mission just east of the river, spotted a platoon of well-armed enemy soldiers

1

hurrying into the jungle site and called it in, an infantry company was flown in the following morning to check it out.

The recon platoon for the Cav grunts had quietly worked its way up through the clinging wait-a-minute vines and the thick, wet vegetation and come to a dead stop ten to twenty meters inside the hillside tree line when they discovered the first fighting position.

The point man was a twenty-nine-year-old staff sergeant named Joe Kline, who called in the find, and then, ever so carefully, cleared the empty two-man fighting position before taking a deep breath, collecting himself, and moving on.

On paper, Kline was supposed to have ten to twelve people in his squad. But in Vietnam a squad was lucky if it had eight soldiers at any given time. Of those, two would be in the rear area recovering from malaria, broken bones, immersion foot, or minor wounds. One more might be on leave, R & R, or emergency leave, and one, well, one couldn't walk and chew gum at the same time.

That left Kline his radioman, a machine gunner, himself, and a new guy who had only two weeks in country. The radioman couldn't take the lead because the radio was important to the team's survival, and if they lost the machine gun, then they'd be shit out of luck. The new guy was still intimidated by the jungle.

Maybe in a week or two the new guy could take the lead, but just then he served as Kline's slack man, following the staff sergeant and covering him as he moved forward.

The fighting position was only the first of several interlocking, L-shaped, earthen bunkers that protected the short trail leading into the large cathedral-like bivouac site. The fighting positions were six to seven feet long and perhaps four feet deep. They were covered with a roof of logs and hard-packed dirt with brush scattered around to conceal their placement. The L-shape allowed two occupants to cover the jungle while protecting the flanks of the fighting positions next to them.

Although Kline had found the first two positions, he had not seen the others until he was only a few feet from the second bunker's opening. The new guy kept his rifle aimed on the next fighting position in line while Kline crawled forward.

While he told himself to stay cool, the staff sergeant's pulse rate climbed as he began to clear the second fighting position. Then someone in one of the trailing platoons tripped over an exposed root, fell hard into his rifle, and cried *"Shit! Motherfucker!"* and the point man barely had time to fall and roll behind a tree before a Viet Cong soldier stuck the barrel of an AK-47 assault rifle through the darkened opening, raking the trail where he had been kneeling moments before. The Viet Cong were screaming and yelling as they fired, and the point platoon was returning small-arms fire as the jungle erupted with the noises and chaos of combat.

The staff sergeant lobbed a grenade into the bunker, and when it exploded, it sent a geyser of dirt, debris, and shrapnel rushing back out of the opening. Even before the dust cleared, he was crawling forward, firing into the bunker, turning the rifle to the left and right as he emptied the magazine. A dead enemy soldier lay splintered and crumpled where he had been pushed against the earthen floor by the grenade's blast. Behind him the NCO could make out a second enemy soldier, who was scrambling back up a small trench line that led into the base camp. Kline fired twice but wasn't sure whether he hit him or not. Other enemy soldiers were firing and falling back, as well, keeping Kline's head down to prevent the American from taking a clear shot.

Within minutes, the firefight was over as the Viet Cong retreated deeper into the jungle, and the enemy base turned quiet again, too quiet. Gunships were coming on station, but they were still a few minutes out. With no targets to attack, they'd circle high up in holding patterns, waiting for a firing mission.

When the order came down to move out again, Staff Sergeant Kline knew that any surprise or advantage was lost, and even as he eased into the opening to the next bunker in line, he knew it would be empty. There were just a half-filled, open canteen and a pith helmet on a crude shelf. Some loose ammunition and a small supply of rice lay where they had been abandoned. The staff sergeant tried to steady his breathing before he moved on. Sweat beaded his forehead and along the sides of his face as Kline absentmindedly squeezed the plastic stock of his M-16, a habit he had obtained over the last ten months in country.

The trees in the jungle base camp had been cleared of most of their limbs and branches, except for the highest ones, which formed a green-and-brown living ceiling. Although the enemy base camp was invisible from the sky, the natural roof let in enough filtered light for the Viet Cong to easily conduct their activities below.

In an elaborate, sunken, outdoor cooking area caved out of the orange clay, an aluminum pot was bubbling with boiling water and a swirl of wild vegetables.

"Where are they?" the staff sergeant said to himself, surveying the jungle camp. The hissing steam brought him quickly back around, aiming the M-16 stomach-high on the enemy fire.

Behind him, the slack man, a twenty-year-old private first class, covered the fighting positions and then moved to keep up with the staff sergeant as the point man leapfrogged from one to the next. The 60 gunner was behind them, setting up the light machine gun on the edge of the open area to provide additional support as the rest of the platoon fanned out.

"Where are they?" the slack man asked when he caught up. The staff sergeant didn't answer him as he kept his eyes on the surrounding jungle.

"Where'd they go?" the private first class whispered nervously. He was studying the boiling water. He felt the same discomfort the point man had only a few seconds before.

The distinct *thump* of enemy mortar rounds in French-made mortars less than a few hundred yards away gave the two American soldiers their answer.

The mortar rounds exploded high in the trees, sending white-hot slivers of shrapnel to the floor below. With calculated precision, the Viet Cong walked the deadly bombs back toward the main body of the infantry company, now caught in the kill zone.

The An Lao was claiming its latest victims.

CHAPTER ONE

The hit-and-run guerrilla war that the Vietnamese employed against the Americans in the Second Indochina War was nothing new to either side. For well over one thousand years, the Vietnamese had used it effectively against the Chinese, the Khmers and Chams, the French in the nineteenth century, the Japanese in the 1940s, and against the French again until 1954, so it was well anticipated by the Americans when they arrived.

Bernard Fall's *Hell in a Small Place* and *Street Without Joy*, chronicling the first Indochina war in the late forties and early fifties, were read and studied by American officers, so there was little naïveté about expectations or the strategies they would face during this latest conflict.

Some Americans even believed that with their own history of Indian wars and the long-term successful campaign against the Apaches in the American Southwest they well understood the challenges involved in guerrilla operations in Southeast Asia and what it would take to overcome them.

Many people viewed Ho Chi Minh as a new Geronimo, and like the legendary Apache leader, Ho Chi Minh became an icon and, as such, took on mythical qualities in the eyes of his followers. After decades of being a revolutionary, he had evolved into the "kindly old uncle." The real fighting chief and primary tactician for the Vietnamese Communists was Gen. Vo Nguyen Giap, and those who studied Giap's strategy and his rise to prominence knew that his ruthlessness and resolve equaled even the most hardened Apache.

By the close of 1966, it was becoming evident in the inner circles of Washington, D.C., that the war couldn't be won by conventional methods, and while the numbers offered at intelligence briefings suggested the Viet Cong and North Vietnamese Army were suffering staggering losses of men and equipment, it had also become apparent that Giap was also ready to sacrifice even more to attain victory.

The Pentagon's best guess was that there were 275,000 Communist soldiers, including 45,000 North Vietnamese Army soldiers operating in the thirty-nine provinces of South Vietnam. There were more in elaborate jungle bases in Laos and Cambodia bordering South Vietnam, a well-established supply line that ran from Sihanoukville, Cambodia, in the south to Hanoi to the north. However, the conflict in and around the Vietnams was also a satellite of the Cold War, and so was closely followed by the Soviets and the Chinese.

The Chinese supplied rifles and ammunition to help the Vietnamese in their struggle while the Soviets were more generous, providing MiG jets and occasional Soviet Bloc pilots to fly them, modern radar-guided antiaircraft artillery, surface-to-air missiles, and light tanks.

On the surface, it was Communists helping Communists; a deeper look revealed age-old distrust and hinted at hidden political agendas. Although some suggested the domino theory would result in Southeast Asia if America lost in Vietnam, others knew the conflict was more a deadly Cold War chess tournament between superpowers, one fought over a jungle-covered chessboard. Early on, President John F. Kennedy understood this and reportedly had said, "We have a problem in making our power pertinent, and Vietnam looks like the place." But the United States could do little to stop the flow of soldiers, munitions, and supplies across the Vietnamese borders other than to conduct clandestine raids or operations against the North Vietnamese Army and Viet Cong in the neighboring nations.

To counter the threat and contain the fighting, in the mid-1960s, U.S. troop strength was increased to 380,000. An additional 60,000 naval personnel served off the coast in combat and support roles. An estimated 35,000 additional American servicemen were stationed in nearby Thailand, mainly air force personnel at the air bases from which tactical aircraft were sent into combat against North Vietnam and against the North's forces in South Vietnam, hitting the enemy concentrations when and wherever they could find them in the five million acres of rain forests and dense jungles spread out over mind-boggling terrain.

From steep mountains to coastal plains and down to the malaria infested swamp that was much of the Delta in the south, Vietnam wasn't one war but a series of little wars with environments and challenges unique to each. The wars in the northern provinces were vastly different from those in the south. The commonality, though, was the sanctuary offered North Vietnamese forces by the forests and jungles that ran from the steep mountains up near the DMZ down to the swamps and flood plains in the Delta region.

Realizing this, the American armed forces looked for methods to aid them in overcoming the natural obstacles. Massive bombing campaigns were applied over suspected jungle bases in the south as well as against military targets in the north. By the fall of 1966, over 128,000 tons of bombs had been dropped, turning whole stretches of canopied terrain into a moonscape. From the skies, these ground zeros looked like dropped egg cartons left out in the rain. Still, the aerial view didn't tell the complete story; the Viet Cong frequently came back, digging deeper tunnels and caves in the area.

To counter the cover and concealment that the jungles provided, the American forces conducted defoliant operations, such as Operation Ranch Hand, which sprayed large quantities of agents White and Orange in order to rob the enemy's natural safe havens of their foliage cover.

The chemicals were designed to strip away the forests and

jungles and to reveal the maze of jungle camps and bases the Communists had built within them.

In top-secret operations, air force helicopters and planes dropped sensitive acoustic and seismic snooping devices along the major infiltration routes to help get a better understanding of just how many soldiers and equipment were being brought into South Vietnam. The acoustic listening devices picked up conversations; the seismic devices accurately identified the trucks and other vehicles driving south. But the sensors provided the strategists only with ears, and until they had several sets of sharp eyes on the ground, they could never be sure of the enemy's intent or real numbers.

New tactics were changing the face of the fighting as strategists sought more innovative strategies to defeat the elusive Viet Cong and their guerrilla war. One of the more successful approaches that caught the notice of the strategists was the Special Forces Project DELTA.

Since the early 1960s, the Green Berets had effectively used small teams, eight to eleven men, to conduct reconnaissance, surveillance, and target acquisition in areas controlled by the Viet Cong and the North Vietnamese Army. Used as an economy-of-force function, small patrols operated out of remote camps and scoured the "areas of operation" (AOs) to locate the enemy. Larger units called too much attention to themselves; such units could be better utilized elsewhere.

A side benefit of the small patrols was that, under the proper circumstances, they also caused a certain degree of fear within the Communist's "safe havens," shattering the belief that the only real threat came from above and that the anonymity of the jungles and rain forests would protect them.

Recognizing the value and benefit that such long-range patrols would have if employed on a larger scale, Gen. William Childs Westmoreland, the MACV commander (Military Assistance Command Vietnam), sent a message to all major U.S. commands in early July of 1966 authorizing the establishment or formalization of LRRP units in the Republic of South

Vietnam. Westmoreland was a strategist born to devil Giap, and this new decision would plague the Communist general for the rest of the war. Westmoreland knew the time was right for taking the war into a new arena, and one of the key players would be the newly formed LRRP detachment of the army's 1st Air Cavalry Division.

CHAPTER TWO

Camp Radcliff
An Khe, Vietnam
November 1966

Maj. Gen. John "Jack" Norton's request to Captain James D. James was brief and to the point. The 1st Air Cavalry Division commander wanted the twenty-eight-year-old, Special Forces–trained officer to set up a long-range patrol detachment, get it up and running in a reasonable amount of time, and produce results.

Norton was a no-nonsense officer, an old warhorse, who had jumped into Normandy with the 82d Airborne Division during World War II, distinguished himself in Korea, and early on recognized the benefits of helicopter-borne operations and championed their cause.

As a two-star general in Vietnam, Norton found himself commanding one of the U.S. Army's hard-charging divisions and the army's premier air cavalry unit in a different kind of war, one that seemed ideal for heliborne operations; the infantry had become "airmobile" and offered a new kind of cavalry to modern warfare.

Major General Norton had been handpicked by the MACV commander, General Westmoreland, to open up the jungle war, and as chief air cavalry officer, Major General Norton selected the people he wanted and needed to do just that, which is where young Captain James came in.

11

Along with a number of other likely candidates within the division, James had been brought in from the field, interviewed for the new position, and then sent back to his unit with a noncommittal "Thank you." James suspected he had a good shot at getting the job but knew a number of others who were being interviewed were just as qualified and just as eager for the opportunity to lead such a unit. By then James had been in country almost five months, and his time as a grunt officer was rapidly coming to an end. Since most officers pulled six months in the field and the remaining six months of their Vietnam tours in staff positions, he wasn't certain whether he would actually get a chance to remain in a combat role. If he didn't get selected for the new unit, then James would do his staff time until he DEROSed home.

A week or so later when the word filtered down to the field that he had been selected, James smiled at the good news. On a helicopter flight back from the field to An Khe to receive the "official" word, James recalled the old warning about being careful about wishing for something, and weighed it against everything he knew and believed about effective small-team operations with handpicked and well-trained people. It can work, he thought to himself as the helicopter bumped its way through the air pockets and high humidity toward the division's base camp.

James had been selected because of his attitude and credentials and because the older, wiser, senior officers knew Vietnam wasn't World War II nor Korea and that it would take a new breed of cat, like James, to do the stalking.

One of the major problems that faced most combat commanders in the war was locating enemy forces and their temporary base areas. The army called it "fixing the enemy's position" in order to fight and defeat him. In the jungles and mountain ranges of II Corps, and with the Viet Cong's strategy of bringing their major units together only for concentrated attacks, "fixing" the enemy's position wouldn't be an easy task, but it was a necessary task if the war was to be won. If Washington wasn't putting its whole heart into the war, at least the soldiers were; losing wasn't an option they were willing to accept.

On arrival, James was briefed on the mission of the new LRRP unit, providing the division and its combat brigades with timely intelligence.

By deploying small long-range reconnaissance patrols (LRRPs) in economy-of-force operations, the unit would conduct surveillance and target the North Vietnamese Army and Viet Cong forces operating in the 1st Cavalry Division's area of operations (AO), which, in Binh Dinh and the southern half of Quang Ngai provinces in II Corps, were considerable.

In the twelve provinces of II Corps Tactical Zone (called "Two Corps") three North Vietnamese Army divisions were operating, the 1st, the 3d, and the 5th, each a veteran unit. That meant there were ten infantry regiments of NVA regulars and six battalions of Viet Cong soldiers. All told, the number came to about thirty-two thousand Communist soldiers. The Cav was itching to take them on, but first they needed to find them.

"Your job in our AO is to find the VC and NVA; find their bases, their fixed positions, or large concentrations so that the division can take over from there," explained Lieutenant-Colonel Ray, the G-2 (division intel officer), going over a large wall map with a pointer to demonstrate the topological problem the division faced: the AO was one thousand square miles of rugged mountainous terrain with dense jungle and remote valleys. To make things more difficult for the 1st Cav, the Viet Cong could easily slip into the general population and move unnoticed through the area's densely crowded towns and cities.

But the LRRPs would be patrolling the countryside. The senior officers studied James who was studying the tactical wall map of the AO. The young captain was quietly assessing the situation and his new role in the equation.

"No easy job, Captain," said the G-2 as the briefing continued. The detachment would operate six-man teams, which would patrol for five to seven days without resupply, fifteen to thirty-five kilometers or farther away from friendly units. Because of the distance there would be no artillery support for the LRRP teams, and if they encountered difficulty, they would be on their own behind enemy lines until the cavalry arrived.

The LRRPs' job would be to conduct surveillance, not combat operations. Five- or six-man patrols made for lousy odds against regiments and divisions. The G-2 stressed that the new unit's sole purpose was to find the enemy and his bases, and then the division would take over. What he didn't say but was well understood, was that was how it was *supposed* to work, provided the enemy didn't discover the patrols and capture or kill them before help arrived.

As he accepted the position, James was confident that the job could be done. And the LRRP concept had proved sound in theory and in practice; the Special Forces had been launching long-range patrols for years with effective results, and other army units and divisions in country were quickly joining the choir. The Air Cav was only one of the latest units to add its voice.

The combined "congratulations, welcome aboard, and briefing" with Major General Norton, Lt. Col. William Ray (G-2) and Lt. Col. George Stotser, the division's operations and training officer (G-3), was pleasant enough, if not straightforward about the job.

The young captain thought it was eye-opening, too; the job came with a few "challenges."

Officially, the new unit would be Headquarters and Headquarters Company—LRRP under operational control of the G-2 in An Khe, with logistics provided by the 191st Military Intelligence Detachment, which sounded impressive enough. The trouble was it wouldn't be on anybody's TO & E, i.e., the table of organization and equipment, which was the army's authorizing and budgeting directive policy. In short, no new funds or equipment would be added to the division's coffers. The official method prescribed for obtaining the necessary items was "to make use of locally available assets." The word *available* left a great deal to the imagination, but in army parlance it meant that James would literally have to beg, borrow, or steal what he needed to do the job.

The fact that the division wanted the new unit up and running by February offered some additional stress; James had a little over sixty days to make it all happen. Making a unit function required a lot of work and the people to do it. There was always special equipment needed, a great deal of training and practice involved, and some occasional sleight of hand just to make it work or look "easy."

Besides finding everything—the right people, weapons, uniforms, and equipment—Jim James would also have to come up with the bunks, tents or hootches, and mess facilities for his new LRRPs. The people he recruited would need to be equipped, housed, fed, and trained before it could be expected that they would produce results. Magic didn't happen in real life, and things didn't suddenly appear with a flash and a puff of smoke in combat. They disappeared, and then only if someone else had zeroed in on the target for an artillery or air strike.

"Headquarters and Headquarters Company–LRRP" was their official title, and they were somewhat assigned to the 191st Military Intelligence unit, although only on paper; the reality was that the new unit would be a self-contained entity, in short, a detachment.

A standard company of soldiers in Vietnam was approximately ninety to one hundred twenty men while a detachment suggested something less; so far HHC–LRRP, 191st MI, OPCON to G-2 was, well . . . just Capt. Jim James.

After the briefing had been concluded and after letting the captain know what he expected, there was only one question Maj. Gen. Norton needed to ask. "Still want the job, Captain?" the general said, already knowing the answer.

"Yes, sir!" James said.

"Good," Norton said, shaking his hand. He added that James could recruit whoever he needed from the division's reconnaissance units and the replacement center, which also meant that

James would soon be unpopular with company, battalion, or brigade commanders. Nobody liked to have their best people snatched or lured away by another command, but that's exactly who James would target.

Since James had been a company commander with the 1st of the 8th Cav, an infantry line unit or "grunt company," he was well aware of the problems large units faced in the rugged mountains and the rolling jungles of the Central Highlands.

Having led one hundred or more rucksack-laden soldiers in the dense underbrush, tall grasses of the savanna-like plains, and steep, jungle-covered mountains, he had immediately discovered that noise discipline was a constant problem. While he had a number of career professionals and gifted volunteers or draftees, he also had a few yahoos who would yell for a cigarette while on operations in the field. Some dumb-ass breaking noise discipline while the platoon on point was quietly and carefully working its way into an enemy bunker complex didn't do anything to help make the patrol a surprise visit. For some soldiers, the gaffe was their survival strategy; they reasoned that if the Viet Cong knew they were coming, then they'd probably run. The trouble with that logic was that it assumed the enemy wouldn't set up an ambush or booby traps or simply help the Communist mortars zero in on their targets.

During the war, more than a few dead-on incoming rounds from the Viet Cong mortars had been as a result of poor noise discipline, which pinpointed the grunts for the VC.

In most cases, the offender was quickly hushed up or given a swift kick in the ass by his buddies, who didn't think the officers' or NCOs' counselings would effectively get the point across. Dying in war was bad enough, but the chance of dying because of someone else's stupidity was something few would tolerate.

Since the Selective Service boards were drafting a cross section of America, it meant that what filtered down to the infantry in Vietnam was a mix of good and bad. At times, that meant giftedly good, while at others, it meant remarkably bad. It was no secret that some courts, believing that a stint in the service would turn offenders around, were giving criminals the choice of joining the service or going to jail.

In some cases, it worked. In others, it just gave a few access to automatic weapons and explosives and an opportunity to use them. For the most part, those who joined the service or were drafted served with pride and honor. Pride, peer pressure, and professionalism would pump up most soldiers for the difficult job of combat, but for others, it would never happen. And some people were not cut out to be soldiers. But during combat, everyone had to carry his share of the fighting or someone would die as a consequence.

James knew that small teams of handpicked soldiers, conducting long-range patrols, could successfully wage behind-the-lines war in the Air Cav's area of operations.

The II Corps area of operations for the 1st Cav was a natural maze of mountainous terrain, a living labyrinth of vast coastal plains, and a remote snarl of jungles. The mountains were part of the extensive north-south range known as the Annamite Cordillera, which rose as high as ten thousand feet. The area was also heavily forested, two-thirds of it covered in dense bamboo and hardwood forests of mahogany, teak, rosewood, and ebony. There were seas of sharp-edged elephant or napier grass and dense interlocking thickets of brush, scrub, and vines that became impassable barriers.

It was terrain that made large-unit operations difficult but was well suited for conducting clandestine warfare. The local Viet Cong and North Vietnamese Army units that had infiltrated the region had long used it to their advantage.

The area was also within reach of one of the major exit ramps for the route the Americans had nicknamed the Ho Chi Minh trail and the North Vietnamese had labeled The Old Man trail. The series of trails and paths that led from North Vietnam across and down through Laos and Cambodia and then into the Republic of Vietnam served as a transit route for the steady stream of enemy soldiers who infiltrated the South.

The Americans knew the route led back to Ho Chi Minh; the young North Vietnamese soldiers who marched over the harsh jungle mountains, fighting malaria, dengue fever, and American B-52 strikes, knew the route would make them old before their time.

For years, the II Corps region had been home to NVA divisions and the Viet Cong infantry, artillery, and *Dac Cong* (sapper, i.e., engineer) battalions, who were trying to take back what the American helicopter soldiers had taken away.

The sappers were perhaps the most feared of all of the enemy units throughout Vietnam since their specialty was the use of explosives and a unique form of commando infiltration to apply them.

Their technique involved working their way through American barbed-wire perimeters, carefully and quietly crawling through the entanglements, stepping over and around trip wires, which, if nudged, would set off antipersonnel mines and flares. Once inside a perimeter, the sappers would kill the guards of nearby bunkers, then blow a hole in the defensive line for the main body of enemy troops to follow as they charged toward command posts or heavy-weapons positions.

If the GIs feared the ghostly sappers, then James knew the Viet Cong and NVA in II Corps would come to fear the LRRPs; the same principle applied. Eventually, when the enemy caught on that LRRP teams were being deployed, when things went bump in the night, even harmless sounds in the night would instill fear or terror in those who thought they should be safe. The American LRRP teams would also take away the element of surprise from Communist commanders.

For the Air Cav, and other divisions, gathering the much-needed "raw, hard intelligence" required to fend off sapper attacks and offensives, major or minor, was always a priority. Raw, hard intelligence wasn't guesswork or speculation but material and information gathered firsthand from reliable sources in the field, both day and night.

Small, long-range patrols, hiding just off major infiltration routes and using night vision devices known as starlight scopes, could effectively monitor enemy strength, troop movements, logistics, and targets during even the darkest night. The hand-held device magnified the faint starlight in the evening sky and portrayed the surrounding jungle in an eerie, artificial green light.

Since the Viet Cong and NVA preferred to avoid the division's scout helicopter patrols during the day, they moved at night. Thanks to such innovative tools as the starlight scope, the viewer could see them coming and going and, occasionally, even hitting their heads on low-hanging limbs in the process. They weren't supersoldiers or ghosts who were able to disappear in the dark, and they could be beaten.

Getting a few of the much-sought-after scopes might take some doing, James knew, and he decided that one of the best places to go looking would be the Special Forces, who, if they didn't have the devices themselves, would probably know where to look.

James knew that the new LRRP detachment could be the division's eyes and ears in the jungle, but he was certain that critics inside the division would say that the 1st Cav already had eyes and ears: the 1st Squadron of the 9th Cav, which had been conducting aerial reconnaissance and ground assaults since the division arrived in 1965.

Since arriving in Vietnam, the 1st of the 9th had been redefining concepts of airmobility and light infantry tactics, and its performance was remarkable; its success unquestionable. The UH-1 helicopter, the workhorse Huey lift ship, the UH-1B gunships, and the small OH-13 observation helicopters were the major factors behind the success, but it was the infantry "Blues"—the Cav's heavily armed quick-reaction platoons—that made it possible. Of all casualties inflicted by the division on Viet Cong and NVA forces, over half were attributed to Alpha, Bravo, Charlie, and Delta troops of the 1st of the 9th.

Because the 1st of the 9th was the division's premier reconnaissance force and since most of the units within the division had their own recon platoons, they could argue that any new company—or even a detachment (especially one without a TO & E)—would only draw on precious assets and resources, tying up aircraft, artillery, or valuable quick-reaction forces that might be needed elsewhere.

It was a valid concern, as some units would now be required to do their jobs with less. However, the LRRP detachment would only add to the division's prowess and combat capabilities by adding a new dimension to the intelligence-gathering mission. The detachment's job and mode of operation would be unlike anything the division had done in Vietnam and, as such, might produce very real and distinct advantages. Patrolling a three-to-six kilometer area, the LRRPs would spend the duration of their missions combing the area for active trails and bases and monitoring known or suspected infiltration routes or border regions.

One of the most obvious advantages was that the detachment would allow the Cav to free up the brigades to operate elsewhere. Even with its unique mobility, the division still could not be everywhere at once.

But small teams could deploy quickly and quietly into suspicious areas and gather intelligence without being seen. An additional benefit, already discovered by other LRRP units in country, was that the patrols were beginning to intimidate the Communists in their strongholds.

Few would argue the tangible benefits of timely intelligence because knowing the enemy's locations, his strength and weaknesses, his direction of movement, amounted to a very real coup. Like playing chess and knowing your opponent's next few moves, such knowledge allowed you to plan your strategy accordingly and shift your forces to meet and defeat the threat.

In one of the 1st Cavalry Division's opening gambits, shortly after arriving in Vietnam a year earlier, in the Ia Drang Valley west of Plei Me in the border province of Pleiku, the division achieved its first major air-assault victory against overwhelming enemy odds. In the vicious and sometimes brutal hand-to-hand fighting, the 1st Cavalry Division took on the North Vietnamese Army regulars and defeated them. However, the 1st Cav lost more than three hundred soldiers, killed in action, with more than seven hundred wounded in the first major battle between the opposing forces. The North Vietnamese Army's 66th Infantry Regiment lost over twenty-five hundred soldiers and suffered staggering numbers of missing and wounded, yet it claimed victory as well.

For the Americans, it was the first opportunity to show they could beat the Communists in conventional battle while proving the value of the airmobility concept. The battle provided the Communists with a hard-earned lesson on how not to conduct warfare against an airmobile enemy. Vo Nguyen Giap was willing to suffer the losses to learn how to fight the airmobile division, and the division would learn to take full advantage of timely intelligence.

So whether Major General Norton was just following the MACV directive to establish a LRRP unit or he truly believed a LRRP unit could provide the division with necessary intelligence didn't matter; the Cav would have its LRRPs.

Regardless of the motivation, James understood his role and welcomed it. He knew that a small group of the right type of people, properly trained, led, and equipped to work behind the enemy lines, could be successful. There was no reason the new LRRP detachment couldn't meet and exceed all expectations.

Reconnaissance of the type carried out by the 1st of the 9th Cav, with its aerial aspects and platoon-size force was quite different from the five- or six-man long-range reconnaissance patrols of the new detachment. The 1st of the 9th's helicopter hunter-killer teams and aerial, light infantry rifle platoons were changing the way the war was being fought, and the success of the aerial reconnaissance and air assaults they provided for each of the Cav's three brigades was unquestioned. They hit hard and swiftly and could cover great distances in a short period of time. When one of the three troops in the squadron's light observation helicopters, flying nap-of-the-earth or treetop level, found the enemy in the open or occupying fighting positions, the scouts engaged them with M-60 machine-gun fire or grenades. When the scouts found themselves in over their heads, the troop's helicopter gunships took over, pounding the enemy with minigun machine-gun fire, rockets, and automatic grenade fire while the infantry platoon landed nearby and worked its way through the jungle to engage the enemy in ground combat.

Their unit motto proclaimed them to be "The Boldest Cavalry The World Has Ever Known," and if success in combat was measured by body count, destroyed fighting positions, or captured weapons, then the 1st of the 9th was achieving its objective and living up to its claim.

But small patrols sneaking around the enemy's jungle camps and territory could quietly guide strategy and frustrate the North Vietnamese campaigns. That the two missions complemented each other seemed obvious to Captain James, but then he was a realist about the war and what it took to win it. The decision to establish a LRRP detachment within the division told him his superiors were as well.

James was the son of a navy admiral and the brother of a naval aviator, but to his family's surprise, he chose to serve in the army instead. Before long, he realized he wanted to make the army a career and started working toward that goal.

By the time he arrived in Vietnam, he was a paratrooper who was Special Forces qualified and who had seven years of commissioned service. As a lieutenant in Italy he had commanded the SETAF airborne recon platoon, and then he served as a Special Forces A Team leader in Ethiopia during the border conflicts with Somalia. Africa had been a harsh teacher, but the lessons learned there had strengthened his resolve for the new war in Vietnam.

His performance as a line-unit "grunt" company commander caught the attention of Major General Norton and the division staff. When the decision was made to select the best qualified officer, from a short list of candidates, to run the long-range patrol detachment, Jim James was the logical choice. His record shone.

However, in combat a sterling reputation only helped you get a job; it didn't ensure that you would keep it. *That* required achieving the objectives division and G-2 had defined.

"You have a blank check, Captain. Use it wisely," Lieutenant Colonel Ray said as he followed James out into the late afternoon gloom. A monsoon's anger had turned Camp Radcliff into a series of small streams and pools. What wasn't flowing or pooling had become ankle-deep mud. During the winter monsoons, the months of September through December, an average of over four and a half feet of rain fell across the region, turning the countryside into a bog and making the going in the base camps an effort at best.

"Thank you, sir," James said, well aware that before he decided to cash it in, he would do well to have a working idea on where and how best to spend it.

"Draw up a working plan and run it by me, and I'll brief the general. While you're at it, you might want to find a place to put the detachment. There's room by the rock quarry, but it's your call. Any questions, Captain?"

The younger officer smiled. "A few hundred or so, Colonel. But I'll save them until I present my plan."

Like any new adventure, it was always good to plant the flag and stake out one's claim. So that's where James began. Even in the downpour, it was easy to see that the G-2 was right. There was room near the old French rock quarry, so the new LRRP commander secured it as his detachment area.

A slight rise between the 1st of the 7th and the 2d of the 8th, two infantry battalions, the space was big enough to fit a detachment, maybe even a company. It needed a little grading to level it off and maybe a bulldozer to do a little selective carving, but it was a good spot to begin the business of literally building something from nothing, a place to begin setting up the basics, like a recruiting tent and, maybe, a sign reading: ORPHANS WANTED. INQUIRE WITHIN.

CHAPTER THREE

Since he wasn't certain how to go about setting up the detachment compound, Captain James's very next act was to secure a first sergeant to do just that. Any good officer knew that a good first sergeant was also a unit's chief architect, attitude motivator, den mother, and the social mechanic who brought everything together and made it work.

James found what he wanted and needed in a top sergeant in Frederick J. Kelly. Kelly was a former Ranger School instructor, a professional noncommissioned officer whom James had liked right off the bat. Kelly immediately set himself to the task. Within days, the newly planted detachment began to unfold. From the expert way he conjured up platoon-size general purpose (GP medium) olive drab canvas tents to olive drab typewriters, olive drab field desks, and olive drab everything else they needed, Kelly immediately proved himself to be a resourceful and capable first sergeant.

Nothing was green in the army except new recruits, powdered eggs, and the envy of other units for acquiring talented personnel. One of the people James received on loan from the Headquarters and Headquarters Company was a veteran NCO, a thin, wiry recon platoon staff sergeant by the name of Joe Kline. At twenty-nine, Kline was a streetwise New Yorker with the accent and attitude that went along with it. Slightly irreverent, cocky, Staff Sergeant Kline also was a competent soldier, and all three combined in him to form the typical, professional NCO. He was brought in as cadre, but to James's and Kelly's surprise, the staff sergeant also turned out to be a pretty good dog robber.

Dog robber is a term used to describe a soldier who can get anything a unit wants or needs so long as those on the receiving end don't look too closely at serial numbers, paperwork (if there is any), or the morning MP reports.

Joe Kline was also a competent soldier. He had to be or he wouldn't have been selected to serve as cadre, even if he was on loan! He was Airborne and Ranger qualified, on his second tour of duty in Vietnam before extending his tour six months to "volunteer" to work with the new detachment.

Officially, Staff Sergeant Kline had acted as his recon platoon's platoon sergeant when the senior NCO was injured by the backblast of a claymore mine when the platoon was being probed by a Main Force Viet Cong assault element. His first sergeant and his platoon leader said Kline took over from the injured NCO and did an "outstanding job." They also said he deserved a seven slot, the next higher pay grade (E-7). They hoped a transfer to division would provide it, so his HHC billet was just a temporary home to help find him a seven slot within the division.

What James didn't know was that the new dog robber had been transferred out of his old unit for beating the hell out of the platoon sergeant, who had been drunk when he thought he heard something out in the jungle. Without checking to see what it was or informing anyone else what he was going to do, the platoon sergeant had purposely set off a claymore mine, nearly killing several of the soldiers in Kline's squad. Since there'd been no backblast injury and no serious injuries to the soldiers, Staff Sergeant Kline would have been willing to overlook the accident, even so dangerous and stupid a one, provided there'd been some sign of atonement. But the platoon sergeant just got belligerent. Kline went ballistic.

The incident was hushed up for the sake of the senior NCO, who had less than thirty days to go on his tour of duty and less than a year before he retired from the army. The E-7 suffered a broken clavicle in the scuffle and was evacuated to Camp Zama, Japan. Kline suffered a broken right hand, so he was mede-vacked out and treated at an aid station. Then he was transferred out of the field because of the broken hand, and because you couldn't have a staff sergeant assaulting a sergeant first class, regardless of the reason. It was bad for morale in a war where morale was at risk to begin with. On paper, the transfer looked kosher enough.

When those in the rear area learned of his other remarkable skills, the staff sergeant was given other responsibilities, which kept him out of the field but deep in demand.

Kline was only on loan, so he'd have no official position within the detachment, but his talents would be put to good use. Kline was an expert marksman who believed that basic marks-manship skills were underrated and whose sympathies lay on the side of the lower-ranking enlisted men. He was in his late twenties and too old to let his hair grow out of a carefully groomed crew cut, which he secretly thought made him look a little like Burt Lancaster. Kline drank Johnny Walker Red Label scotch in the rear area, preferred Sinatra over pop music, and swore as a matter of course, the word *fuck* being the most fre-quently used.

His biggest career drawback was Stateside training duty and where he had been reprimanded for what he said were "stupid fucking rules designed by stupid fucking people." The one inci-dent that burned his ass most was when he dismissed his pla-toon in an advanced infantry training company from guard duty after a twenty-mile forced march only to discover that his ex-ecutive officer, a sorry-ass second lieutenant who'd somehow been unable to make the march, had established a guard duty roster for Kline's platoon. To add insult to injury, the guard mount was for an empty storage area. The XO thought the "ad-ditional training" would help the men stay alert since most of them were going to Vietnam soon anyway.

When the newly commissioned officer discovered that the staff sergeant had dismissed the detail and overridden his orders, Kline was brought before his commanding officer, a twenty-four-year-old first lieutenant who had only recently returned from Vietnam and was finishing his time in the service in a training capacity. The CO only gave the XO the time out of courtesy to a fellow officer, even if he was a second lieutenant who seemed determined to flaunt his own authority.

"The men were beat, sir," Kline explained when the CO asked to hear his side of the story. "They did twenty miles, and since we have a live-fire exercise scheduled for tomorrow, I told them to clean their weapons, turn them in to the arms room, and hit the rack. Besides, it's an empty fucking warehouse anyway! What? Are we afraid somebody's gonna break in and fill it up?"

Up until that point Kline's reasoning was sound, and even the XO was having trouble arguing it. Now, though, the CO had a new problem to deal with—ego.

"That's the not point, Sergeant!" said the indignant second lieutenant.

"That's precisely the point, Lieutenant," Kline said and then added to the commanding officer, "Tell him, sir. Tell the silly little shit it's about taking care of your people, valuing them so they value the mission you ask them to do."

"The trainees are tired, and if some of them have to stay awake most of the night guarding an empty building before we send them into a live-fire exercise, then we're only asking for a problem. You want that problem, Lieutenant?" the CO asked.

A short time afterward, Kline volunteered for a second tour of duty in Vietnam. He believed that the trouble with the U.S. Army was that it was divided into two camps, the Warriors and the Administrators. He strongly suspected this had always been the case and that when David was getting ready to go out to slay Goliath, some "pissant administrator was standing on the hill counting fucking pebbles!"

He also believed that the only true administrator was a good company clerk and that the rest were pissants.

He hated pissant rules and regulations administered by "pissants who seem to take great delight in keeping us from getting what we fucking need." Kline wasn't well read, but he liked to quote something he had once come across about Winston Churchill who, when told that his people were doing their best, snorted and harumphed and said, "You can't just do your best. You have to do what is necessary!"

Kline was loyal, brave, and occasionally hardheaded, especially when it came to keeping him from doing what he felt was necessary, all traits his rabbi and court thought would make him a good soldier or mobster.

"Jail or the army. Your choice," the judge said after Kline was picked up as a passenger who was "joy riding" in a vehicle that wasn't his own.

"If I were you, I'd lean towards the military," his rabbi confided. "Leaning is preferable to falling, and so much easier to straighten out."

Joe Kline went reluctantly only to discover in basic training that he had a knack for soldiering. What's more, he liked it! In advanced infantry training he received recognition for marksmanship and physical training. Upon graduation, he volunteered for basic parachute (Airborne) training and graduated among the top three in his class.

He hadn't attended Ranger school until he reenlisted for a second three-year hitch. In the mountains of Georgia and the swamps of northern Florida, he had blossomed into a real soldier and someone who loved what he was doing. However, he was constantly confounded by the bureaucracy he knew only detracted from the army's mission.

While others, including commanders and supply sergeants, would beg, bully, or plead to get equipment or supplies, a good dog robber would simply get it, firmly believing that the end always justified the means. Kline was a very good dog robber.

Red tape was always blasphemy, and by-the-book paper shufflers were heretics. A dog robber's amen to the late-night missions was usually "fuck 'em" aimed at the bureaucrats. No one wanted to ask the particulars as to where or how things were obtained or how their prayers were answered but instead found it easier to change the subject and talk about sports or the weather.

When a new jeep or two turned up in the motor pool, a motor pool sergeant might suddenly show some interest in Mickey Mantle's quest to break the five hundred career-home-run mark while the dog robber painted over the old unit designation on the front and rear bumpers.

"I'll be a *son of a bitch*! Mantle's gonna do it! I don't fucking believe it!"

Or when a pallet load of beer was sling-loaded into the company area by an unmanifested helicopter flight, ground guided by a dog robber, officers and senior NCOs suddenly noticed a monsoon sky clouding over in the distance.

"I'd say there's a case for rain," a first sergeant might say, while another senior NCO looking over his shoulder at the beer might smile, adding, "A few cases each, actually."

Dog robbers were one of the reasons why the Inspector General's office conducted annual inspections and investigations. The inspectors checked unit inventories and stores to make sure the companies had what they were required to have and nothing more. So when the calls came down that the IG personnel were on their way, parades of stolen vehicles filled with equipment began, usually with the dog robbers as the grand marshals.

Every unit valued its dog robber, and even early on, the LRRP detachment was beginning to appreciate the talents of theirs.

As the captain was about to embark on his fact-finding trip, the first sergeant briefed him on the disposition of the detachment.

"We have a shower point set up over there," the first sergeant said, pointing to a large, hanging canvas bag with a screw-in nozzle. "I'm working on getting the sandbags we'll need for the commo section and bunkers," the first sergeant added as Captain James nodded. Staff Sergeant Kline was listening and nodding along with the first sergeant.

"Not a problem," the dog robber said, smiling. "The engineers have a whole shit load. I've got a friend over there; I'll talk to him. Maybe he'll let us have a conex container or two while we're at it. Maybe we can borrow a chain and a lock too!" Steel conex containers made great storage sheds for grenades, claymore antipersonnel mines, and any other explosives or weapons the detachment needed to secure.

"Good," James said, obviously pleased. He was pleased, too, that the dog robber had actually used the word "borrow."

Rocket and mortar attacks posed a real threat to any position that wasn't protected; Viet Cong 60mm and 82mm mortars could easily take out a helicopter, and the Soviet-supplied 122mm rockets delivered over forty pounds of explosives that could take out a hootch and everyone in it while sending hot pieces of shrapnel into others nearby. Three-foot-high sandbag walls were an excellent buffer against the impact of the mortars and the danger of flying shrapnel. The division's five hundred helicopters were a tempting target, and although the Viet Cong were aiming to knock out the aircraft with the mortars or one-hundred-pound rockets, they'd settle for American lives.

"Division says anyone we pull from another unit will have to eat at their old mess hall," Kelly said, informing the company commander of the latest challenge.

"What about the new arrivals?"

"We'll have to shop around," Kelly said.

"How about C rations?"

"No problem, sir," Kline said. "We'll also see what we can do about setting up a barbecue in case any steaks should happen to fall like manna from heaven or something."

"Or something?" James echoed, staring at the dog robber, not really expecting a more detailed answer. The NCO grinned and went back to his hootch as James and Kelly watched him walk away.

"Should we be worried?" asked the captain while the first sergeant shook his head.

"The engineers, maybe."

Sometimes the shortest route through military red tape and an overburdened supply system was someone who knew how to work around the system, which dog robbers did with fervor.

Top Kelly and Staff Sergeant Kline knew the ropes, and their talents left Captain James with the necessary time to begin his homework.

The new detachment would need a standard operating procedure, or SOP, which would literally outline and define every item and routine the long-range reconnaissance patrol unit would require to get up and running. The SOP would determine who and what he would need to do the job; realistically, before he could begin any recruiting, Jim James decided that it was time to pay visits to other LRRP-type units already in country to learn what was and what wasn't working so that he could understand the best approach to use and start his new unit out with a workable SOP.

The Maine native understood the value of a blueprint, but he was aware that what might work for some LRRP units wouldn't necessarily work for the Cav. But the other LRRP units were spread out across the Republic of South Vietnam. When he ran his proposal to visit them by Lieutenant Colonels Ray and Stotser, and the officers briefed the commanding general, he expected some reluctance. When the G-2 and G-3 came back with the response, James was ready for the rejection.

"The general thinks it's a good idea," said Ray. "He also thinks you'll need your own helicopter to do it properly, so we'll get you one to use temporarily to call on the units you need to visit."

"Thank you, sir!" James said, unable to hide his enthusiasm. He had hoped they might give him time to visit one or two LRRP units and maybe a jeep to do it with, so he had been ready to hop cargo flights and do a little hitchhiking to visit the units he had in mind.

"Keep in mind it's only on loan. You can't sell it or trade it away," Stotser said. "We'll round up a crew for you, and the rest is up to you. Keep us informed."

"Yes, sir," James said, thanking the senior officers again.

"No company yet, but I have my own helicopter," he said to himself, pleased with the briefing. "It's a start."

CHAPTER FOUR

For his schooling, the Cav captain began with the 1st Brigade of the 101st Airborne Division stationed up north in Phu Bai. The Airborne infantry "Screaming Eagle" LRRPs were headquartered at Camp Eagle and ran long-range patrols in I Corps (pronounced "Eye Core") military region, tracking and monitoring the North Vietnamese Army units that plagued the area. While U.S. Marines were primarily responsible for the demilitarized zone that separated the two Vietnams, with their forces stretching from Dong Ha to Khe Sanh, the lower half of the I Corps region was staked out by the 101st. Thanks in part to the division's LRRPs, the 101st had its share of success and stopped up the gaping holes in the area the NVA had once breached from nearby Laos.

The 101st had formed its initial LRRP platoon down south in III Corps in 1965 and operated out of the Bear Cat–Bien Hoa area, working the region that protected Saigon. As the division moved north, the LRRP platoon fine-tuned its skills and abilities. So when James arrived, he found a working blueprint to study.

After calling on the unit commander and first sergeant and introducing himself, he went to work picking their brains and listening to their comments and suggestions as they gave him the grand tour.

James talked with the operations and intelligence NCOs, team leaders, and team members, and any and everyone who could answer his questions. He listened, took notes. They had their problems, but then you could learn from those as well.

He studied their weapons and equipment and watched with keen interest as they demonstrated immediate-action drills and patrolling techniques. He sat in on several briefings and observed several patrol debriefings.

James took in every aspect of their training and disposition, attitude and physical characteristics, weapons and uniforms, right down to the black baseball caps they wore with obvious pride.

James grinned, unique headgear seemed to be a hallmark of special operations units, whether unauthorized baseball caps or authorized berets. Even before President Kennedy authorized the use of green berets for the Special Forces soldiers in the early 1960s, berets were the unofficial headgear for the SF. Initially, there was little uniformity in their design or use. However, it wasn't long before every graduate of the qualification course, the Q course, knew the right way to wear the green beret and which precise angle made him look like one handsome son of a bitch! The LRRPs, who adopted the black beret as their unofficial headgear, wore it with the same amount of pride and defiance.

Most LRRPs would say that the army's standard field headgear, the helmet, was hot, heavy, rattled, and obscured both vision and hearing; it was discarded for the more practical floppy hat, a "boonie" cap or beret. In the rear areas, the units wore distinctive black headgear like badges of honor. To most LRRPs, the beret was a matter of principle and pride, and mocking the beret could lead to all-out bar fights.

He had seen young paratroopers get into fights with infantry soldiers simply because the "legs" made fun of the Airborne jump wings or because they had committed the cardinal sin by reminding the Airborne troopers that only two things fall from the sky—birdshit and paratroopers. Rivalry was strong, and even in a warzone, the pride of the elite units was always worth fighting for, even against other GIs who obviously didn't comprehend the depth of that pride.

From Camp Eagle, James flew south to Dak To to pay a visit to the 173d LRRPs. The 173d was actually the 173d Airborne Brigade, which was stationed in the triborder region of II Corps. The 173d stood squarely across the major infiltration routes from neighboring Laos and Cambodia; because of its proximity to the Ho Chi Minh trail and because it was in a border region, the 173d was constantly under attack by the Viet Cong and North Vietnamese Army.

The VC and NVA openly operated base camps and supply operations in strength inside Laos and Cambodia so they could launch attacks against the American positions, then retreat back across the borders, knowing that, for the most part, they wouldn't be pursued.

Dak To was an easy target and some believed that it was intended to be since it drew concentrations of enemy forces that the air force then targeted. In a war of body counts, the Communists were losing, but in a prolonged war where the North didn't care how many had to die, the soldiers they lost attacking the Americans at Dak To were just the cost of doing business.

Dak To was also home to the 4th Infantry Division, and as the 1st Cav helicopter flew into the sprawling army base camp, James saw the damage from the enemy's latest large-scale attempt to take it back. In November, the ammunition dump had been destroyed in an all-out assault, and as the Huey made its approach, the scorched, blackened rock and earth and the rain-filled indentations and crater holes from the exploded ordnance attested to the accuracy of the enemy's mortars and rockets.

The scars of war in Vietnam sometimes lingered for decades. In Italy, the scars of medieval campaigns were considered tourists attractions; their real meaning and value lay in reminding the generations who followed of the cost of their heritage. In Somalia, James had seen the clans carry on grudges and fights over causes and reasons long forgotten and poorly defined.

Throughout Vietnam, there were old shell holes and the

remains of colonial forts that even the brown water runoff and underbrush could not reclaim. Their outlines and perimeter patterns were still visible from the air, the ghosts of wars past, still haunting the countryside.

The 173d, better known as "The Herd," had been the first ground combat unit to arrive in Vietnam, the first to make a combat parachute jump in the war, and the first to realize the value and to reap the benefits of small behind-the-lines patrols. Like the 101st, all of the 173d's LRRPs were Airborne qualified and generally considered to be a cut above the average soldier.

The ballsy attitude and don't-give-a-rat's-ass enthusiasm were apparent even to the casual observer because the Airborne units were all-volunteer, and the LRRPs took their can-do spirit one step further. They said they had brass balls, and they had to believe it to go behind enemy lines in such small numbers.

Most of the 173d LRRPs looked to be in their early twenties; their NCOs were older career soldiers who had either served with the Special Forces or as Ranger School instructors at Fort Benning, Georgia. James took note of everything, and from time to time wrote down the things—good and bad—that he didn't want to forget, stuffing the notes into his jungle fatigue pockets for later review.

In some LRRP units, team members cooked C rations in their night halt positions or copped a quick smoke on patrol, which was something James wouldn't allow. The glow and the odor from a cigarette or small fire was unmistakable as was the smoke emanating from it. But such discoveries proved the value of James's window-shopping trip.

From Dak To, James flew south, toward the coast on the South China Sea, to the 5th Special Forces Group in Nha Trang. Nha Trang was a key logistical center for the supply of American military forces and was just fifteen miles north of the white-sand beach areas of Cam Ranh Bay. It was all very scenic, tropical, and deceptive.

The 5th Special Forces Group was actually the headquarters for the approximately three thousand five hundred or so Green

Berets and their forty thousand irregular forces operating throughout Vietnam. From Nha Trang, they ran projects and programs that would directly impact the captain's new detachment. James knew very well that, more than any other military unit in Vietnam, the Special Forces had defined the art of long-range patrolling, starting with the Project DELTA teams and the Delta's training of other soldiers selected from units arriving in country. This training later became the Recondo School. The name Recondo had been created by the MACV commander, Gen. William Childs Westmoreland, from the three aspects he felt best defined the course: reconnaissance, doughboy, the nickname of the infantry, and commando, for the special soldiers they would become. If Major General Norton was an old warhorse, then Westmoreland was the charioteer.

In an impressive military career that began to reveal itself when he was made the first captain of his class at West Point, the South Carolinian, Westmoreland, soon afterward earned battle ribbons in campaigns from North Africa to Germany during World War II.

During the Korean War, he commanded the 187th Regimental Combat Team, and after the gunfire had finally ceased, his career spiraled upward steadily in a way few other officers would ever equal. Long before he took over the Military Assistance Command in Vietnam, Westmoreland was an ardent student of the history of Vietnam as well as of French military tactics and strategies and those of the Viet Minh. Because he was keenly aware of the reasons for which foreign armies had failed in Vietnam and understood the strengths and weaknesses of the Viet Cong, Westmoreland was able to plan his strategy from a sound knowledge of the requirements for success.

The Brits had been fighting a small war of their own in Malaysia long before the American buildup in Vietnam, and the lessons learned and experience gathered had come at considerable cost.

Since the early sixties, the Green Berets had been sending their people to Kota Tinge, Malaysia, from Vietnam for the unique training the British could offer. The jungle-operations knowledge that they brought back made it possible to offer a shortcut to a wealth of insight and practical skill to their own people and programs.

The Special Forces Recondo program was an idea borrowed from the British Jungle Warfare School in Malaysia. The Special Forces adopted the skills taught by the British and added to them new skills and practices learned in Vietnam, and then helped set a new standard for conducting or countering guerrilla warfare.

It was time for James to call on some old SF friends, ask a few favors, and maybe call in a few IOUs. By then, he had decided to set up a training program in the detachment, modifying it to meet the tasks of the division, before sending his people through the Recondo course to sharpen their skills.

Over a few drinks at the officers club, he sought advice and made deals, and when he left, he remembered why he missed the Special Forces from time to time. They made things happen. A handshake and promise were better than contracts to most Green Berets. When he left Nha Trang, a few more items on his shopping list had been taken care of.

From Nha Trang, it was south toward Vung Tau on the coast where the new LRRP commander paid a visit to the Australian SAS squadron. The Special Air Service offered another dimension to the solution of the LRRP equation; the Brits were good at jungle warfare, but the Australians excelled at it. In World War II, they had fought successfully in Borneo and on numerous other islands against the Japanese. Then they spent a dozen years afterward in Malaya, with the British forces, perfecting their jungle warfare skills.

The Australians had been in Vietnam since 1962 when a thirty-man force of instructors well versed in guerrilla tactics arrived to train and assist the South Vietnamese. By late 1966, with a task force of nearly six thousand men serving in Vietnam, the Aussies had gone from serving in a training capacity to taking an active combat role. One of the stand-out weapons in their arsenal was the SAS, which played havoc with the Viet Cong and North Vietnamese Army units they tracked and ambushed.

In calling on the unit's commanding officer and staff and working through the introductions, the U.S. Army captain opted for his usual straightforward approach.

"I'm setting up a long-range reconnaissance unit with the 1st Air Cavalry Division up north and would appreciate any suggestions you might have on how best to go about the task, sir," he explained to the SAS officer in charge.

"The 1st Cavalry Division," a staff officer repeated. James nodded. The fact he had shown up in his own, private helicopter wasn't lost on the Australians. "You're the ones with all of the helicopters." His tone was all admiration as he eyed the helicopter. Airmobility in combat was a key to winning battles, and to others, it sometimes seemed the Cav had most of the keys.

"We hear you have the largest helipad in Vietnam?" another officer asked, smiling.

"The known world," James replied, picking up the good-natured momentum.

The squadron officer sighed audibly. "Then, I suspect you're off to a fine start, Captain. I think a quick in and out is the best way to deal with the Viet Cong. We'll be delighted to assist you in any way we can."

James thanked the officers and was given the grand tour, doing a little admiring of his own.

They were talented professionals with a raucous spirit and low-key sense of humor, which James enjoyed. Many GIs made the mistake of trying to drink the Australians under the table only to wake up with a good view of the bubble gum beneath their rounded ceilings.

As LRRPs, the Aussies were true innovators. They had developed the "Australian peel" method of breaking contact with an enemy force and most other special operations units had added it to their own repertoire of quick-reaction drills ("immediate action drills," "IADs").

The peel was a remarkably simple routine that allowed a patrol in contact to concentrate its fire as the men broke away from the enemy. The soldier in contact would empty his magazine at the enemy and then peel away, with the next man in line following suit, repeating the process until contact was broken.

James had heard on many occasions that the Australian SAS were "remarkably good" but after studying their operations and procedures, interviewing their officers and enlisted men, and taking a hard look at every aspect of their training, combat drills, and readiness and performance, he came away thinking "remarkably good" didn't adequately describe them. They were damn "bloody" good! Anyone who underestimated their capabilities would be sorely mistaken. When he was ready to go, he thanked the SAS commander and the others who had offered their help and left with a new admiration for the Aussies.

From Vung Tau and the south, it was back to An Khe and the noticeably cooler Central Highlands. The low-lying lands around the Bien Hoa area were stifling in the hot Vietnamese days, and while the temperature was perhaps only a few degrees lower in the Central Highlands, it was enough to offer a small amount of relief.

The working trip had proved productive. At each stop, Jim James had gained a better understanding of the kind of people, training, and resources he would need to make the Cav's LRRPs effective. Along the way he saw a few things he didn't like and logged those as well.

More than once he had been pulled aside and told the "real secret" to successful long-range patrols by the officers and NCOs who commanded them. "Find the best people you can and train them well," they said. "They'll do the rest. They won't let you down. That's all there is to it."

James had been in the army long enough to know this simple maxim was true. Special units are made up of special people; volunteers who constantly demanded something more of themselves and who were willing to push their own limits to get it. That was the common denominator. The rest was training, leadership, logistics, and attitude. A little good luck thrown in wouldn't hurt either.

So with a working plan in mind, his outline for the new unit's SOPs, courtesy of some of the best long-range patrol units in the war zone, Captain James returned to An Khe.

Now it was time to go recruiting.

CHAPTER FIVE

It was referred to as "The Highway"; its official title was National Route #19. In the best of weather, the highway was little more than a potholed, dusty macadam road, which ran from the coastal city of Qui Nhon on the South China Sea, snaked its way west through Binh Dinh Province for fifty miles through the steep and deadly An Khe mountain pass, into the highlands, and continued on through the infamous Mang Yang Pass, to the remote border provinces of Pleiku and Kontum. The two passes were the targets for enemy ambushes bracketing the highlands. While An Khe Pass opened up the region to the coastal plains, Mang Yang Pass was the main route that brought Highway #19 and the much-needed logistics and supplies by convoy to Pleiku.

While the highway was reasonably smooth and level in the larger towns and cities, once beyond the outskirts, the route deteriorated dramatically. The high cliffs and ledges, nearby jungles, and vast countryside made it ideal for ambushes that frequently began with command-detonated mines, which didn't do anything for the condition of the road. Road maintenance was unheard of, so the scars left by the fighting tested springs and suspension systems as well as nerves.

There were an estimated thirty-seven thousand miles of roads throughout Vietnam, less than 16 percent paved. That made the going slow, at times hazardous, even without the possibility of getting blown out of your jeep or truck by an enemy B-40 rocket.

On remote stretches of the neglected road, National Route #19 became a turnpike for the Vietnamese civilians who were forced to pay tolls or "taxes" to the Viet Cong or the Saigon government soldiers who set up money-making blockades. Crooks weren't about to let a war get in their way.

Midway on the route, about one klick from an abandoned French fort, stood Camp Radcliff, set on the edge of the dilapidated village of An Khe. Huts and small neglected buildings lined the highway to form An Khe, but there was no discernible pattern for the other hootches, animal pens, and structures that made up the rest of the village. It was an isolated community that relied on the nearby American base camp for its existence and growth. An Khe fed on the division like a leech, getting fatter as the camp went about its business and growing with the war.

The U.S. Army base camp, with its collection of protective bunkers, fixed gun placements, guard towers, tents, modified tents known as hootches, and mammoth man-made helicopter pad, lay beneath the towering and impassive Hon Con Mountain. As one engineer officer remarked, "Camp Radcliff was a constant work in progress."

Besides the perimeter or "green line" defenses that were designed to help thwart enemy ground assaults, Camp Radcliff was carefully wrapped in thousands of feet of rusted razor-sharp barbed wire and ringed with antipersonnel mines and trip flares to deter intruders.

Camp Radcliff was the home for the 1st Cavalry Division and its enormous fleet of helicopters, and that investment had to be protected. The 1st Cavalry Division was the war's first completely airmobile division, and its nearly five hundred observation, lift ships, transports, and gunships added a new dimension to its cavalry origins. From their Texas beginnings in 1921, the horse soldiers fought dismounted in World War II and Korea; in Vietnam they saddled up once again, this time on helicopters, and rode across the Southeast Asian skies toward their campaigns and battles. Nicknamed "The Cav," the division referred to itself as "The First Team," with a motto proclaiming it to be "the first in and the last out."

An Khe was the Cav's hitching post on a combat-zone base camp that was a modern-day Fort Apache. For well over one hundred years, An Khe had stood as a distant colonial outpost, holding the mountain passes and region between Qui Nhon and Pleiku, in an area consumed in conflict and carrying the scars of decades of fighting. The new base camp was strategically placed, this meant that besides being distant and remote, the area was also home to Viet Cong units. The army's use of the word *strategic* sometimes meant "in the enemy's face." In combat terms, the words *distant* and *remote* translated into being on your own for a while when enemy mortars, rockets, or ground assault attacks began.

Several years earlier, the small, sleepy village of An Khe had been the site of a Special Forces compound specifically designed to serve as a toehold into the region, and when the 1st Cavalry Division deployed to Vietnam in 1965, it was decided that the small outpost would be expanded to meet the needs of the entire division and the huge flotilla of transport, observation, and attack helicopters it needed to conduct its combat operations. The toehold suddenly echoed to the cadence of thousands of pairs of boots and the *whop-whop-whop*ping of myriad twirling helicopter blades.

The base camp had been named for Maj. Don G. Radcliff who, shortly after the arrival of the division, was the first member of the 1st Air Cavalry Division to lose his life in the war. It was an honor for the fallen soldier, but it was also an omen for those who remained.

Radcliff was positioned so it would be a thorn in the side of the Viet Cong and North Vietnamese Army regiments and divisions that inhabited the region. Binh Dinh Province was the heart of Vietnam's Central Highlands, and Camp Radcliff was designed to monitor its pulse.

The ground cover on the huge helipad was handcut, and when the two-kilometer-by-three-kilometer parking lot was completed, it was properly dubbed The Golf Course because from the air that's what it resembled.

Whenever a new arrival asked where the eighteen holes were, some veteran would tell him to "wait until the sun sets," which is when the Viet Cong rocket and mortar teams targeted the camp.

Initially, the camp was little more than the helipad, but later it was expanded, growing to encompass nearby Hon Con Mountain, partially to avoid providing the enemy with higher ground from which to launch sniping and mortar attacks.

Near An Khe village, the forgotten French fort, with its battered thick walls and antiquated defensive positions, housed a small community of bars, whorehouses, and other enterprises that catered to GIs. Several klicks from Camp Radcliff, the fort was better known as Sin City.

Rock 'n' roll, rhythm and blues, funky soul music, and country music spewed out of the many shanty bars, while blue-white clouds of spice-rich meat smoke from open-pit grills sent unusual and frequently enticing smells tumbling over the surroundings. Streetwise young vendors and old, toothless hawkers offered a variety of legal and illegal merchandise as prostitutes in Vietnamese and western garb sized up prospective customers, zeroing in on their military payment certificates, ready to take the soldiers for whatever they could get. You could buy warm Coke, beer, and cigarettes for outrageous prices, get massaged and laid, or listen to favorite songs in smoke-filled bars.

It was said that you could break any number of commandments in one afternoon in Sin City. As always, life was cheap in a war zone; Sin City simply provided a place to barter over the price. Everybody was hustling something, and GIs were always the primary targets. It was the dog robber who pointed out that Sin City and Camp Radcliff offered ". . . all of the comforts of home provided you lived a real shitty life."

There were pockets of profit all along Highway #19, and although An Khe's Sin City was growing prosperous because of the war, the war would overshadow the profiteering.

Because of frequent and intense enemy activity spanning the province, and because the high mountain terrain offered many natural ambush sites, Highway #19 seldom remained open for consistent traffic. Those not protected by military escort or in convoy were at the mercy of opportunity. Ambushes, land mines, and Viet Cong tolls were frequent and had proved costly for American and Vietnamese forces, and civilians as well.

Just eleven years earlier, during the French Indochina War, the highway had been a miserable, winding route of death for the French. There were Vietnamese on both sides who claimed it was haunted and that the ghosts of many who had died violently would forever be confined to that highway of grief. Old beliefs die hard, but on Highway #19 those beliefs were reinforced by repeated violent encounters.

On June 24, 1954, in perhaps one of most costly conflicts of their war, Groupement Mobile 100, nearly thirty-five hundred combat veteran French colonial and legionnaire forces, their artillery and armored vehicle cavalry were caught in ambush by the Viet Minh's 803d Infantry Regiment.

The French had only evacuated their fortress at An Khe earlier that morning and were heading toward Pleiku for safety when, less than ten miles from the column's starting point, their drawn-out line had been ambushed to slow its escape. The Viet Minh used the ambush and follow-up attacks to delay the mobile force until their main body was in place. Maneuvering took time, and the Viet Minh had used tactics, the clock, and terrain to their advantage. When their trap was set and their forces in place and ready, they sprung hard near road marker PK 15. It was there that the real battle began.

The Viet Minh used a command-detonated mine to blow up one of the column's lead vehicles and block the road. From the hillsides, they raked the lead vehicles with heavy machine guns and recoilless rifles. As the rest of the column began to back up, the Viet Minh sprang their next surprise. From concealed spider holes and hastily constructed trenches over several hundred meters the Communists advanced en masse and assaulted the French column.

In the bitter struggle that followed, the Viet Minh savagely overran the lead vehicles and French soldiers as they raced on toward the next vehicles in line. When they were pushed back by Colonial forces, it was only briefly since the Viet Minh's rockets and mortars tore apart the column's remaining vehicles and secondary explosions rocked the trapped mobile unit and the soldiers within them.

Again and again, the Viet Minh soldiers charged, over-running armored cars, tanks, jeeps, trucks, and towed artillery until they retreated, leaving behind French forces desperately trying to hold on.

Time and the terrain were against the defenders, and there was little the French could do but withdraw in confusion, back the way they had come, while those who could not escape and those who were to cover the French retreat fought heroically on in the lost cause.

The battle wasn't lost because the French forces lacked combat experience or because they were not brave or devoted. Many in the destroyed units had distinguished themselves in combat during the Korean war and were proven, field-tested soldiers. They had demonstrated time and again their collective heart and courage. The simple truth, and the main factor in their defeat, was that the Viet Minh 803d Infantry Regiment had waited until the French column was well within their natural trap before they sprang the attack. They had used the terrain of the highlands to their advantage, and their victory had been aided by the sullen populace of the countryside along the miserable highway.

In the aftermath of the battle and the gruesome sporadic firefights that followed, over nine hundred of the French forces lay dead or dying. Eight-five percent of all of their tanks, armored cars, and vehicles were captured or destroyed. The French force also lost all of its artillery and nearly 70 percent of its radio equipment and heavy weapons and machine guns to the Viet

Minh. It was a stinging loss for the Colonial Army and a pivotal victory for the Vietnamese Communists. The First Indochina War was coming to a rapid end, and the Viet Minh relished the win.

A small plaque had been erected at the road marker post to commemorate the battle, and while some viewed it as a reminder of the valiant fight between two armies, the Vietnamese Communists knew it would serve as a warning to the Americans or anyone else who came after the French. It was their country, their fatherland, and they would do whatever was required to keep it.

MACV, the Military Assistance Command Vietnam headquarters, knew the region's history and significance. An Khe had been selected for the 1st Cavalry Division base camp to keep open the highway and to serve as the pivotal point for operations in the region.

But even as the 1st Cavalry Division was setting up the base camp, enemy opposition was frequent and furious. Sniper fire, mortar and rocket attacks, and ground probes had become a part of the price tag for the new business.

To counter the attacks, the 1st of the 9th Squadron assigned to the division rear area sent out Pink teams, teams that consisted of the light observation (LOH, pronounced "loach") helicopters from the White platoon (better known as scout birds), and the gunship helicopters from the Red platoon, working in a high-low configuration, conducting daily and last-light reconnaissance flights around the camp, looking for enemy activity in the immediate area. Flying at low level, the LOH birds would search out the Viet Cong, engage them with M-60 machine-gun fire or grenades while they marked the site with a smoke grenade, then quickly veer away to safety. That is, if they could escape in time.

The Viet Cong were adapting to the air-cavalry tactics, and more and more of the scout helicopters and their crews were being shot down in the process. Crew-served .51-caliber machine guns threw very large slugs that left gaping holes in machinery and bodies. That is, when the rounds didn't hit a fuel tank and turn the Loaches into fiery balls. If the aircrews survived the impact of the heavy machine guns and somehow managed to keep the aircraft in the air, they still had to fight the crippled birds back to safety.

Those scouts who survived climbed back into new or patched-up helicopters, a little shaken by the ordeal, and went back out to find the enemy once again.

The smoke grenade thrown from the Loach gave the gunship, which was circling high above, a target to roll in on with its rockets, automatic grenade launchers, and miniguns. The gunships would let loose their fury and circle back for another run. They, too, took hits, and all too often paid the ultimate cost for their bravery.

At night, division artillery conducted H & I fire, harassment and interdiction cannon fire on likely avenues of approach. Pink teams and H & I, combined with the barbed-wire barriers, trip flares, antipersonnel mines, manned and sandbagged guard bunkers and towers, ensured that the base camp would remain reasonably safe.

While Camp Radcliff was more self-contained than other division base camps, it was best suited for the division's needs. Despite its smaller size, Camp Radcliff was heavily fortified and well laid out. It was specifically designed to be the smallest practical size, its true strength resting squarely on the large Golf Course, the surprising airmobility of the division itself.

With the helicopters at its disposal, the 1st Cav could press any offensive or counter any enemy activity with swift and deadly response anywhere within the tactical corps area. Camp Radcliff would serve the airmobile division as its home, and the large yellow and black division patch that was carved and decorated into the mountain served as its welcome mat.

At least for James, it felt that way. When the UH-1 Huey helicopter touched down on the Golf Course the captain smiled at what the 8th Engineers had done with the mountain; the top was sheared off and used for radio communications. He thought the Cav patch was a nice touch. After reporting in with G-2, he thought about finding a shower, then getting something to eat, but instead decided to take a quick detour to personnel to make an appointment to review personnel files. Whoever said "the job wasn't done until the paperwork is complete" didn't know the half of it when it came to recruiting LRRPs.

In personnel, his objective was to painstakingly go through the records of every infantry lieutenant in the division and then to scour the files of the enlisted men, searching for qualified soldiers from the infantry, artillery, signal, medical, or military police specialties. He'd also send out a call for qualified applicants who were interested in the new unit and were willing to volunteer for an interview.

That was his plan, and after making an appointment to begin the drawn-out review in the morning, he thanked the personnel officer and the NCOs who had said they would help any way they could. This meant they'd open their files and offer him a table, chair, and a cup of coffee; they'd also retrieve the files he requested; the rest would be up to him.

But that would begin the next day. It was late, and James was tired. He'd head back to the detachment area, check in with the first sergeant, and find out if there were any major fires to put out after he reported in to division. If everything was okay, he'd take a shower, if the canvas bucket was filled, then choose dinner from a half-filled case of C rations, hoping to find a compressed pound cake or a can of peaches, and with the sound of artillery firing in the background, write a few letters home.

When he had left, the living conditions for the fledgling unit were spartan at best. But he was delighted to find several platoon-size hootches in place, an outhouse and shower area, and a first sergeant who was overseeing the placement process. The hootches were actually large tents covering boxlike basic wood frames. Raised floors kept the streams of rainwater from pooling in the hootches. Rope lines secured the canvas, and the tents' side panels were rolled up and tied off to let in any breeze.

"It looks good," the captain said to Kelly.

"It's getting there, sir," he replied as the deuce-and-a-half truck rolled into the compound area and came to a braking halt. An orange cloud of dust trailing the vehicle rolled up and over the rear wheels.

"Any new fires to put out?" James asked.

The first sergeant shook his head. "Sparks, sir, but no real blazes."

They watched as Kline, the dog robber, got out of the passenger's side of the truck, thanked the driver, and then walked back to the rear of the deuce-and-a-half and dropped the tailgate. Climbing into the back, he began to unload its cargo of folding cots, mosquito netting, pillows, and a half dozen or so rotating electric fans.

"So how was the weather down south?" the first sergeant asked.

"Hot and wet," he said, staring at the electric fans. "How was it here?"

"Hot and wet, but I suspect it's about to cool down some, especially if we can get another generator."

Like the rest of the troopers in the detachment, the captain's living quarters were basic. His home was a hootch with a canvas cot, a field table, a wooden footlocker for his uniforms, hastily constructed furniture and storage units, and an all-utility empty ammo box that acted as a stool, a cache for letters, and, occasionally, as a footrest. The lighting was bare bulb, which operated at the whim of a testy generator. The tents smelled of mildew and dust, and although it wasn't much, it was home.

That evening, several mortar rounds fell on the base camp, and division artillery immediately countered with an outgoing barrage that made deep sleep problematic.

While he slept, his .45 automatic was habitually close at hand, as were his web gear, knife, and rifle. Preparedness training he'd picked up in the Special Forces and carried into combat as a company commander applied to the LRRPs as well. Lying back on his cot, he drifted off to a light sleep, knowing that the war was never all that far away and, often, closer than he'd like.

CHAPTER SIX

The following morning, after plowing through the records, the search at personnel yielded a short list of twelve to sixteen people Captain James wanted to interview. From those, he hoped to come up with a handful who might fit the bill as field LRRPs, with others designated for rear-area support. He had to have good commo, medical, and logistical support to keep the teams functioning in the field.

With the names in hand, James checked in again with the G-3, talked briefly with the G-2 to let him know what he was doing, and made sure the helicopter was still available to him.

In Vietnam, priorities changed from moment to moment, so flexibility was the key when using borrowed resources. It was also the key to tactics and surviving combat where the soldier was frequently reminded that the only things set in stone were the letters on flat white grave markers.

Several units he needed to visit were assigned to remote fire support bases or in the field. James would visit the units to talk to his candidates, but the process would take a good portion of the week. He began with the 1st Brigade. Once he had secured the helicopter, he informed First Sergeant Kelly of his plans, then headed for the flight line.

The rains had ceased, and a white-hot sun had pushed its way through the tumbling clouds. Steam was rising from canvas tents as the heat of the morning welled up and pushed back off of the ground; ground that had once been pools of orange ooze was quickly drying and cracking under the sun.

As the temperature rose, it shimmered in waves and lingered heavily across Camp Radcliff and An Khe. The strong, lingering odor of human waste and burning kerosene flowed from a nearby outhouse where several bored GIs were standing beside three metal tubs of burning excrement. The tubs were actually the bottom thirds of fifty-five-gallon metal barrels that were used as collection tubs for the army's outhouses.

The black, acrid plume of smoke rose lazily into the sky, dissipating very slowly into the morning air. All across the base and across every forward military base across Vietnam, that daily ritual was being carried out for sanitary purposes by GIs. Their jobs were to pull out the tubs, mix in the kerosene, ignite the mess, and occasionally stir it. Downwind, the smell was overpowering and gagging; GIs didn't have to be told twice where to stand while the mess burned. For some GIs, Vietnam was a country that tasted of kerosene and excrement in the morning, dust in the afternoon, and mildew and insect repellent at night.

As James walked to the helipad, he came across a small, jagged trough in the soil that looked as though someone had dragged a thick rope over the ground but lifted it away just as it came to an opening in a sandbag drainage ditch. But it wasn't a rope that had left the trough, it was a snake, a five-to-six-foot-long common cobra, probably chasing a rat breakfast before sunup, before the heat had taken over and caused it to look for someplace cooler. James shook his head and kept walking. The rats were everywhere, so it was only logical that the snakes weren't all that far behind.

There were many hidden dangers in Vietnam, and not all of them had political motivations. The British naturalist Charles Darwin had theorized a century earlier that it was all based upon the survival of the fittest. In the outposts of Vietnam, his theory seemed to take on new and significant meaning.

When the Huey helicopter lifted off from the Golf Course at An Khe, dipped its rounded nose over the barbed-wire perimeter, then gained altitude, the heat became more reasonable. Cool even to outright cold, depending on how high the helicopter flew and how thin the air became.

As they flew over the rich patchwork of green and brown countryside, the captain thought that if it wasn't for the war, the ridiculous heat, and the snakes and rats, Vietnam wouldn't be such a bad place to visit.

As his recruiting trip progressed, James was more surprised when the unit commanders greeted him with "Glad to help you out, Captain. Take your pick!" than when the greetings included cold stares and veiled and not so veiled resentment for stealing their best people.

In training environments, losing an experienced noncommissioned officer or promising young soldier to another unit was one thing, but in a combat zone it was something else entirely. Besides, Vietnam was proving to be a different kind of war, an unpopular one, and the ranks of experienced senior NCOs was thinning dramatically. Those career NCOs who came to Vietnam and opted to return for another combat tour of duty were few and far between; this only fueled the frustration of some commanders. This problem of the availability of experienced NCOs was made worse by their loss in combat and their loss to the commissioned ranks as college-educated commissioning-fodder became harder to recruit.

However, James didn't look upon it as stealing resources as much as transferring them to another account, one that the entire division would draw from and benefit from with interest. So if a unit lost a good staff sergeant to one that would save more lives, the trade-off was worth it—in James's view—even if the "losing" unit didn't want to admit it.

James was wise enough to know that NCOs were the backbone of any army and that how tall any unit stood depended on its officers' trusting their judgment and instincts. He laughed when it occurred to him that if NCOs were the backbone of the army, then a heavy-handed commanding officer might just be a real pain in the ass.

As a career officer, he had learned early on—as so many career officers had learned before him—you had to trust your NCOs and let them go about the business of running the army.

For his executive officer, Captain James chose a tough, hard-charging lieutenant named Ron Hall and immediately put him to work scouring the rosters for other likely prospects. Home for Hall was North Bend, Washington, a small logging community at the foothills of the Cascade Mountains. He was commissioned out of ROTC, Airborne and Ranger qualified, and had been serving as a line officer with A Company, the 1st of the 7th Cav, when James caught up with him. From an interview with Hall and his unit commander, James learned that the lieutenant was tough, confident, and the type of officer and soldier needed when things got tense in the field. The LRRP teams would need someone like Hall to make quick, capable decisions. XO in James's detachment wasn't a staff position. It was operational and hands-on. The executive officer would be responsible for setting up a training program for the new unit and overseeing its effectiveness. Hall would also be the detachment commander's right hand, so James wanted and needed someone he could rely upon to make the tough calls and make them in time.

Because of the vast area the division had to cover, it was likely that the executive officer would be in charge of half of the detachment at some distant location or, at the very least, be inserting and extracting six-man teams under hostile enemy fire and in other less than desirable conditions.

James didn't need anyone who couldn't or wouldn't carry his own weight, and in the initial days of building the unit, he also opted for those who weren't afraid or unwilling to carry more than their share if or when it came to that. And it would; the burden of combat was always heavy, and behind-the-line units *always* seemed to shoulder more than their share of the load.

CHAPTER SEVEN

To fill out his cadre of noncommissioned officers and team leaders, James also targeted former Ranger school instructors, "RIs," he had found in the division's infantry units. The interviews were casual and calculated to get a look at the candidate in the field or work environment. He could tell a lot about a field soldier by observing him in the field, from the condition of his kit to the cleanliness of his weapon.

From a grunt company in the 2nd of the 8th Cav he picked up a squad leader named Patrick "O.B." O'Brien. O'Brien was a twenty-seven-year-old staff sergeant and ten-year army veteran who had served at the mountain Ranger camp in Dahlonega, Georgia, before Vietnam. According to all accounts, he operated well in combat.

Older than most of the other soldiers, O'Brien was a professional who had found his calling. He had also found the South and, although not a southerner by birth, he was certainly becoming one by choice. At least his assignments made it home, and the climate was more to his liking with the warm, sunny days of fall and winter scoring high over the dreary subzero winter days of his native Motor City.

"O-B-R-I-A-N?" James asked, writing the name down as he spelled it out for verification.

"That's O'Brien with an *E*, sir," the staff sergeant said as James began the informal interview. His accent was deep south, but the feisty side to him was all Irish.

"Where are you from?"

O'Brien smiled. "Detroit, Michigan, sir," he said, although he pronounced the city as "DEE-troit," which caused the captain to smile. The accent seemed to have been adopted by most of the Ranger Instructors. If they weren't southern by birth, then they became southern by acclimation and intense training.

O'Brien had enlisted in the army at seventeen, had become a paratrooper in 1956, in the days of the brown boot army, had successfully completed the Ranger school at Fort Benning, Georgia, and later had been handpicked to serve as the one of the cadre in the elite and extremely tough training program.

O'Brien was not content to be an average soldier or to follow in someone else's footsteps. But then, neither were most of the other Ranger instructors. To say that many kept beat to a different drum would not adequately explain the difference. In another time, the RIs would have been adventurers, mountain men, or explorers. O'Brien preferred to make his own tracks, and his 201 file (i.e., personnel record) showed he had done a pretty good job at it. Captain James was impressed. Of course, as a veteran professional staff sergeant, O'Brien was duly skeptical when the captain came calling. After all, when a Special Forces captain came looking for volunteers in the field, a prospective recruit could be reasonably certain it wasn't to offer him a comfortable, safe, rear-area job.

"I understand you're recruiting for the Special Forces Recondo School, Captain?" he asked matter-of-factly.

"No, not at all. Where did you hear that?" James said.

O'Brien shook his head, swore, and laughed. "Actually, I was *told* that's why you're here, sir. Looks like I was misinformed." A small smile formed at the corners of his mouth, giving the staff sergeant's face a sarcastic bent.

"I'm here because I'm putting together a LRRP unit for the division," James said.

"Sneaking around behind the enemy lines, you mean?"

James nodded and looked O'Brien in the eyes. He wouldn't soft-pedal his sales pitch. Soldiers like O'Brien preferred you to get to the heart of the matter. "That's right, with four or five other team members, and finding out where the Viet Cong and NVA are and what they're up to."

"A small team makes a lot less noise than the ninety to one hundred we have here in Charlie Company, Captain." O'Brien turned his head toward the soldiers who were busy cleaning weapons or working on their fighting positions.

"Most of these men are draftees and have maybe all of six-teen weeks of basic infantry training before they got here. Don't get me wrong, sir. Some of these soldiers are pretty good sol-diers. I mean, they're doing a good job considering everything, but some . . ." The staff sergeant sighed and shook his head dis-gustedly before he continued. "Hell, I got some who forget to remove the pin from grenades when they throw them. Tough to take out bunkers or spider holes when the damn things only go *thunk*." O'Brien shook his head again and sighed. "It's tough to fight a war, let alone win one, when you have to suffer silly little shits like that."

James agreed. "Which is why I'm handpicking my people. We'll send them to Recondo School and then train them ourselves."

"How long are the missions, sir?"

"Seven days with two, maybe three days off in between," James replied which only caused O'Brien to smile.

As a grunt, O'Brien was forced to live in the odious muck and the wet, spongy, insect- and leech-infested jungles for *weeks* on end. During the monsoons, the dry, cracked ground turned to an orange ooze that made walking slow and very diffi-cult. Hot, wet boots and socks fell apart in no time in the jungle and became the breeding ground for trench foot and jungle rot. Once-healthy feet and toes wrinkled, whitened, and split, caus-ing great pain and suffering; left untreated, that led to more seri-ous problems.

Like most good NCOs, O'Brien spent an extraordinary amount of time reminding his men to change their socks—if they wore any—and to keep their feet dry.

Much of the fight in Vietnam was against the elements.

When the rains let up, the mud caked and cracked, leaving small pools where swarms of mosquitoes bred and flourished in small, dark clouds. When they settled upon a soldier, they attacked en masse. If he didn't cover up or use enough bug repellent, then the mosquitoes feasted upon the exposed skin. Dozens could be killed in one swat while others hovering near the nose and mouth would be accidentally inhaled or ingested.

If the plague of bites wasn't bad enough, then after several weeks, the symptoms of malaria would begin to show: the fevers, the chills, diarrhea, vomiting, dehydration, which left untreated led to certain death. In that part of the world, malaria was a serious threat that claimed thousands of lives each year and had plagued invading armies for several millennia. Nearly a thousand years previously, Kublai Khan's army had been driven back by malaria, and in the wars that followed, it had been a consistent ally of the Vietnamese.

For O'Brien, two to three days off in a rear base-camp area was a rare luxury. As for sneaking around in the woods, that was just a bonus. "For that much time off, I'll sneak around Hanoi for you! How many people do you have in the company, sir?"

James hesitated. "We're not a company, yet," he said sheepishly. "Provisional company at best. More like a detachment, really. So far counting you and me, oh, say . . . about a half a dozen." A slight smile formed on the corners of the captain's mouth, but the captain never gave another indication that he wasn't serious.

The staff sergeant stared at the captain, waiting for the punch line. When it didn't come, he realized the recruiter was serious. "Six men?" O'Brien said, laughing.

James nodded, still smiling.

"You bullshitting me, sir?"

James shook his head and laughed along with the NCO. It was funny, even if it was true. "Like I said, Sergeant, I'm handpicking my people. We're new, but we're not inexperienced. So far most of the people we have are former Ranger School instructors like yourself. I'm also only selecting qualified RTOs and medics as well. You know, people like you who don't think pulling a pin is too technical." James then outlined his plans for the new unit and how he intended to make it work.

O'Brien listened with interest, and when he asked questions, James answered them honestly, if not always favorably, which told him something about the captain. Not one for bullshit, O'Brien liked what James had to say and that he didn't offer it up with smoke and mirrors. That impressed the NCO. Vietnam was a dogfight, and pretentious strutting didn't work when the snarling and the real struggle began. The army had its share of poodle officers, but when it came to the fight, O'Brien preferred junkyard dogs, scrappers who could hold their own without tucking their tails and running.

There was something about James that O'Brien understood. James was more than just a career soldier looking to get his ticket punched in the appropriate combat slot so he could move on to his next promotion. O'Brien had heard too many NCOs and officers in the past talk about "duty, honor, country" without knowing what the fuck the phrase really meant and who seemed to care little for the soldiers who were asked to provide them with meaning.

It was clear to a career NCO that the captain had decided on the tough track through the army by choosing Special Forces as part of his career path. In the upper echelon of U.S. Army senior officers and generals, only a handful had served for any length of time with Special Forces or Ranger units; the rest were drawn from the conventional or traditional fields such as aviation, armor, artillery, signal or straight-leg (non-Airborne) infantry. Among them, the snake eaters were few and far between; politicians in uniform were plentiful.

When the captain had finished his briefing, O'Brien nodded. The idea had merit and appeal.

"Half a dozen, huh?"

James shrugged again. "Almost that many," he said, "but they're good people."

"There *will* be more, right, sir?"

James nodded, paused. "Eventually." He grinned.

"When do you want me, Captain?"

"Glad to have you, Sergeant!" James offered his hand, which O'Brien shook. "It will probably take a day or two, but as soon as I can arrange the transfer."

O'Brien nodded, knew better than to salute an officer in the field, and told the captain he needed to talk to his squad, to let them know he was leaving. The smile was gone as his face registered obvious concern. "Some of them are pretty good soldiers, sir," he said.

James nodded and watched the NCO leave, thinking that O'Brien was exactly the kind of soldier he wanted as a team leader. If an NCO didn't care about his soldiers, then he wouldn't be of much use to a LRRP unit, let alone the army. The trouble was, there were NCOs who didn't care for their men, and weeding them out took one-on-one interviews. James liked to think he was a pretty good judge of character, and what the personnel records missed, he hoped he could pick out in person.

In a similar interview at another line unit, James recruited S.Sgt. Ron L. Christopher, another veteran noncommissioned officer who had the qualifications he was looking for and a good background. From his old unit, he selected Sgt. John Simones, a twenty-seven-year-old former Marine who had served with Force Recon before joining the army. Simones, who was from Middleboro, Massachusetts, had volunteered for Vietnam service while he was stationed in Vicenza, Italy. While others were doing their best to get out of going to combat, Simones was doing what he could to go. Soldiers fight wars, and Airborne soldiers fight better.

Besides the Force Recon and the army training he brought to the detachment, he also brought a love for the Boston Bruins in particular and hockey in general.

With each new pick, things were shaping up. James was satisfied with himself, realizing that it was all coming together.

Even to the casual observer, the recruiting pattern the captain used was obvious. It was no coincidence that the cadre James selected were career NCOs who "happened to be" former Ranger instructors from the Ranger Department. The RIs were the lifeblood of the Ranger school at Fort Benning that turned new officers and NCOs into halfway decent woodsmen and qualified, tab-wearing Rangers.

During the eight-week Ranger course, the RIs ran their students ragged, deprived them of sleep and food, taught them how to rappel down the cliffs of Georgia and to negotiate the swamps of northern Florida, and to fight well when they got to where they were going.

RIs were more than outdoorsmen, they were professional soldiers who were modern-day Daniel Boones. They could sneak through the jungles or swamps, survive off the land, and feel at ease or at least reasonably comfortable in environments that would cause other soldiers to shudder. They didn't rattle easily, if they rattled at all, but when they did it was with what Hemingway once described as "grace under pressure." Few of the candidates who James recruited would ever describe themselves as having grace, but their fluidity in the field could not be denied.

James also chose qualified personnel for the operations, intelligence, and commo positions. Over half of his choices were top NCOs and soldiers with more than four years of service.

To fill in the teams, he found several lower ranking enlisted volunteers at the 1st Brigade's LRRPs, a quasi–long-range patrol detachment made up of grunts who worked the brigade's AO and on occasion assisted the Special Forces on recon operations out of Plei Me.

PFC James Ross, a nineteen-year-old from Vero Beach, Florida, was one of the two he recruited from the 1st Brigade. Ross had been with the brigade LRRPs at LZ Oasis for his first three months in country, working the Chu Pong Mountain area, and had even pulled several cross-border missions into Cambodia out of the Vietnamese province of Kontum.

The borders between Vietnam, Laos, and Cambodia were ill

defined and frequently disputed, and the maps the GIs used left a lot to be desired, so cross-border operations were not as uncommon as some people liked to believe. Or as secretive. In running battles or in hot pursuit with the Viet Cong, who used the neighboring nations of Laos and Cambodia as safe havens, unofficial border crossings became the way of dealing with a frustrating threat that otherwise would have been unopposed.

There were those who knew you didn't stop a foxhunt just because the chase brought you into a new field. While generals and senior officers would have to follow the rules, the younger and more aggressive officers, NCOs, and soldiers found logical ways to work around them. "This can't be Cambodia? The NVA say they don't have any soldiers in Cambodia, so this must still be Vietnam. Let's chase the sons of bitches for another klick or two, then turn back!"

The occasional 1st of the 9th recon patrols and squadron helicopter gunships or other recon units that ventured unwittingly or on purpose into Cambodia and Laos were addressing the shadow war, although that wasn't officially acknowledged or sanctioned. Of course, the CIA and Special Forces were deep into *that* fight while those like young Private First Class Ross were hammering away at the edges.

Ross had just returned from Recondo School run by Special Forces in Nha Trang when James caught up to him for the interview. He had done well in the course and impressed several of the cadre who had suggested that he might want to give the Special Forces a try when he completed his tour of duty. The private first class had replied that he'd think about it. With eight and a half months left to go on his tour of duty, completing it might take some doing.

Captain James's first impression was that the young soldier had a lot on the ball for someone who was only a private first class. The interview confirmed it.

After the preliminary questions and after the lanky private first class had offered his background material, his impressions of the Recondo School, the training, and Special Forces soldiers he had come in contact with there, James asked a few carefully aimed questions that required more honest, gut-level responses.

"You've been with the brigade patrollers for, what, three months now?" James said, reading from his notes.

"Yes, sir."

"How would you rate them?"

"Sir?" Ross was surprised by a captain's asking for an evaluation from an enlisted man. Ross wondered what he was after.

"You've just completed Recondo School, and I know that they take you on actual combat patrols to see what you've learned. Now you have something to compare it to, so how would you rate Recondo patrols against your unit patrols?"

"The Special Forces run a good school," Ross said cryptically, and then unfolded his response. What the hell? The captain was asking for his opinion, so he might as well give it to him even though he might not be happy with what he got. "I think at brigade we played at being L.P.R.Ps, only I didn't realize it until I went to Nha Trang."

"What do you mean?" James asked.

"As I said, I think the Special Forces run a good school, maybe too good," Ross explained. "In fact, I don't think anyone ought to go out on a long-range patrol until they've been through it or something very much like it. At brigade we were lucky. It's that simple. We made a lot of mistakes out there, only we never knew it at the time. Stupid mistakes that should have gotten us killed."

James was surprised and impressed by the private first class's insight and candor.

"I'm setting up a LRRP unit for the division, and we're going to have our own training in An Khe. Anyone who comes into the unit will have to go through it before they get assigned to a team."

"How long is the course?"

"Two to three weeks, if there's time. We'll go into everything, starting with map reading, identification of enemy weapons and equipment, marksmanship, terminal guidance, helicopter landing zone selection, medical training, language training, and whatever else we feel is essential. After that, it'll be continuous training, too, whenever something comes up that we might need to know. We have some good NCOs and instructors lined up. All of them combat vets."

"They Special Forces, too?" Ross had noticed the Arrowhead patch on the captain's jungle fatigues that marked him as a green beret.

"Ranger mostly. The kind who don't like to rely on luck."

Ross grinned. "My kind of people, sir." He added that he'd like an opportunity to work with the new detachment and hoped the captain would consider him. James said he would and made arrangements to that effect. By then, James was almost used to the frowns and glares he received when he informed a unit of his intentions.

With each new interview, he came away knowing that he was setting a strong foundation that the detachment could build upon. These are good soldiers, he said to himself, dismissing the resentment company commanders might feel, knowing that he'd be more than a little angry, too, at whoever came around to steal them from him.

When he was reasonably satisfied that he had his core of NCOs and a number of potentially excellent team members, he turned his attention to the division's replacement station for the rest of the enlisted men needed to fill out the unit roster.

Getting volunteers, he suspected, would be a problem since there wasn't much to offer. It was no secret in Vietnam that the army was paying cash bonuses for soldiers who reenlisted in the combat-arms fields because those positions were otherwise difficult to fill.

James didn't have any cash bonuses, and couldn't offer quick rank or even extra R & Rs for anyone coming to the detachment. All he could offer the new arrivals was a chance to belong to a well-trained, highly motivated unit, a special unit doing a special job behind enemy lines. Not just recon work but *long-range* recon.

At the division's replacement center when the dozens of new arrivals gathered around to listen to his sales pitch, James was honest and up front. A job as a LRRP didn't appeal to everyone. Most of the new arrivals were draftees who only wanted to do their 365-day tour of duty and then go home. Being a draftee and a grunt and going out to fight a war with over one hundred other draftee grunts was one thing, but adding more training and then playing hide-and-seek, with five other gung ho volunteers, with an enemy who was determined to kill you, he suspected, wasn't much of a carrot on a stick.

"It takes special people," he said to the assembled soldiers, detailing what the detachment was all about, describing the kind of person, the job, and the dangers involved. James was blunt, and he wasn't painting the kind of picture that appealed to everyone. But then, he didn't want it to.

"What do you mean 'special,' sir? Like football jocks or something?" a thin-faced specialist with lean arms and frame asked from the audience.

"I want soldiers who are in top physical condition," James replied. "Because you'll be carrying everything you need for five to seven days on your back without resupply."

"No resupply?"

"No," he said, but then added, "Well, maybe water. Maybe not. Some AOs are pretty dry out there, and the only watering holes are usually controlled by the Viet Cong. Keep in mind that the job of a LRRP is not to let anyone know you're there. A patrol member will carry everything he'll need on his back for the entire seven days. An infantry company can't very well sneak through the jungle without the enemy eventually catching on because with that many people, noise discipline is low, and you have platoons strung out over a long distance. Also, that many soldiers can't work their way through an area without leaving something behind, a C-ration can or cigarette butt or a rifle or two."

"A rifle?"

James shrugged. "It has been known to happen."

"How many people go out with the LRRPs, sir?"

"Six," said James. Faces in the crowd began to look as though they had somewhere else to be. "But that's six *good* people who know what they're doing and won't let each other down," he said. "Besides, it's much easier to hide six people in thick jungle than it is to hide a platoon or company-size element."

"So you're looking for supersoldiers?"

"No. I'm looking for good soldiers who want to be better soldiers," he said, knowing he also wanted those who were physically and mentally tough: volunteers who were honest, disciplined, and loyal to something, whether it was family, friends, country, or sports team. Loyalty went hand in hand with teamwork.

The response seemed to answer more than the one question, which led to another concern.

"So what's in it for those who do volunteer, sir? I mean, what do we get out of it?" The question seemed to be one most of the assembled soldiers had on their minds because as it was asked other soldiers leaned forward to make sure they heard the answer.

"You get to be a LRRP, and when you look in the mirror at the end of your tour of duty, you'll know that you have done a man's job, that you survived as a result of the training you received and the skills you developed because of the equally talented people working beside you. Gentlemen, this is an unconventional war, and those who best understand unconventional warfare will do better than those who do not. It's that simple." James saw obvious disappointment in some of the soldiers' eyes, but one or two nodded in understanding. To the thoughtful, it was a sobering speech.

Of those who came to listen to what he had to say, he knew that some showed up out of curiosity and some were genuinely interested in becoming members of the detachment. A few were looking to barter their service for whatever they could get in return.

James talked to them all, but he knew his real target audience. Even in an army comprised mostly of draftees, there were those who stood out, those who some might label gifted amateurs, whose raw skills could overshadow those who claimed to be professionals. Sergeant York and Audie Murphy had been gifted amateurs as were so many of those who had died fighting in Vietnam. There were also a few career enlisted men in the audiences, back for another tour of duty, and they were also targets of the talks.

Afterward, James went one-on-one with prospective recruits, and then examined their personnel records, weeding out unlikely candidates while taking note of those who showed promise. He repeated the process many times during the first few weeks, and when the interviews were completed and his other duties were through for the day, he'd lay back on his cot amazed at the quality of soldiers he had found.

Talk of the "good old days" and "real army" always came up when professionals got together for a drink. Usually, someone lamented that the "new army was going to shit," but because of his daily interviews, James came away with another view. Things only went to hell if you let them. There was nothing wrong with the new generation of soldier. They were a little more skeptical perhaps, but the heart and desire were there. The balls, too!

The first time he addressed the new arrivals, he expected that perhaps eight or ten would stick around for more information and of those a handful might request an interview. To James's surprise, over half the audience came forward when he had finished his sales pitch, something that said something about the caliber of those who had volunteered or who had been drafted to come to Vietnam.

It was well known that back home opposition to the war was growing, and while some important and impressive voices— from Barry Goldwater to Bobby Kennedy—were being raised against the proliferation policy, those actually fighting the war weren't allowed the luxury of debate; they had duties and responsibilities; in that distant, dismal war zone, the more immediate concerns took priority.

However, time and again, new arrivals came forward, and Captain James came to realize that the detachment would have a continuous draw from the replacement station.

Of course, there were those who walked away, and the reasons that they walked were sometimes stated loudly enough to be heard nearby, at times purposely so.

"That's fucking crazy!" one soldier had said to another member of the audience. "Going out with five or six people."

"It's suicide," a second soldier had said loud enough to draw attention.

The second soldier nodded, siding with the first, believing there was safety in numbers, and since an infantry specialty in Vietnam guaranteed combat, it made no sense to some to increase the odds against them by thinning their numbers. On the other hand, to others the small numbers added up to survival.

Those who volunteered got the one-on-one interview, and although many offered interest and enthusiasm, only a few percent were selected for LRRP training. James had his own stringent criteria and wasn't about to waive them. But then, he had good reason.

If a LRRP team made contact with the enemy, the odds wouldn't be in the Americans' favor. There would be close and fierce firefights, in which the recon teams would probably be heavily outnumbered—running battles and daring escapes where each team member had to rely on the others to survive. Daring was one way to describe their missions; foolhardy might be another.

There was another reason James wanted only the best people he could find, a very personal reason. Perhaps one of the most difficult jobs any commander faced had to do with writing letters to the families of soldiers under his command who had been killed in action. While his goal was to send all of his people home walking, talking, and in shape as good as when they arrived, he knew that given the nature of the job in a combat setting, that would be impossible.

But the odds would be better if the quality of people he recruited was high and their training and SOPs were excellent. Within a few weeks, he had eighteen people in the new unit. Half were veteran soldiers in their mid to late twenties; the remaining were nineteen- or twenty-year-olds who were on their first and, perhaps, only hitches in the army. All had skills the unit needed, and the detachment would jell with training, support, time, and good experience.

To complete his roster and personal wish list, James planned to send out Lieutenant Hall to recruit montagnards (non-Vietnamese highland tribesmen) and Vietnamese scouts to form a platoon of indigenous LRRPs, another practice he picked up from the Special Forces. They would be essential to the new detachment as it developed. Besides, who else to better employ against the enemy than the Vietnamese and the montagnard (often abbreviated to "Yards") tribesmen who lived in the region and knew just as well as the enemy how to fight in the jungle. Most of the native peoples, if not all, had been involved in tribal, ethnic, or other battles for survival on a continuous basis for decades. In the not so distant past, the Vietnamese had hunted the montagnards for sport.

Although small and slight, the Yards offered courage and heart that belied their physical size. They were just plain good fighters.

Montagnard, or mountain people, was the French term, which the former colonialists attached to the indigenous tribes like the Bru, Rhade, Sudang, and Jarai who called themselves the Dega, or "Sons of Heaven." The montagnards were not Vietnamese. In fact, it was believed by anthropologists that they were of Melanesian and Australoid origin while the Vietnamese themselves were of Chinese and Indonesian descent.

Many Vietnamese referred to montagnards as *Moi*, or savages, and treated them with contempt and open hostility, which is something Captain James wouldn't tolerate in the detachment. Nor would he allow any discrimination on the part of his people.

He knew that the montagnards and Vietnamese would bring to the unit the jungle experience and understanding that would be the catalyst and key to the LRRPs' success. Training for jungle patrols is one thing, but knowing the jungle and the war on intimate, lifelong terms were something else entirely.

Until he could get slots to the Recondo School for his people, James had the lieutenant and the dog robber set up a program that was realistic and applicable to the theater of operations. The detachment's own training would be three weeks long, followed by the MACV Recondo course in Nha Trang.

The detachment training schedule included plenty of physical conditioning, a quick and dirty course in ambush techniques, radio and communications procedures, combat-reaction drills (aka "immediate action drills"), language training, first aid, map reading, explosives training, weapons familiarization, and any and everything James, Hall, and the cadre of Ranger school instructors could think of.

One method of breaking contact with the enemy was psychological. The teams would use only tracer rounds in their magazines so that when or if they were suddenly discovered the retreating LRRPs would send a literal shower of fire back at the enemy soldiers, making them believe they were up against a larger American force. Normally, tracer rounds were placed every fifth round or so, and the VC and NVA knew that very well. So with a wall of fire coming back at them, the Viet Cong and NVA might very well balk at pressing an attack, thinking that the team was a platoon or even a company. Of course, a ruse like that would work only so long. But until the enemy caught on, the ploy would probably allow an outnumbered recon team the chance it needed to break contact.

The LRRPs' battle dress would be tiger fatigues, the unique black and green camouflage uniforms favored by the Special Forces for the jungle patrols, but it was also decided that the team members would carry specially tailored black pajamas in their rucksacks, which the team members practiced getting in and out of as well. The pajama-like Vietnamese shirt was cut large enough to slip over the rucksacks, too, so from a distance or in a monsoon downpour, it would be difficult for even Vietnamese to be certain if the LRRPs weren't just gung ho Viet Cong; something that the LRRPs were counting on if it came to trying to escape and evade.

Meanwhile, one problem seemed to be in requisitioning the equipment needed to get the detachment properly functioning. Trading "enemy flags" for weapons proved to be an effective way of fulfilling some of the requirements, but the dog robber was still using his talents to obtain the more difficult to find items. Several of the younger NCOs and lower-ranking enlisted men also seemed to be taking part in the practice, which didn't really come as a surprise to Captain James. The real problem was that the unit was in danger of acquiring too many hard-to-hide items. They shopped the army first when it came to arms and equipment, but they practiced their LRRP skills on the air force when it came to the luxuries. To the dog robber, clandestine procurement was a higher calling; to the younger LRRPs it was a personal challenge.

Several even joined the dog robber on his outings or branched out on their own. Taking off toward the coast, to the vast rear-area supply depots, in an empty two-and-a-half-ton truck; a truck that suddenly appeared one day sporting one unit designation on its front and back bumpers and the detachment's designation.

To some, the "outings" or "midnight requisitions" were just one unofficial method of reallocating government property while others preferred to call it "grand theft." But to the LRRPs, it was just a matter of putting goods to better use. Lots of goods.

After the first trip, when they returned with the truck filled to capacity and satisfied grins, James had the good sense not to ask where or how they acquired the goods.

"They were donated, sir," the dog robber volunteered, as the detachment commander nodded warily, unconvinced of the kindness of strangers in that strangest of strange lands. Lieutenant Hall didn't even try to conceal his amusement.

"Uh-huh," the captain said, walking away while reminding himself that one of the necessary skills of a good LRRP was stealth, a grasp of which his NCOs demonstrated in interesting ways. Other acquired skills seemed to involve the use of a paint brush, a file to file off serial numbers, and knowing when to fill up the truck quickly, then drive around while keeping away from those who came to do "unannounced" inventory checks. A heads-up phone call from someone at division usually provided them the ten- to fifteen-minute lead time needed to get the truck loaded and rolling.

For other special wants and needs, Captain James called in a few favors from old Special Forces buddies, who managed to come up with exotic weapons, the latest in radios and generators, and rucksacks. At the officers club in Nha Trang, he found a C-123 pilot who was willing to transport the larger and heavier items back to An Khe for him. There was just a little bartering involved—scotch and war souvenirs—but it was enough.

Slowly, like a jigsaw puzzle, pieces of the detachment were beginning to come together, and James was pleased with what he saw. Someone had brought in a grader and leveled the ground in the detachment area, providing a flat, even surface for hootches and tents. It looked good, and the captain said as much to his executive officer, who nodded, then said, "The MPs stopped by a little while ago. They wanted to know if we'd seen a grader. Seems one is missing from the 8th Engineers."

"A grader?" James said, surveying the level detachment area again.

"Yes, sir."

"We haven't, have we? Seen their grader, I mean?"

"Not permanently, no," Hall said, suddenly finding interest in a cloud formation.

"Maybe it'll show up back at their area or say, close to it. Real soon?"

"That wouldn't surprise me at all, sir. In fact, I bet whoever borrowed it is doing that right about now. And, it wouldn't surprise me if whoever took it had been advised or even threatened that should he ever decide to borrow it again, then he damn well had better ask the engineers first and maybe bring along some-one officially qualified to operate it, say next week or so."

"A wise move," James said.

"Scholarly."

"Any chance of getting a bulldozer in, too?" the captain asked.

"Anything's possible, sir," he said. "By the way, we had sev-eral pallets of LRRP rations show up today."

"LRRPs?" James replied. He was genuinely impressed; the new freeze-dried, dehydrated rations were lighter than canned C rations and brought new variety to field foodstuffs, adding beef and rice and spaghetti to the well-known roster of Cs. Just add water, shake and mix, and in a few minutes you had a meal. With hot water, the rations tasted fine. With cold water, they took on a crunchy breakfast-cereal quality. The lighter weight meant the teams would carry a lighter load in the field—or more ammo and water.

"That's outstanding!" James said.

"Yes, sir, it is."

"Outstanding" was the highest official compliment and rat-ing an officer or enlisted man could receive since "out-fucking-standing" didn't read well in print. When it came to promotions, even back then "grade creep" had forced rating officers and NCOs to fill out a good soldier's efficiency report in glowing terms, filled with as many "outstandings" as would fit in the re-marks section. Some rating officers and NCOs considered it a challenge to be creative in their hype.

"So and so is a really outstanding thoroughly professional soldier who stands out among outstanding soldiers for his outstanding skills, outstanding attitude, and outstanding performance on guard when he's quite frankly, outstanding."

As a result, outstanding became the compliment of choice for most GIs, and more creative types added their own colorful qualifiers.

The captain noticed the four men of an aircrew standing near the first sergeant's tent with their baggage in tow.

"Who are they?" he asked.

"Another present. Division sent them over. They're your new helicopter crew, sir. We now have our very own command and control helicopter."

The helicopter and crew meant, rather than having to depend on another unit's resources or a loaner, Captain James had his own UH-1 Huey helicopter at his disposal twenty-four hours a day. That was great news, and it was hard to hide his excitement. James walked over to the aircrew with the XO in tow.

"Where do you want us, sir?" the aircraft commander (AC) asked, saluting. James grinned broadly and returned the salute.

"Right beside me every hour of the day," James replied. "You eat when I eat. You sleep when I sleep. And when one of our teams gets in trouble, *we* respond. Clear?"

"Roger that, Red Stag Six."

"Say again, Mister?"

"Your new call sign, sir, is Red Stag Six, at least that's what I was told at operations."

"Red Stag, huh? Well, that makes it yours as well. You're my C & C bird," James said, holding out his hand. "Welcome to the LRRPs!"

"Thank you, sir. Where do we bunk?"

"We'll have something for you soon," he said as the two-and-a-half-ton truck returned from yet another shopping run and men bustled over to unload it. If there weren't yet tents or bunks for the aircrew, James suspected there soon would be.

The pilot started to salute the captain again only to have James wave him off. "We'll save saluting for the VIPs. You're going to be here for a while, and I don't want your arm getting tired."

The pilot grinned, said "Roger that, sir," and then turned and followed the XO as he showed the crew where to store their things.

Not long afterward the LRRP pilots' tent went up, along with a hand-painted sign that read: GOD BLESS THIS GODDAMN HOOTCH. No one bothered to ask where the paint came from either.

CHAPTER EIGHT

The new LRRP detachment suffered its first capture before the patrols were deployed. Staff Sergeant O'Brien, one of his two newly acquired team leaders, and several other sergeants in the unit had been drinking and then got a little too ambitious on an equipment reallocation foray and had been apprehended by the air police at Phu Cat Air Base. For stealing the base provost marshal's jeep.

They might have made good their escape if an air police patrol hadn't noticed three drunken army personnel in an air police officer's jeep. Drinking and driving never mix well; drinking and driving stolen vehicles didn't go over well either. At least that's what the three LRRPs were thinking as two air police jeeps closed in to arrest them.

The first sergeant soon retrieved the errant LRRPs, promising the offended parties that action would be taken against the three misguided passengers from the detachment.

"You damn well better!" an air force senior NCO said to his army counterpart while Kelly glared back at the man.

"I know my job," he said quietly, but with a look that shut the senior NCO up. Kelly led his men out of the provost marshal facility toward the flight line where they'd catch a helicopter back to An Khe.

"The provost marshal's jeep?" Kelly asked O'Brien, trying to get a handle on the situation, controlled disdain resonating in his tone and demeanor.

"It had the prettiest radios you ever seen, Top! We could have reached Fort Benning with those damn things!"

"Looks like you reached jail instead."

O'Brien shrugged and seemed indifferent to the situation. His real problem was coming on like a drummer in the distance who was marching straight toward him. The hangover was beginning to kick in, and it definitely wasn't as much fun as any beer commercial he had ever seen on TV. He was certain that by the time they reached An Khe there would be more misery in store. He had figured on an Article 15 for sure—nonjudicial punishment in which extra duty and the loss of part of the soldier's pay usually were the punishment for an offense. They might even bust him a rank or two, but he doubted that they would court-martial him. At least he didn't think they would since he'd probably be asked to pack his bags and be sent back to a line unit, which would be punishment enough.

"You fucked up," the first sergeant lamented.

"I got caught," O'Brien said, in partial agreement.

The first sergeant didn't offer an opinion one way or another about the punishment, and when they got back to An Khe and the Rock Quarry, he called an impromptu formation. It was time for a lecture. When the eighteen LRRPs were assembled, he called out the offenders and chewed their asses.

Royally.

Kelly wanted to make certain everyone got the message, even the dog robber, who studied O'Brien and the others with new admiration. It wasn't just any jeep, he thought warmly, but the provost marshal's jeep! Like a shit-faced Robin Hood stealing the Sheriff of Nottingham's favorite steed, a big, white horse with a gold trimmed horse blanket and the king's royal crest. A worthy try.

When Kelly had finished, he told O'Brien the Old Man would want to talk with him, that is, when the Old Man had the time. Only when a few days went by and nothing happened, O'Brien took it as a good sign. When a week went by and still nothing happened, O'Brien figured he was home free. But in war nothing is free, and the price paid is always more than expected.

The air force provost marshal eventually sent a letter through division demanding to know what kind of punishment the staff sergeant had received. Captain James had the unpleasant duty of informing him that the soldier in question had been sent back out to combat and was unaccounted for. Since the reply was signed by the unit's commanding officer, the air force officer saw no reason to pursue the matter further. The matter was closed. Well, sort of.

"You wanted to see me, First Sergeant?" O'Brien asked after he had been summoned to the orderly room. The tent was warm, and the bare bulb used to provide light to the makeshift office wasn't helping matters any.

"The Old Man does," First Sergeant Kelly said. "Oh, by the way. Keep away from Phu Cat Air Base for a while. They don't like it when dead people do a quick recovery."

"What?" O'Brien answered. He was confused by the remark, but the first sergeant just waved him forward.

"Never mind," Kelly said.

When O'Brien reported to Captain James, the Old Man locked his heels and chewed him out for action unbecoming a noncommissioned officer. When that was done, James kept him standing for a few minutes before he finally dismissed the errant staff sergeant.

O'Brien didn't move. "You're not busting me in rank, sir?"

James shook his head. "Not this time."

"No extra duty either, sir?" Confusion was obvious on his face.

The Special Forces captain stared at the NCO for a moment before offering his reply. "I need you in the field," he said finally. "You can screw with the Viet Cong or the NVA but leave the air force alone. For the most part, they're on our side. You understand me?"

"Yes, sir."

"By the way," James added. "LRRP missions are extra duty.

Some people might look upon being sent behind the enemy lines as punishment enough."

"Legs, maybe," O'Brien said disdainfully, referring to non-Airborne personnel.

"Maybe," James said. "But if you do something like this again, I will pull you from the field and keep you back here filing morning reports."

O'Brien's shoulders sagged at the thought of being a rear-area soldier. He said, "Yes, sir," one more time and saluted as he turned to leave.

"Top says the jeep had great radios. Is that right?"

"The best, Captain," he said, turning back with a grin.

James shrugged. "Don't do it again, Sergeant."

"Steal radios or get caught, sir?"

James stifled a laugh but didn't respond. As he watched the NCO leave, the first sergeant walked back in shaking his head.

"You know what they call themselves, don't you? The men, I mean?"

"LRRPs, I hope," James replied.

First Sergeant Kelly shook his head. "At times. Mostly though they call themselves the James Gang," he said, without expression. "They even have a sign. I think they stole the wood."

"The James Gang?"

Kelly nodded. "That's right, sir. Only our cowboys have automatic weapons and grenades. I'll rein them in tighter."

"Thank you, Top."

"No problem, sir. I'm just glad the Cav has helicopters instead of horses. Otherwise, they'd probably be out rustling water buffalo."

James shrugged and laughed briefly. "Thank God for small things," he said to himself more than to his first sergeant.

Every day was a juggling act, trying to keep it all in the air. The rear-area concerns were fairly minor; the real challenge would come when the six-man patrols took to the field.

CHAPTER NINE

———

Nineteen sixty-seven was the Year of the Goat, and although the Vietnamese Communists were believed to be atheists and nationalistic, they understood the significance of the symbols of the Chinese zodiac and were influenced by their meaning.

Those born in the Year of the Goat were said to be kind-hearted but timid; defenseless and generous, especially to those less fortunate. Because of that gentle nature, they were also expected to be taken advantage of. They were not Tigers or Dragons but instead animals to be subdued or sacrificed. To the Viet Cong, the Goat symbolized the Americans, and 1967 would be the year to assert their power over the stubborn but weaker foreigners.

By January, the LRRP detachment, even with its "provisional company" status, had grown to twenty-four U.S. personnel, twelve of whom were divided between two teams; the rest supported headquarters functions. An average U.S. Army Airborne infantry company in Vietnam might run from 90 to 120 people, usually with three platoons of 24 to 30 soldiers each, plus rear support personnel so detachment probably best described the new unit after all.

On the other hand, the Airborne company roster of 90 to 120 personnel never told the full story anyway; few units fielded that many soldiers. At any given time, soldiers were out because of combat wounds, sick or ill, on emergency leave, R & R, or in "transition"—rotating in country or going home. The numbers always varied.

The LRRP detachment was in a unique position, since many of the people James had recruited had similar DEROS dates, which meant cohesion for the teams and since, by then, they had only had four weeks or so before deployment there would be no leaves or R & Rs for a while. Although there was little anyone could do to stop the LRRPs from getting sick or ill, their training helped reduce the odds of their getting wounded or killed. There were no guarantees other than a commanding officer who constantly watched over the training to make certain his people were getting what they needed.

The initial training class for the LRRPs was conducted in the detachment area by Hall and the veteran NCOs. Consistency was the key, and they were looking to create team players who would know their roles in coming events—whatever they might be.

Kline, the dog robber, was one of the designated instructors, as were the others whose combat specialties had already been tested and proven. Among the cadre there was a wealth of knowledge to draw from, and James was banking on the training to get those with little or no jungle combat experience the specifics they would need to function properly as LRRPs.

"Where's the XO?" James asked the staff sergeant during a break in the training.

"He's running an E and E [escape and evasion] course up on Hon Con Mountain," Kline said. "I think they'll have an easier time with the Viet Cong. The lieutenant's a real fire-breather."

James nodded and grinned. "That's why he's our XO. So how are they doing?"

Kline shrugged. "As well as can be expected, I suppose . . ."

"But?"

The dog robber grinned like a used-car salesman whose customer has just figured out that maybe the odometer had been turned back a bit. "But we won't really know until they get out in the bush. Bullets coming at you change everything. I know I became a more devout student of basic combat skills after my first firefight. Damn near religious." He pulled out a cigarette, lighted it, and inhaled deeply.

Blowing out the smoke, he picked a piece of tobacco off his teeth and then added, "When we're done, they won't be able to heal the sick or cure the lame, but they'll be pretty damn good at calling in fire and brimstone."

By the time the initial training cycle had been completed and after the men had graduated from the Recondo training, the new LRRPs had jelled into workable teams. How well they jelled would become clear when they took to the field. Glancing at the small roster, Captain James was reasonably satisfied with his recruiting efforts and the people selected. Almost smug.

He had his teams leaders in O'Brien and Christopher; two medics, PFC Johnny Suggs and PFC Geoffrey Koper. He also had a solid list of enlisted team members, including Jim Ross, Richard Lopez, Rodolfo Torres, Richard Spina, and sergeants Douglas Fletcher, Gary Biddle, Arthur Guerrero, and John Simones.

Because of his talent with communications equipment and procedures, Torres—of McAllen, Texas—would also head up commo training. Torres, like Staff Sergeant O'Brien, had a knack for making things happen and creatively improvising in the process. The teams would use PRC-25 backpack radios, as well as a small, lightweight HT-1 AM voice radio for backup communications.

The detachment would need someone to run the operations center, and eventually Captain James settled on S.Sgt. Tom Campbell, whose skill and talent impressed both him and XO Hall.

The early patrols relied on the PRC-64 and HT-1 radios. The TOC, or tactical operations center, would monitor the patrol frequencies twenty-four hours a day. The radio was a team's link to the outside world, while the team's weapons would secure that link. It offered the team members some degree of comfort, then it was taken away with the understanding that both the radios and the weapons were usually provided to the government by the lowest contract bidder.

For the most part, the equipment was up to the task. In the case of the radios, precautions would have to be taken to ensure they would work when the teams needed them. Since the radios were battery operated, the teams would need to carry extra batteries during the week-long patrols. The team's radiotelephone operator (RTO) would be responsible for maintaining the radio in the field, keeping it free of dirt, dust, and excess moisture. He'd also carry a folding long-whip antenna when he needed more range to maintain contact with the TOC. Transmissions by the patrols would be limited to five conditions: (1) after the team was inserted, it would send the LRRP detachment headquarters a status report, usually that it was not in contact and that the patrol was proceeding as planned; (2) the patrol would transmit situation (i.e., status) reports twice daily according to a prescribed schedule; (3) they could radio in an emergency call, such as enemy contact, a deadly snakebite, or other such incident; (4) if they had significant information to report, (5) they would call in prior to the team's extraction to notify the LRRP detachment headquarters that they were in place, ready, and the pickup zone and surrounding area was secure.

Torres was credited with creating the brevity codes used to keep the transmissions as short as possible. Torres knew the less time the RTOs talked, the safer it was for the teams; it was harder for the enemy to get a radio fix on their location, or even to overhear the RTO's voice if they happened to be within earshot.

James stared at the roster again. "A good start," he said to himself. When the Vietnamese and montagnards arrived, the roster would jump considerably. Lieutenant Hall was slated to bring in the Yards and the Vietnamese and had run his recruiting plan by James, who approved it.

Tactically, it wouldn't be a bad idea to have two Vietnamese or montagnards per team. The Vietnamese and Yards could walk point and wear the black pajama-like clothing the Viet Cong favored. Carrying AK-47s, the Kalashnikov assault rifles, they would easily confuse enemy patrols they came up against for the few seconds it would take to seize the initiative in any point-to-point contact.

An American walking around a bend in a trail and suddenly coming face-to-face with a Viet Cong point man would immediately provoke a gunfight and then a running escape. With the Vietnamese or montagnards on point, the Viet Cong or NVA would lower their guard momentarily only to realize their mistake much too late.

The same tactic worked well for Special Forces, and James and Hall didn't see any reason why it wouldn't work for LRRPs. Recruiting locals might prove difficult, so it was decided to look farther south, Yards and Vietnamese whose loyalties were a little better defined and proven time after time on the battlefield. While it was certainly true that there were cowardly or extremely "nonaggressive" South Vietnamese soldiers, there were also those whose heroism rivaled any nation's best.

Hollywood hadn't recognized Asian heroes, but then they seemed to have a hard time with heroes of any nationality. Besides, this was the era of the antihero, so how could the real-life John Waynes ever expect to get a fair shake? Stereotypes were easier to sell, but then, there were a lot of sales jobs going on.

One of the real difficulties Captain James discovered came in defining the LRRP mission to the soldiers who had to carry it out. During training, he noticed that some veteran NCOs were having great difficulty with the notion of sneaking around and "hiding" from the enemy as opposed to just ambushing them. Several of those NCOs were brown-boot-army types, real hard chargers who knew that a soldier's job was to close with the enemy and kill him. Period. Since they were also Rangers who were trained in special operations warfare, avoiding combat was a difficult pill to swallow.

"Reconnaissance is our primary mission. Granted," O'Brien

said to James during a detachment meeting. "But, if we get a target of opportunity, we take it. Right, sir? I mean, if the circumstances permit for a good ambush, we blow the fuckers away?"

"No, Sergeant. You don't," James said adamantly. "*The* mission, *our* mission, is reconnaissance. Long-range reconnaissance in places we don't want the Viet Cong or NVA to know we visited. We gather intelligence, and that means observing the enemy without being observed. If they don't know we're there, then they also won't know how they're being targeted, how we'll know their direction of movement, strength, whatever else they have up their sleeves. The division needs hard intelligence, and that's our primary objective. That's our job. You understand that, Sergeant?"

"What if we're compromised?"

"Then everything changes. If you're compromised or in contact, you fight back with everything you have and every trick you can use. Once you call in a contact we'll race to get gunships and extraction helicopters to you as fast as we can."

O'Brien nodded, even though he clearly had reservations; that much registered on his face. He'd go along with the order precisely because he was a career professional soldier.

James knew some wouldn't like it, but that was the task they had been given, and it was the task they would do. "Again. I want you to use your own better judgment in tight situations only; I don't want you instigating a firefight. Our job is reconnaissance," James added, while O'Brien and the others reluctantly agreed.

"And since we're on the subject, let's talk about false contacts or calling in to say you're compromised when you just want to get out of the field. Gentlemen, I won't tolerate it," James said, cautioning the assembly while looking over the room of solemn faces. "Now, I know how miserable it gets out there and how easy it is to get shook when you're behind the lines and the VC are all around you, but don't radio in saying you're compromised and in contact unless you are."

The captain's gaze went from face to face for emphasis, so the point was well understood before he continued. "Once you radio in that you need help, we're going to do everything we can back here to get it to you. I promise you that we'll get gunships and artillery diverted from other missions and at your call. I'll also promise that Lieutenant Hall or myself, along with the helicopter crew, will bust our asses getting out there to you. All we ask in return is that you don't put our lives or the lives of those who might also need those gunships or artillery in jeopardy by calling in false contacts. Have I made myself clear?"

"Yes, sir," several of the LRRPs said as other heads nodded in unison.

"Good," James said, turning the class back over to the dog robber. Kline began passing out the detachment's SOIs—signal operating instructions, the radio communications code handbook for a team in the field. It was their bible and lifeline.

"Sergeant Torres has devised a state code for any immediate concerns," he said, tapping the small plastic encased books. "You use the state codes to convey things when you're in contact and you have to escape and evade or you need air support."

"What code state do you use if you're in a running battle, and you have the entire North Vietnamese Frigging Army hot on your trail?" someone asked while the others chuckled.

"Don't laugh," Kline said. "We actually have a code for that. It's 'California' and should you come up against an enemy company- or battalion-size element and they're after you, then yell 'California' into the radio, and that will tell us you may need some help."

"May?"

Kline shrugged. "Depends on how fast you can run," he said, grinning.

If they didn't get discovered on patrol, then there was always the risk of getting in and safely getting back out of the landing zones. Then their training and professionalism would take over, provided the teams weren't overrun upon insertion or their PRC-25 radios didn't fade out during the torrential downpours or become blocked by the terrain when they've suddenly found themselves in an occupied enemy bunker complex and have to fight their way out. Since the teams would usually operate outside artillery range, the radio was the teams' only link to the outside world and to a quick extraction. The LRRPs would plan for the worst and hope for the best, and on occasion, the worst just might happen. It was the nature of the job.

Well, it was the Year of the Goat. Maybe that was appropriate; the new LRRPs might very well become a Judas goat that lured in the tigers of the rain forest and set them up for the kill, provided that everyone else was in place to shoot the tigers before they could pounce on the bait.

CHAPTER TEN

By early February 1967, the two teams were ready to deploy to the field to support continuing division operations along the Bong Son Plains and coastal valley regions. The Tet (lunar New Year) truce, which all sides had agreed to in theory, had been broken by the Viet Cong and North Vietnamese Army, and the war was back on—if it ever had ceased at all. That didn't come as a surprise to anyone who had been in Vietnam for any length of time. Few cease-fires or truces ever seemed to hold longer than it took for the official word to come down that there was going to be a cease-fire.

The Viet Cong and NVA had used the time to maneuver into position for their next strike and to make necessary repairs to damaged facilities.

In a press conference in Washington, D.C., Secretary of Defense Robert Strange McNamara said that the air strikes in the North were accomplishing their objectives and that the Communist buildup in the South had leveled off.

If, in the philosophical sense, truth is indeed the first casualty of war, then half-truths were the walking wounded of the political struggle. However, for those caught up in Vietnam's bloody arena, the posturing and political strategies being played out by those who never got their hands dirty didn't really matter; for the grunts, there was only the war. When it came to casualties of war, truth was measured by the anguished moans and cries of the wounded or those who would be haunted by the sounds.

Any truths the new LRRP teams discovered would be

learned one patrol at a time. Brigade G-2 would assign the detachment specific areas to patrol, selecting them based upon the brigade's intelligence-gathering requirements. After patrols' areas were assigned, the teams began their planning phase, usually forty-eight hours prior to insertion. Little was left to chance.

Captain James and Lieutenant Hall issued "warning orders" (formal notification of a patrol assignment) to the team leaders and assistant team leaders, who would then conduct an aerial reconnaissance of the specific areas of interest. The maps showed one view of target areas, but overflights provided another reality check.

A proposed dry landing zone on a map could very well be a rain-forest lake in the monsoons, filled with muck and mud and making the team struggle just to get into the jungle for cover. A forest on the map might have been logged or even burned away by artillery strikes. A small hamlet or village might have sprung up too close to the proposed insertion or extraction points.

The unit's command-and-control helicopter was utilized for the overflight reconnaissance. Typically the on-board complement would be the aircrew (pilot, copilot, crew chief, and door gunner), Captain James, the patrol leader, and usually the assistant patrol leader. Lieutenant Hall would lead the overflight reconnaissance mission for the second team.

One high pass was made over the area of operations to select the proposed landing zone, an alternate landing zone, the pickup zone, and an alternate in case anything went wrong.

After the team leaders, assistant team leaders, and officers had a good look at the insertion sites, extraction locations, and the general AO, they returned to brief the rest of the team.

Once satisfied that a flyover had provided enough information about the AO, the single helicopter would make its way back to the brigade headquarters. Initially, at least, observers on the ground would be indifferent to the occasional lone, high flying helicopter since it didn't offer a visible threat or repeat any pattern.

Back at the designated brigade, the patrol leaders finalized their patrol orders while the detachment headquarters coordinated the necessary resources such as fire support, reaction forces, aviation support, and any additional communications requirements the LRRPs in the field might need.

Meanwhile, Staff Sergeant Christopher and Staff Sergeant O'Brien issued the five-paragraph field order to their assembled teams. The patrol orders included the proposed route of movement and areas of special interest, the LRRP points of origin for ease of position reporting and proposed locations for overnight halts, locations of the communications checkpoint for aircraft, and the escape and evasion azimuth in case the teams were compromised and forced to call for an early pickup.

The patrol order for a given mission was usually given to team members as well as to selected members of the LRRP detachment headquarters, selected brigade headquarters personnel, and the aircrews who'd fly them in and seven days later pull them back out again.

Premission rehearsals would be conducted as well as "briefback" sessions to ensure those charged with carrying out the mission knew the order and intent as well.

When the equipment and weapons were checked and rechecked and when anything metal on the LRRPs' equipment had been taped down and secured, the team leaders shifted their attention elsewhere. They slowly walked around each LRRP, checking the green and black camouflage paint covering their hands and faces for bare spots of skin that might give them away in the jungle. A variety of shades of greens, browns, and blacks were natural in the jungle; shiny pink flesh would attract attention and bullets.

When the team leaders had finished their inspection, they checked and rechecked again, leaving nothing to chance. Then the teams were loaded into jeeps and driven to the helipad to climb aboard the aircraft. Even though the helicopters were only a sixth of a mile away the LRRPs rode because of their heavy packs, camouflage paint, and festooned LBE ("load-bearing equipment").*

Christopher's call sign would be Wise Owl Six while O'Brien's would be Moby Dick Six; the Six designated the team leaders; Wise Owl and Moby Dick were the baptismal patrols. Christopher's team would be first out; O'Brien's would go out the following day. Both would work the AO around the Bong Son Plains and the coastal mountains and be attached to the brigades working the area, which needed to get a better look behind the lines. The two targeted sites were the An Lao and Kim Song valleys, both enemy strongholds and safe havens.

Each team would be inserted in an identical manner. The aircraft supporting the insertion would arrive thirty minutes prior to liftoff, and the crews would be briefed by James. Both insertions would be done at last light, in the twilight minutes just after sunset and before total dark. This was done for three reasons: (1) it was harder for the enemy to observe the insertions; (2) if detected, it was easier for the team to avoid contact; (3) it was easier for the team to detect if it was being followed.

The aircraft formations would consist of three slicks or Huey lift ships and two Huey gunship helicopters. The three slicks would take the lead. The gunships and their impressive array of cannons, machine guns, and rockets would follow. Both Alpha and Bravo troops of the 1st of the 9th had their Blue (infantry) platoons waiting to serve as quick reaction forces (QRFs) if anything went wrong.

The team would be in the lead helicopter, with two decoy helicopters in the second and third positions. James would go out on one of the two insertions, his C & C helicopter serving as the second decoy aircraft.

The formations would then conduct false insertions in other

---

*The LBE consisted of a shoulder harness and pistol belt, on which were carried magazine pouches, grenades, first-aid pouch, canteen, bayonet or bush knife, and McGuire-rig rope and D-ring. A soldier could drop his ruck and continue to fight wearing his LBE.

landing zones to throw off any enemy in the immediate area. They'd fly low level, just above the trees, and as they neared the real landing sites; the team helicopter would touch down briefly, and the patrol would quickly scramble out of the helicopter's bay and disappear into the wood line.

Meanwhile the second and third lift ships would overfly the LZ, with the insertion helicopter popping back onto their flight path to give the appearance that the three helicopters were still flying their low-level formation. Since many of the natural grass fields or breaks in the jungle that they selected were only big enough for one helicopter at a time, the insertions might not be noticed by the Viet Cong.

On the ground, the teams would leapfrog their way into the jungle, several team members moving as others covered their advance. Once into the cover, they would establish commo and then "lay dog" for fifteen minutes or so to see if there were any signs that they had been observed (warning shots fired nearby, movement in the brush, sighting of NVA or VC, etc.), then the teams radioed the relay station or the command-and-control helicopter that all was well and that they were moving out.

The point man, following the unit's SOP, would then take a new direction of movement to throw off anyone who might have spotted them when they landed and set up a welcome on their line of departure into the bush. Since the Viet Cong weren't aware that the 1st Cavalry Division was employing behind-the-line patrols, they hadn't bothered to monitor potential landing zones or take any other countermeasures. Even so, it didn't mean that a soldier who was getting water or chopping wood might not see what was happening and report his discovery. The Viet Cong would soon learn to monitor the potential landing zones in their areas, since the airmobile division needed the open fields to insert their forces.

By changing their direction of movement, the teams gained a small advantage, a head start. Usually detachments' LRRP team leaders took the point and led their teams three hundred or so meters into the rain forest before establishing their first night-halt position. The six-man teams would then form a tight, wagon-wheel perimeter—each man facing outward to cover sixty degrees, their feet touching at the center—and using two-man shifts, two LRRPs would provide security while the other team members slept.

In the morning, prior to first light, the patrols would depart the overnight halt positions and begin reconnaissance. It would be a long first night, but the 1st Cav's LRRPs were officially in business.

CHAPTER ELEVEN

The first few patrols went off without any significant problems or incidents. The LRRPs were cautious and decidedly tense, since they had nothing to gauge the missions by, no yardstick to measure them against. The standard was still waiting to be set.

Christopher's Wise Owl and O'Brien's Moby Dick teams both completed their week-long reconnaissance missions and brought back information that G-2 requested,* as well as a few critical observations that would help fine-tune future patrol SOPs. Classroom instruction was one thing, but the knowledge that came from combat patrols was something else entirely.

Prior to missions, the team leaders would talk to their teams about noise discipline and why they needed to move slowly on patrol, but the lectures took on more significance once a column of a hundred or more armed enemy soldiers was observed walking down a jungle trail only a few yards away. Sudden movement or even a little sneeze could give the Americans' position away, and they would be forced to fight it out against odds that were always against them in terrain the enemy knew like his own backyard.

---

*Such as the presence of new enemy units, whether they were VC or NVA; what kinds of weapons they were carrying, their strength, direction of movement, etc.; were there new trails in the area, new bunkers or fighting positions. G-2 also wanted documents, because those could give hard data about enemy activities, units, assignments, and morale.

"Superman, John Wayne, and Tarzan could probably wipe out a hundred heavily armed Viet Cong, but unfortunately, they're not on any of the teams!" Kline explained during the premission training. "That's Hollywood. Vietnam is another movie entirely."

Day after day, during the week-long patrols, the LRRPs discovered better ways to pack and repack their equipment to keep it from making noise, and to shift it around so that it became more comfortable. Once those lessons were learned, the information was passed along officially in the debriefings or unofficially as the LRRPs helped one another.

As the teams patrolled they found ways to better negotiate the difficult terrain, and numerous other little things that could only be learned in the field, or maybe trying to get to the field. Some things you could only endure. But the field taught you the value of a clean rifle and a carefully hidden claymore, and that the sound of metal-on-metal carries. The field taught you the value of fear, because fear kept you alert and frequently stopped you from doing something stupid.

The monsoon season, which ran from October through April, brought heavy rain and wind, and the runoff from the coastal mountains swelled streams and rivers and flooded the coastal plains. Open field landing zones became mud sumps, and during the monsoon season, Vietnam often seemed in danger of floating away.

On an early mission insertion near Ba Le, in the coastal mountain range above An Lao, O'Brien's team and the rest of the five-helicopter formation were bounced around and pummeled by a really miserable storm. The sky was black and churning, and the lift-ship pilot fought to keep the giant tadpole of an aircraft in formation and, once, even to keep it from flipping over. The team helicopter rocked and rolled in the turmoil, much like the generation of soldiers in its belly, only they weren't keeping beat with any music; they were just trying to hold on without being slammed into one another or against the airframe.

The formation flew out over the South China Sea to make their turn back toward the coast and their mountain objective. They were fighting the weather every inch of the way; clearly, it was going to be anything but a comfortable night.

"Get ready!" the crew chief yelled to Lieutenant Hall, who tapped O'Brien on the shoulder and repeated the call as the coastal mountains grew in the open helicopter doorway.

There was no touchdown, just a low, gut-wrenching flare to a hover as the Moby Dick team jumped from the helicopter's skids and formed a quick perimeter while the aircraft lifted away, struggling against the weather to work back into formation.

The helicopter wasn't the only one struggling. Staff Sergeant O'Brien took the point and turned up the jungle-covered hill to get away from the landing zone and had to choose his footing carefully in the downpour. The rain was falling in heavy sheets and immediately drowned out the noise of the helicopter; anyone watching would have had trouble pinpointing the insertion area, let alone spotting the team on the jungle mountainside.

PFC Marvin Johnny Suggs, of Calhoun, Georgia, was the team's medic and maybe weighed all of 122 pounds soaking wet, which he was just then. Suggs followed O'Brien's lead, or tried to; like the team members behind him, it was a struggle to keep up with the team leader. Even in the heavy rain, mud, and despite the steep grade, O'Brien effortlessly worked his way up the hillside. At least it seemed that way to Suggs.

Missing a foothold in the dark, the medic slipped into the mud face first as the seventy-five-pound rucksack slammed into his shoulders and head, driving his face into the muddy hillside. A stream of brown runoff water pushed into his mouth and nose, and the medic spit it out.

"Shit!" he said to himself and quickly pulled himself up with the help of an exposed tree root and continued up after the team leader. It was like trying to climb a mud slide; mud clung to his knees and elbows where he fell, making his tiger fatigues look patched and worn. The green and black camouflage paint that had covered his face washed away, leaving only small patches that made him look like a pissed-off frog.

The team's rear scout didn't have to worry about trying to cover their trail, since the monsoon winds and torrential rains erased their tracks within moments. When Suggs reached the crest of the hill, he found O'Brien sitting on his rucksack beneath several trees that offered a little protection from the rain. O'Brien was studying the surrounding terrain and shaking his head. Between the dark black sky, multiple columns of rain storms, Suggs could see that the region consisted of heavily forested mountains and deep, lush green valleys. They were lush and green because of the water that fed down from the mountains, and Suggs imagined the valleys would soon begin to flood.

Somewhere in the seven-klick patrol area was supposed to be a Viet Cong battalion hospital. The LRRP team's job was to find it. Intelligence said it might be underground and that the LRRP team might very well walk over it without noticing it during the patrol. Looking around at the rugged terrain with its huge granite boulders and rocky crags and ledges, O'Brien concluded that the hospital would likely be in one of the valleys, burrowed into a mountainside, screened by the dense vegetation and other natural cover. And it would be well guarded by enemy soldiers who, like the LRRPs, would be hunkering down, trying their best to stay dry—and not having any luck.

Small streams of rainwater fell down his boonie cap, but O'Brien seemed unaffected. As Suggs pulled himself up, O'Brien turned and grinned at the soaked medic, who was breathing heavily.

"Doc, you one mountain-humping son of a bitch!" he said, opening a can of C-ration peaches while surveying the territory, as much as could be seen, which wasn't much at all since the cloud cover had dropped dramatically and left only an occasional hole. Even then, the heavy rain obscured any important view. "Might as well grab some chow," he added.

The team leader could sense Suggs's hesitation. He laughed.

"We're in the middle of a real motherfucker of a monsoon, and right about now, the VC are out trying to collect two of every kind of animal, to ready for the big-ass flood that's going to wash out everything in the province. In this wind and rain, you don't have to worry about anyone getting a whiff of your cold C rations. Just keep a nostril open for anyone coming toward us who smells of *nuoc mam* fish sauce. When you're done eating, you can keep watch for the others while they eat."

Suggs nodded, and the team leader turned his gaze and immediate attention back to the AO.

One by one, the remaining team members came up behind Suggs and began to spread out in a wagon-wheel perimeter while trying to find that perfect spot under tree limbs and branches, the one that would be free of rain.

"We'll set up a night-halt position here," he said to the assistant team leader, who took a quick look around and saw that the position O'Brien had picked out offered cover and concealment from the enemy at least. The weather, well, that was another problem. They were on the high ground, which would be good for keeping an eye on the valleys below and on the other hilltops—providing that the weather improved, which wasn't likely.

If anyone came up the same trail after them, they would have to struggle as the LRRPs had. Sneaking up on the LRRPs was out of the question, too. The six LRRPs eased into position and made themselves as comfortable as possible, considering the miserable circumstances. The wind was howling and ripping at the underbrush and tree limbs, while the monsoon rains turned the ground into muddy streams that slipped and fell back down the hillside. The sky was a roiling mass of black and gray clouds, and if the Viet Cong were not thinking about building an ark, then one or two of the Americans were considering it.

The team members weren't allowed to carry ponchos (too noisy), but a small piece of poncho liner was carried to keep the mosquitoes away in the field; all the LRRPs could do was pull their boonie caps down and huddle into themselves as the angry night closed in around them.

It rained seven days straight and threatened to go on longer. The team found trails and occasional fighting positions, but the latter were unoccupied, filled with rotting leaves and pooling or stagnant rainwater and an occasional frightened rat; the area was quiet. But the team had covered five to seven klicks, a considerable area considering the circumstances, and had little to show for it. Only the monkeys and birds, huddled in the treetops to survive the storm, watched as the drenched LRRPs moved on.

On the last day of the patrol, the morning they were to be extracted, O'Brien got a call saying the detachment couldn't get a bird out to pick them up. O'Brien rogered the message and relayed the news to the others, not that it came as much of a surprise; clouds and fog were hugging the mountains around them.

"They can't get a helicopter out to get us in this weather, so we wait," O'Brien said, taking a look around their perimeter. They were on the crest of a hill, tucked into a good location, the claymores were out, and the rain had obliterated any sign of their trail.

They'd have to divide up what was left of their rations, in case the cloud cover held and the rain continued. If that was the case, then O'Brien would move the team the next day, set up a new perimeter, establish commo, and wait some more.

However, by late afternoon the cold blanket of clouds was lifting itself skyward, and they were visited by more cold rain. But around five in the morning the team was told that the extraction helicopter was on its way.

The team's RTO rogered the call, and O'Brien told his people to get ready. As they pulled in their claymores, they watched the surrounding hillside while the rain pelted them mercilessly.

The extraction helicopter hovered briefly as the cold, wet, hungry, and tired LRRPs leaped aboard, glad to be in from the rain. As they were lifted out, O'Brien laughed to himself, thinking that at least the monkeys, birds, and Viet Cong were smart enough to stay out of the cold fucking rain; LRRPs were a whole different kind of animal. Judging from the expressions on the faces of the door gunner and crew chief, that animal wasn't high on their list of intelligent species.

CHAPTER TWELVE

Less than a week after the debut of the detachment's two LRRP teams, the 1st Cavalry Division launched Operation Pershing, an aggressive offensive designed to hammer the Viet Cong and North Vietnamese Army units within the Cav's area of operations and take away any sense of security the enemy might feel in the region.

As a result, the two teams were rotated for deployment among the division's three brigades, sometimes for periods long enough that the teams made temporary homes with the brigade elements.

Captain James didn't like the idea of having his teams loaned out or scattered and made his case for a unified, centralized command. However, the physical geography of the division area of operations didn't allow it. Not for efficiency nor for adequate response time in a rapidly shifting battlefield.

Initially, Team 1 went to the 1st Brigade at LZ English, which was working the An Lao Valley northwest of Bong Son and the rice-rich Bong Son Plain. The region was primarily coastal plains, but vast stretches of rain forest and dense jungle carpeted the mountain range known as the Tiger Mountains, which offered sanctuary and concealment for enemy activity in the area. Division intelligence said a number of Viet Cong battalions were known to be working the area, and VC tax collectors openly traveled from village to village to collect revenue for their cause, and VC assassination teams kidnapped and murdered police, village chiefs, and anyone opposed to their political views or goals. The VCs' own family members were not excluded from the organized terror.

Assassination was nothing new to the Viet Cong, nor their forerunners—the Viet Minh; it was viewed as an effective tool in their physical and psychological struggle against first the French then the government of the Republic and their American allies. The Viet Minh's Battalion 905 comprised thugs and murderers and was responsible for a series of brutal assassinations and other vicious crimes in the Saigon area. The Viet Cong continued the brutal legacy, employing similar tactics, and their teams had proved to be just as odious.

However, while the tax collectors and assassination teams could—with effort—be neutralized or rendered much less effective, the enemy regiments and divisions were another matter. For many years, the jungles and mountains had protected their base camps, and locating the enemy's safe areas and resupply depots was where the 1st of the 9th and the LRRP detachment came into play.

LRRP Team 2 went to the 2d Brigade to work the Kim Son Valley, which was southwest of Bong Son and just north of Phu My. The 18th NVA Regiment of the 325th NVA Division, which had previously worked the area of Quang Tri, a province north of Quang Ngai, was then conducting combat operations in the region. Assisting them were the local Viet Cong companies and battalions who viewed the area as a safe haven. And why not? Historically it always had been under their shadowy control, and neither the French nor the Japanese could dislodge them.

When they had taken hits or lost battles, the Vietnamese would use the jungles and mountains to regroup, lick their wounds, and plan new offensives to win their war, the protracted war.

The French had referred to these areas as the massif region, from the old French word that means massive. It is used to designate a large mountain mass. In Vietnam, this area was a compact group of mountains unconnected to any real range, as though it had sprung up on its own, as independent as the people who inhabited it. The massif region provided the Viet Minh—and, later, the Viet Cong—with hideouts and escapes so they could conduct a protracted hit-and-run war with success.

Gen. Vo Nguyen Giap officially set the strategy for North Vietnam when he said, "The enemy will pass slowly from the offensive to the defensive. The blitzkrieg will transform itself into a war of long duration. Thus, the enemy will be caught in a dilemma. He has to drag out the war in order to win it and does not possess, on the other hand, the psychological and political means to fight a long, drawn-out war."

His strategy was clear. Giap would use his forces to strike at the Americans and eat away at their resources and resolve, just as he had done against the French. In Asian warfare that strategy was nothing new. More than two thousand years earlier, the strategy had been defined by Sun-tzu, a Chinese warrior-philosopher who wrote, "When you do battle, even if you are winning, if you continue for a long time, it will dull your forces and blunt your edge; if you besiege a citadel, your strength will be exhausted. If you keep your armies out in the field for a long time, your supplies will be insufficient."

What Sun-tzu advised more than two thousand years earlier, Giap had reinforced from his own combat years, and although many in American uniform knew that as well, either from their own combat experience or their studies, the war was being fought from Washington, D.C., by some who apparently thought Sun-tzu was an animal farm in Florida, and that tactics and strategies applied only to pork-barrel politics and pay raises.

Operation PERSHING was intended to attack the enemy's sanctuaries and safe havens with relentless helicopter-borne operations and to force the enemy to fight when and where he wasn't prepared. The mobility of the helicopters was changing the way war would be conducted. The 1st of the 9th Cav was spearheading the reconnaissance aspects of the operation, the

LRRP teams adding a new edge to the job. The 9th Cav two-aircraft hunter-killer teams, utilizing the small OH-6 observation helicopter paired with either the UH-1B gunship helicopter or the new AH-1G Cobra attack helicopter, could cover remarkable distances and discover the enemy when he least expected it. The unit's motto was "The Boldest Cavalry The World Has Ever Known," and the airmobile teams and light infantry reconnaissance platoons were providing it with new meaning day after day.

On the ground, the LRRP detachment's initial long-range patrols were proving their worth to the brigades. Besides correcting U.S. Army maps, which were sometimes based on earlier French military maps, which were sometimes based on even earlier Japanese military maps, the teams were finding numerous hidden "runners" and well-concealed high-speed trails that the enemy used to move throughout the region. They also discovered bunker complexes and base camps, cache sites of weapons and rice, and jungle hospitals. The teams even monitored the comings and goings of enemy units and the occasional enemy general. Mission by mission, the LRRPs were providing vital pieces of the overall puzzle of the war in the region.

On one early patrol, they found a large jungle trail hidden beneath the dense foliage of trees that rose 120 feet in the air. The patrol leader waited before setting out sentries as he and the ATL studied the hard-packed orange trail and the strange lumps of dark material on one side.

"Elephant shit," the team leader said while the ATL took a closer look and wondered how in the hell he knew what it was.

"It means Charlie's packing heavy," he said before slipping back into the safety of the dense underbrush. "Probably mortar plates and tubes or 122s." The 122s were the 114-pound portable Katyusha rockets that could deliver a forty-pound explosive payload up to a distance of ten miles.

The Cav LRRPs set out claymore antipersonnel mines, and it wasn't long after that when they heard the noise of an enemy unit working its way noisily down the trail. With their weapons ready, the Americans watched from only a few yards away as the first pack elephant, led by a Viet Cong handler, turned the bend in the near distance. Moments later the others followed. On their backs, the elephants hauled the heavy base plates and rounds needed for 81 mm mortars, along with large .51-caliber antiaircraft machine guns. The number of elephants and heavy weapons would give the brigade a heads-up on a battalion-size force that was moving to attack.

"Call it in!" the team leader said to the RTO, who nodded and radioed in the findings. The cannon cockers or air force could handle the battalion, he decided. He knew the claymores would work against the Viet Cong, but they might only piss off the elephants, who might turn and stomp the shit out of the team.

Even Tarzan knew when it was better to watch from the trees and assess the situation before challenging the enemy with *aw-ee-aw* and swinging into action. Besides, in those mountains, Jumbo was working for the bad guys.

The warning from the LRRPs provided the necessary details to hit the Viet Cong and North Vietnamese Army soldiers hard where they lived and operated.

Air force B-52 air strikes were quickly diverted to the new target of opportunity, and a flight of bombers dropped loads of 250-, 500-, 750-, and 1,000-pound bombs from a high altitude onto the unsuspecting enemy soldiers. Each aircraft carried up to twenty-seven *tons* of bombs. The Viet Cong and North Vietnamese Army operated from deep tunnel complexes and natural caves. In the months ahead, the presence of B-52s ensured they would dig in deeper.

Those caught aboveground in the explosions and who somehow had survived them tried desperately to regroup but they became the target of the division's helicopter gunships, who struck from the air as the airmobile infantry platoons and companies were ferried in for bomb damage assessment (BDA) and mop-up operations. It would take weeks, if not months, for the Viet Cong to carry in the heavy weapons and supplies—not to mention to replace personnel—needed to mount another such attack. Despite the NVA's seemingly tireless efforts and the endless train of Soviet and Chinese weapons and supplies that flowed down the Ho Chi Minh trail, it still took a long time to replenish.

Soon it was clear to the enemy that in addition to the threat posed by the swift observation helicopters and by the devastating attack helicopters, he now had a new danger to consider. There wcre rumors that the Viet Cong referred to the LRRPs as ghosts. If that was true, the LRRPs were intent on proving that the ghosts in the highlands could lead them to the doors to hell.

CHAPTER THIRTEEN

The village was just to one side of the mud-color river and consisted of a handful of thatched huts, a pen or two for the pigs, several open-fire cooking areas where small wisps of smoke rose toward the sky, and a network of rice paddies carved into the nearby hillside of the coastal mountain range. The plain of paddies and community gardens supported the small hamlet and quite probably enemy soldiers who, Staff Sergeant O'Brien suspected, often came to call.

Two large water buffalo stood in the brown water of the paddies, their massive heads lowered, unconcerned with anything more than foraging. There were a half dozen scrawny chickens pecking out breakfast in no discernible pattern, and the scene was a bucolic picture of early morning village tranquillity as the inhabitants went about their morning rituals.

From their vantage point on a small brush-covered rise, the LRRPs could see the village clearly and identify those within view. A Viet Cong soldier, dressed in black pajama-like clothing, carried an AK-47 slung over his shoulder as he chatted with another soldier, who was adding wood to the fire.

A soldier wearing a khaki uniform walked from a doorway to one of the huts, yawned and stretched, and then walked around behind the hut to relieve himself.

O'Brien looked back to the rest of his team, pointed to his eyes, then back to the village, holding up one finger indicating he had one enemy soldier in sight. A few moments later his fingers were tallying up a new score. He stopped at fifteen or so, which was all he could confirm visually. It wasn't a village as much as it was a barracks site.

The rest of the team came on hyper alert, eyes and weapons on the brush to their front. The village was a garrison point, which meant the Viet Cong felt comfortable enough to make it their laager. Of course, it also meant they probably had guards posted to make sure no one disturbed their comfort. The Americans weren't sure where the guards were, but sooner or later the shifts would change, and the VC on duty would move back down to the village, which was when the LRRPs would get a fix on their positions.

O'Brien's team had moved in without notice, so after calling in their find, they remained in place to monitor the situation. The village sheltered a platoon-size element, at least; only time and monitoring would tell.

An hour or so later, a tired guard, shoulders hunched, made his way down the rise two hundred meters to their left as another guard walked out to take his place, which meant with little or no movement the LRRP team was in a good position to observe the village. However, although their position offered good concealment, it offered little in the way of cover. The area was all brush and grasses down in the small valley; the jungle started at the hillsides.

A small boy, no older than ten or eleven years of age, walked out to retrieve one of the two water buffaloes and lead him back toward the rise. The small boy and the lumbering beast seemed in no hurry as they walked toward the grassy area. But even at a good three hundred yards distance their direction and probable destination were unmistakable.

"We're going to have company," O'Brien whispered as the rest of his team brought their weapons up. If the six-man team had been on alert before, then their senses shifted into overdrive as the small boy and the animal walked on.

Two hundred yards.

One hundred yards and then seventy yards away. The large

beast suddenly stopped, lifted its massive head, and flared its mud-brown nostrils.

"Shit!" O'Brien said to himself, knowing what the beast was sensing even if the little boy did not.

When the boy tried to urge the animal forward, the water buffalo balked, which is when the boy began to suspect something was wrong. In a land of tigers, deadly snakes, and other feral animals and where a war always loomed just over the mountains, the boy turned his attention away from the animal and studied the brush in front of him. He couldn't see the Americans, but the beast's agitation told him something was wrong.

The boy turned back to the village, yelled, and finally caught the attention of someone in the village. When the guard on the rise to their left walked down to see what the yelling was about, O'Brien ordered the team to get ready to move out, which proved to be the right move. The soldier brought his rifle off of his shoulder and prodded the water buffalo forward.

When the angry beast stopped again, the guard figured that discretion was indeed the better part of valor and sent the boy back to the village for support.

O'Brien pointed in the direction he wanted the team to move, and after the first man slowly crept away, Jim Ross followed with the radio on his back. One by one, the others followed; O'Brien kept his rifle centered on the Viet Cong soldier until it was his own turn to escape. Before the Viet Cong were able to locate the spot from which the Americans had watched the village, the team had disappeared in the underbrush.

The enemy soldiers were shouting as the village bustled with excitement. Another soldier brought up a second water buffalo and, the second beast leading, a line of enemy soldiers pushed through high grass and brush. By then it was late afternoon, and the Viet Cong were having little success.

As the black curtain of night began to close in on the jungle, the first lights flicked on in the distance behind the LRRPs. Within moments other flashlights came on, and several dozen armed enemy soldiers were methodically working the surrounding areas. The LRRPs were being stalked.

"Gooks!" a team member behind him had whispered, watching the show while O'Brien quickly devised a makeshift strategy to counter the ploy. "Call it in! Let them know things are about to get tense," he whispered to his RTO as Ross radioed the team's situation back to An Khe.

The team leader knew the enemy soldiers would have trouble zeroing in on the team's location in the dark. If he could move his men quickly and quietly back to where the enemy had already searched, then the team might just keep the VC at a comfortable distance.

The trouble was the enemy soldiers were doing more than just moving forward. They were determined to flush the Americans out, using the same methods they used to hunt game. The Cav LRRPs were their trophies, and there was no doubt they wanted their horns.

Spreading out on line, they fixed their bayonets, and as their officer and NCO gave them the order, they moved out. They came forward slowly poking and probing the thicker underbrush where they thought the Americans might be hiding. The Vietnamese moved carefully, covering every inch of the black field in front of them before turning in a new direction. In the difficult spots, in the thick bamboo clumps or heavily foliated thickets the hunters chucked in rocks or fired single rounds.

"What are they doing?" the assistant team leader asked as O'Brien analyzed the scene. His response wasn't rushed or worried.

"Trying to get us to fire in places they're not willing to go into." Bamboo vipers and other deadly snakes like the banded kraits, common cobras, and even the huge king cobras frequently nested in thickets. Since the snakes were all active at night, hunting small rodents, frogs, lizards, and other snakes, the Vietnamese were none too willing to venture in. Since most, if not all, snakebite victims in Southeast Asia died horribly shortly after being bitten by a venomous reptile, the Vietnamese had good reason to be cautious. Snake venoms generally attacked the central nervous system, leaving the victims to claw and scratch for life as it slipped away. Besides, the single shots and rocks hitting an American or something metal like a weapon or canteen would be enough either to provoke a response or make a giveaway sound. *Nothing* in nature sounds like a canteen struck by a rock.

The LRRPs used the darkness to their advantage. While the enemy was concentrating his efforts on one site, O'Brien hurriedly had the team quietly slip away to another area, covering their trail as they moved.

When the hunters thought the team was hiding in a field of waist-high grass, they brought out the water buffalo again and drove them through the field. They well knew that the water buffalo were disturbed by the smell of Americans, and if they got a whiff of the Americans, the "boos'" black nostrils would flare in anger or alarm, then they would either charge the LRRPs' position or make enough noise to indicate the team was nearby.

The LRRPs hugged the ground, and the water buffalo lumbered away from them, unaware of their presence. It was all cat and mouse, and with each frustrating search, the Vietnamese were growing more tired of the game. But the stakes were about to be raised.

Visibly angry that they weren't having any success, the NVA officer in charge yelled at the line of Vietnamese and decided to change tactics: the hunters were split up into smaller groups and began working several areas at once. After that, the Americans had to be doubly careful. O'Brien kept his people moving, shifting their positions only when one group of VC was about to close in on the team and there was no other way to avoid detection.

As an enemy soldier spread out the underbrush in front of him, he never saw the rifle barrel that was pointed at his chest nor the team leader lobbing the grenade in a high arc. In the dark, no one would see it fall.

The explosion killed the soldier and wounded another behind him, but the Viet Cong concentrated their small-arms fire in the direction of the perceived threat, not knowing the Americans had once more slipped away.

A second round of grenades caught another cluster of Viet Cong who had tried to close the team in as the exchange of rifle and machine-gun fire brought on more confusion in the dark. The LRRPs were moving quickly toward a designated pickup zone and covering their escape as they ran.

The running escape was difficult enough, then the Moby Dick team had another problem: the team's radio, the backpacked PRC-25, couldn't penetrate the surrounding hills. When listening for the TOC's comforting ID, they heard only the rush of white noise.

Later, back at An Khe when they were retelling their story in the debriefing, the team's radioman offered a detailed technical assessment of the problems the teams were beginning to encounter with their equipment.

"We were being chased by the Viet Cong who were hot on our trail and more pissed than ever, and I can't get commo because of the hills. For a while there was nothing but white-noise static. The radios are shit!" Ross was more than a little pissed. Then he laughed, thinking about a joke he had heard during parachute training. Two new paratroopers getting ready for their first jump were told by their sergeant that there was nothing to worry about. That it would all go smoothly.

"You'll climb aboard the plane, get to about eight hundred to one thousand six hundred feet, and when you exit the aircraft, your parachute will pop open into a nice canopy," he explained. "But if they don't, then you'll deploy your reserve chute, and you'll land safely. When you do there will be a truck to bring you back to the company area." The two new paratroopers nodded nervously and climbed aboard the aircraft. When their turns came, they jumped. Their parachutes didn't open, so they immediately tried their reserve parachutes. But they didn't work either. As they were falling to their deaths the first paratrooper

Captain James D. James, the 1st Cav's first LRRP detachment commander, An Khe, Vietnam, 1966. (Photo courtesy of James D. James)

Staff Sergeant Patrick O'Brien and Specialist Jim Ross. (Photo courtesy of Patrick O'Brien)

Ross with the detachment's new mascot puppy, Lurp. (Photo courtesy of Jim Ross)

Pre-operational detachment, January 1967. (Photo courtesy of John Simones)

Left to right: Sergeant Dick Spina, Private Hup, Sergeant Rodolfo "Rudy" Torres, Corporal Klong, Sergeant Doug Fletcher, and Sergeant John Simones. (Photo courtesy of John Simones)

Patrol insertion. (Army photo)

Sergeant James "Spanky" Seymour and montagnard Corporal Blol. (Photo courtesy of Jim Seymour)

A detachment LRRP and an "entertainment specialist" in Sin City.

Cav B Model gunships firing on an enemy position. (Army photo)

A battlefield award certificate taken off the body of Major Nguyen van Khach after a LRRP ambush. (Photo courtesy of Jim Seymour)

The destroyed railroad bridge at Bong Son. (Photo courtesy of Jim Seymour)

Warning sign in the Bong Son telling travelers that the road is closed due to mines and Viet Cong activity. (Photo courtesy of Jim Seymour)

Staff Sergeant Rodolfo "Rudy" Torres, the detachment's multitalented NCO, who would come to signify the heart and soul of the Cav's LRRP/Rangers. (Photo courtesy of Rudy Torres)

LRRP Team Leader Jim "Spanky" Seymour (right) and Assistant Team Leader Lee Hennings (center) coming in from the field. (Photo courtesy of Jim Seymour)

said to the second one, "You know, I bet the truck won't be there either."

It was gallows humor, the kind soldiers loved to use when talking to their buddies. The trouble was, when it was happening for real, the soldiers didn't laugh with any humor. Usually it was nervous laughter and accompanied by swearing. It wasn't funny, just dangerously ironic, because while NASA and the U.S. government could put astronauts deep into space and were readying a mission to the moon, and while those same astronauts had radios that could reach Houston from deep in space, the army couldn't come up with a decent field radio that could reliably reach ten miles or so in a jungle combat zone!

When Ross was finally able to contact the exfiltration helicopter, letting the crew know the VC were right on their heels, he breathed a little easier. By then, the Viet Cong had figured out the LRRPs' ploy and were rapidly moving to intercept them. There were only so many landing zones within reach of the Americans, so the Viet Cong divided their force and raced toward them.

In the deadly game of hide-and-seek and perhaps the ultimate game of tag, you're dead, the long-range patrol made their escape to the sound of the ticks of the enemy's bullets hitting the awaiting hovering helicopter. Firing and moving, several LRRPs jumped into the waiting helicopter as the door gunners tore up the tree line.

"The truck's here," Ross said to himself, laughing at the absurdity of it all. "The truck's here!" But the extraction helicopter turned out to be carrying an incoming reaction force, and as the fresh grunts came out the open bay of the helicopter, O'Brien ordered the LRRP medic, Private First Class Suggs, into the aircraft. Suggs started to protest, but the team leader wasn't listening.

"We'll see you back at An Khe," he yelled to Suggs. "We're leading them back in." O'Brien motioning toward the grunts. Suggs wanted to stay with the team, but O'Brien wanted the 122-pound private first class on the outbound aircraft. The grunts had several medics with them, and he was giving Suggs a break. O'Brien was smart enough to know you took care of your people, especially your medics, since they were the ones you relied upon the most when everything went to hell in an instant.

Going to hell slowly was another matter and one that fired up the veteran soldier enough to draw heat from the higher-ups. During the early stages of Operation Pershing, the LRRPs were used primarily for intelligence missions, but occasionally they found themselves just outside the bases, acting as early warning observation and listening posts (OPs and LPs), gate guards, or pulling perimeter sweeps around the base camps. Some of the jobs were chickenshit, and the LRRPs knew it.

Staff Sergeant O'Brien didn't like it and said as much. The base-area security tasks could easily be handled by the grunts or military police, and besides, it was a waste of the team's talent and time. Immediately after mission debriefings, the teams needed time to repack their rucksacks and web gear; drawing grenades, claymores, rations, and ammunition and making sure everything was ready for the next patrol.

They also needed time to practice their reaction drills (aka immediate action drills), not to mention a little downtime. It wasn't a question of shirking duty or responsibilities, but the men of the detachment were drawing more than their share of the shit details and were made to feel like bastard children in the process.

You don't use hound dogs to fetch papers and don't abuse them without occasionally discovering that they have shit in your favorite shoes. O'Brien also wasn't too thrilled about the way the brigades treated his team, pushing them aside after the mission and using them for whatever until they were needed again. It was the "whatever" tasks that offended them the most.

O'Brien vented his frustration with brigade and with the detachment back at An Khe and was told the situation would be looked into. Shortly afterward, his team was back in the field on patrol, which satisfied O'Brien. But even then other problems had to be ironed out, such as defining the LRRPs' function to those who didn't understand the LRRP mission.

After one seven-day mission on which his team had monitored an unarmed twelve-man enemy force and returned to brigade with the information, a startled staff officer asked why O'Brien didn't ambush the twelve Communist soldiers.

"Excuse me, sir?" the team leader said incredulously. The postmission debriefing was usually for intelligence purposes, but at times it took on another function.

"I said, why didn't you ambush the enemy soldiers or capture them, especially since they were unarmed?"

O'Brien felt like chewing the dumb shit out, but offered a more diplomatic—and legal—answer instead. After all, a part of the debriefing process was devoted to filling in the gaps in the division's understanding of the situation, and this silly son of a bitch didn't seem to know a whole hell of a lot.

"What's our job, sir?"

"Excuse me, Sergeant?"

"I will, sir. But first, I'd like you to tell me what you think the job of a LRRP is, sir?"

"Are you being insubordinate, Sergeant?"

"No, sir, just enlightening," O'Brien said, not so sure he wasn't being just a little bit insubordinate. He *was* more than a little pissed off. Risking his life and the lives of his team members wasn't something he took lightly, and as a professional soldier, he resented the implication that he had somehow failed. "Our mission, as defined by the division commander, is to gather intelligence by not making contact with the enemy. I say again, sir, by *not* making contact with the enemy, by not engaging in battle unless we're discovered. We've been ordered to observe and monitor the enemy only, even when the silly little bastards are right in our rifle sights, so if you think it makes me happy to watch them walk by, and then walk away, then you have another think coming! The fuckers don't offer us the same luxury! Besides, sir, I know you're well aware how the NVA are also known for walking into friendly villages, taking rice and whatever other food they can find from the people, and then forcing them to serve as pack mules for the ammunition and equipment they're bringing into the province. Since these people weren't carrying weapons and only carrying equipment, it's easy to see they might have been forced laborers."

The staff officer started to respond, decided against it, and instead walked away, gritting his teeth. His clamped jaw and the pulsating veins in his neck accented the frustrated look.

"That went over well, Sarge," someone behind him said, and when the team leader turned he found the smiling face of his young radioman, Spec Four Jim Ross.

"Fuck him," O'Brien said, snorting and then pulling out a cigarette.

"You ever think about going into public affairs? You have such a way with words and people."

"Fuck you, too," O'Brien barked, only this time he was smiling as he lighted the cigarette, inhaled deeply, and then blew out a cloud of light blue smoke. "Come on. Let's go see if anyone else wants to hear the rest of what we have to say."

"You think they want to know about the terrain, trails, and the rest of the things that aren't on their maps?"

O'Brien shrugged. "It's what they pay us to do; hopefully they'll be smart enough to listen."

CHAPTER FOURTEEN

Since the detachment was new, the LRRP mission was yet to be understood by some within the brigades. In the "ironing out phase" there were a few other rough spots as well, rough spots that would make themselves evident, at times in dangerously frightening ways.

One of the first incidents occurred on a week-long mission in the densely forested mountains north of LZ Two Bits. On the third day out, O'Brien's team pushed through the underbrush of a small natural valley and discovered a well-used enemy trail, which in LRRP jargon was a "high-speed runner." It was maybe six feet across, of hard-packed soil, lying well concealed beneath hundred-foot-high trees.

Up in the trees, birds were talking to each other. A small creek paralleled the trail, and the setting was disturbingly tranquil, a Disneyland of the damned. Directly across from where the team crouched in hiding, Specialist Four Ross could see a fighting position, which they watched until they were certain it was empty. Farther down the trail, another bunker covered the opposite approach, and once again the team watched and waited. Ten minutes later, O'Brien moved out to inspect the site while the others covered his advance.

It was a major infiltration route and a good find. Ross watched as O'Brien studied the trail and then motioned the team back up the way they had come. When they had pulled back far enough, O'Brien explained his plan.

"We'll call it in and monitor it," he whispered. Heads nodded in unison, acknowledging the team leader's order. "There are sandal prints, and they're fresh," which was all the others, including Ross, needed to set the team in motion. While the RTO set up the long whip antenna on the PRC-25 to call in the discovery, O'Brien looked around for an optimal vantage point to watch over the route. From the small valley, the long whip antenna enabled them to reach the brigade's TOC; the short antenna proved useless. The trouble was, the long antenna made moving slow and difficult because it got caught in the vegetation, so after calling in the report, Ross quickly replaced the antenna.

O'Brien decided on a rock ledge on an adjacent hillside. The ledge offered both concealment and a place to monitor trail activity with the starlight scope. Good protection, too. The leaves and vines offered good concealment from the air, and natural breaks in the rain forest revealed segments of the trail. As good as it got.

As they made the difficult trek to the high ledge, climbing and pulling themselves up using roots and holds, several of the team were breathing hard. O'Brien was on point and leading the way, Private First Class Suggs thought, like a possessed Swiss mountain climber. Suggs was a few team members behind O'Brien, and he was convinced that by the time he reached the ledge, he'd find the team leader working on a good long yodel. Suggs's rucksack and aid bag were killing him, but he kept going until he reached the ledge.

Sure enough, O'Brien was sitting on his rucksack, surveying the view, and although he couldn't make out O'Brien's face, Suggs was pretty sure he was smiling. As the team began to settle in, planting claymore antipersonnel mines and fixing avenues of fire, Specialist Four Ross tried a commo check and was pleased when the TOC came in loud and clear. Red Stag relay was on the job. Their satisfaction was short-lived; the team leader motioned for the team to remain still as a line of NVA soldiers came into view below and continued on through the valley. Within minutes, they were gone, and the shadows of the late afternoon began to limit the view.

The team leader and assistant team leader each counted ten then verified the count with each other after the enemy soldiers had passed. Each count would make for a more accurate picture, even taking into account the "pucker factor," that could make one lose count, as might a sudden rush of adrenaline when the first enemy soldier was seen clearing a bend in the rain-forest trail. Then, when cool professionalism took over, the LRRP would pick up the count and compare it with his teammates.

Of course, there were a few like O'Brien, who picked up the count immediately as he carefully held his right index finger on the trigger behind his blackened rifle sights and breathed slow, steady breaths.

Fifteen minutes later, a second line of enemy soldiers appeared on the trail below, unaware that they, too, were being watched.

As evening set in, the rich greens and decaying browns of the rain forest began to fade to gray, and soon the jungle had been drained of all color, become little more than a puzzle of shadows. Night would bring total darkness unless there was a moon, and even then until it rose in the sky, the small valley would disappear. In the jungle, total dark was just that, a deep, intense blackness that hid myriad dangers, at times within an arm's reach. But maybe not that night.

The terrain was to the LRRP team's advantage. The NVA or Viet Cong wouldn't be able to sneak up on the team because of the site O'Brien had selected. If they tried in the dark, they would slip and slide and make enough noise to give the six Americans more than enough advance warning. It wasn't much of a haven for snakes either.

Guard duty would be rotated, each of the team members taking turns pulling guard. That provided adequate time for sleep, that is if the LRRPs could sleep at all. The jungle often made for a poor campground. Lines of ants and termites, poisonous spiders, scorpions, and centipedes made a home of the jungle floor, as did larger, more familiar reptiles and animals including a variety of lizards, venomous snakes, Asian leopards, tigers, civets, wild boar, monkeys, and elephants.

For the LRRP, guard duty was a battle against swarms of malaria-carrying mosquitoes. Just breathing brought some of the pests into the nose or mouth while others focused their assaults on exposed flesh. Then, too, during the monsoon season, the heavy rainfall soaked the LRRPs to the skin, and the elevation of the mountains and the proximity to the South China Sea made for a muscle-shivering chill that only the intense afternoon sun would diminish.

Surprisingly, after the climb up the hillside through the thick jungle and after the buildup and slow release of adrenaline, the team members were able to sleep in spite of these natural irritations and annoyances.

On the midnight shift Ross was huddled up with his small piece of olive drab poncho liner so when brigade called and told him to prepare to copy a message, the RTO said, "Red Stag relay. This is Moby Dick. Wait one." Then he ducked beneath his poncho with his SOI (the signal operating instructions code book), a black grease pencil, and a red-filtered flashlight along with the radio handset. Light and sound carried in the jungle, and Ross was taking the precautions necessary if he was to remain unobserved.

When he was ready to copy, he asked the caller to identify the day's code from the SOI. When that was done, Ross told the caller to transmit the message.

When the brigade TOC had finished, the spec four read the coded text back to confirm it. Satisfied with the confirmation, the young soldier began to translate the message.

Halfway through the process, Ross grew suddenly cold, sat bolt upright, and said, "Oh shit!" to himself. This can't be right, he thought. He then completed the translation and quickly went back to verify the message. He had been tired before, but he was wide awake and hyperalert by this time. The adrenaline was rushing through his body as he conducted the task. When that was done, he said, "Oh shit!" again and hurriedly switched off the flashlight, threw off the poncho liner, and then shook his team leader violently awake, startling O'Brien and the team member next to him.

"What?" O'Brien whispered, facing out and bringing up his rifle as he studied the dark jungle waiting for the enemy to come through the underbrush. Why else would the spec four wake any of them like that? O'Brien got his answer immediately as Ross passed him the message and repeated it almost verbatim. The obscenities were his own. They were colorful, descriptive, and appropriate considering the news.

"Brigade says there's an Arc Light planned in this area for 0600 and we need to get the fuck out of here," Ross explained. Arc Light was the code name for the air force B-52 (eight-engine bombers) strikes, which would drop massive amounts of deadly cargo over the Vietnam target site, then turn back for Guam.

"You verify it?" O'Brien asked. He looked at his watch. It was a little past midnight.

"I read it back, and they verified it," the RTO replied. "The bastards."

"Shit!" O'Brien grabbed the radio handset and called brigade to get them to cancel the air strike or change the target site, but he quickly discovered that it couldn't be done. The planes were enroute. Someone had screwed up and screwed up big time, a classic case of one service not knowing what the other service was doing. Maybe the air force had a target of opportunity too good to pass up, some rear-area "strategist" not really understanding the ground situation. How difficult could it be to move a few inches or so on a map?

A few inches or more on paper translated to a real effort in the Central Highlands, let alone anywhere else in country. Moving in the dark through enemy ground would normally be slow just for safety. Throw in the mountains and rough terrain, and the problem was compounded. Adding in the jungle and a time factor raised the stakes again. O'Brien didn't even want to think about the possibility that, for all its high-technology aura, bombing wasn't yet an exact science. If they were within the impact zone, white-hot, exploding shrapnel was indifferent to those who thought of themselves as "the good guys."

When the B-52s dropped their bombs, not all of them remained within the primary target areas. As if by shotgun blast, the main target would be taken out, but a few pieces of the "edges" might go along with it. So how far would the LRRPs really have to move and how big was the buffer zone? What about an "oops"? Earlier that month, a friendly artillery shell had accidentally hit a friendly position, killing seven Cav troopers and wounding four. Fuckups happened, and people died.

"Okay, then what about an extraction?" Moby Dick asked. The answer wasn't what he wanted to hear: weather prevented it; the fog was closing off any avenue of escape.

"Roger. Moby Dick out." O'Brien turned to the team. "Saddle up! We're getting out of here. *Now!*"

Even in the dark, the expressions on the faces of the team members showed confusion and concern, so O'Brien whispered, "B-52 strike." He shook his head.

"Where?" asked one of the members of the patrol.

"Right the fuck here!"

Within minutes, the claymores were pulled in, the rucksacks shouldered, and the team was ready to move out.

"Nice of them to tell us," Specialist Ross said. But O'Brien wasn't listening, his mind was on other matters. Five miles might be enough. Four would probably put them on the edge of the kill zone. One more would, he hoped, be a good buffer, provided they weren't delayed by a firefight with enemy. Five miles in six hours, through mountainous jungle, at night, in enemy territory.

Great. Just fucking great.

The going was slow as the team snaked its way down the hillside. From time to time, O'Brien would call a halt to listen for anything out of the ordinary; sounds of metal on metal that carried in the night, like a sling guard hitting against a barrel or maybe a loose canteen. The broken fog had prevented their extraction, but at least it muffled their movement. He also sniffed for wood or tobacco smoke, *nuoc mam* fish sauce mixed with wild garlic. When he was certain it was safe to move out again, he'd move the team forward.

Two hours later they were at the valley floor. They would need to follow the stream down the valley, paralleling the trail very closely for a while before the terrain allowed them to veer away.

The going got even slower. That the bunkers and fighting positions were empty the previous day didn't mean much that night, since they had seen enemy units moving along the trail throughout the day; the bunkers were, more than likely, occupied. Caution just made sense under those conditions.

The Viet Cong and NVA units moved from jungle base camp to jungle base camp with great frequency. An enemy battalion could be scattered over vast sections of countryside, moving in squads or platoons to avoid detection from the air, and coming together only to attack at their convenience.

For decades they had dug fighting positions and bunkers throughout the region. As the squads, platoons, companies, or battalions occupied the bunkers and base camps, separately or together, they would work on improving the existing fortifications, to ensure they always had a ready camp available. It was time saving and convenient and a natural part of the way they waged war. So it was safest to assume the bunkers were occupied; deadly stupid O'Brien was not.

The LRRPs approached the bunker sites with weapons ready, choosing their steps very carefully. If they were challenged, a sudden firefight would only complicate and delay the team's escape. That is, if they weren't pinned down, wounded, or killed.

O'Brien picked out his footing carefully as each of the men behind him moved cautiously, weapons ready, waiting for the cry of the inevitable Viet Cong sentry.

With a CAR-15, several M-16s loaded with only tracer rounds for a distinct psychological advantage, an M-79 grenade launcher for additional punch, and even a shotgun aimed at the bunkers in the dark shadows, surprise would be in their favor. If a groggy Viet Cong guard challenged them, it'd be his last.

But no order to halt came; the bunkers immediately next to the trail were empty. Clearly, no one expected Americans in the area. Two and a half hours of careful moving later they had gone perhaps two miles. Three, at best. There was no way they'd make safe ground at that rate.

O'Brien knew what he had to do. He turned his team toward the trail. It would break two of the unit's three cardinal rules, which were: one, stay off trails, and two, don't move steadily. A third rule had to do with never setting up a night position before sunset. In this case, it didn't apply, but they were sure as hell breaking the first two. The trouble was, there wasn't a choice. The trail was the fastest way to leave the area, also the most dangerous.

Calling a halt when he reached the edge of the trail, O'Brien peered out of the surrounding vegetation and waited a few minutes for his eyes to adjust. When he detected no movement, he stepped out on the mountain path. With little natural light filtering through to the jungle floor the staff sergeant was studying the shadows for movement.

"Follow me," he whispered back toward the team members. Hugging the edge of the trail, O'Brien moved out considerably more quickly, with the rest of the team in tow. He picked up the pace after they passed several empty bunkers. Their getaway was gaining momentum. It wasn't a run, but it was definitely a quick march, the kind the enemy used.

The Vietnamese knew the American units didn't move at night nor in that area, so if a sleepy Viet Cong or NVA guard noticed five or six soldiers moving quickly past his position, then he would assume they were comrades. At least that's what the LRRPs were counting on.

The tactic worked, and if O'Brien's pace count was right,

they had moved a considerable distance, only they still had a way to go. Ross nervously checked his watch and turned his head toward the sky that was up there somewhere above the trees. Way above the trees.

The B-52s would arrive on station so high above them there wouldn't be a warning of the pending Armageddon until the first bomb fell through the trees and blew earth and whatever was on it into oblivion. The crater left would be the size of a swimming pool, and the terrain immediately around it impassable.

At 0500, it would still be a while before the sun could work its way into the mountains, even longer before it could filter through the jungle's dense foliage and the maze of tree limbs. But total darkness gradually dissipated as though layer after layer of gray screen was being lifted as the morning moved on. Colors and shapes gradually began to return. In the distance, a bird screeched its morning call.

At 0530, O'Brien broke into a run urging the team to follow. "Move people! Move!" he whispered back to Ross and the others, but there was really no need. They were running as well and were right on his heels. It had become a foot race for survival.

They were breathing hard, and rivulets of sweat ran down their faces and necks, spreading beneath their armpits and lower backs in dark rosettes. Their rucksacks strained at their shoulders and slammed hard against their backs, but as the first murmurs came through the trees behind them, any immediate pain or fatigue was forgotten. O'Brien quickly turned the team off the trail and a few yards into the underbrush.

"Get down! Get down!" He was yelling, but the order was being drowned out by the bombing. Chicken Little had been an optimist. This sky was falling! Worst of all, it was his own chickens who were dropping the five-hundred-pound eggs.

The morning calm was swallowed by an immediate deafening roar, a rolling thunder that came from behind them and overtook the morning. The frightening explosions rumbled and roared as the team covered their heads and dug themselves into the earth as uprooted and splintered hundred-foot-high trees flew through the underbrush like giant spears. A roiling cloud of dust and searing shrapnel whooshed through the jungle as the ground rose and fell continuously, carrying and bouncing the LRRPs with it. They were jounced and battered, but there was nothing that they could hold onto for support. The continuous air strike was like an earthquake combined with a volcano's spewing hot metal shards and splinters.

The concussion and heat were unbearable, and the splintered bomb fragments that embedded themselves into the trees would hiss with searing sap when they hit.

The attack seemed to go on forever, and when the terrible noise suddenly ended and the earth stopped shaking, neither registered at first. The dust clouds were still rolling over the jungle, and the sudden silence was overpowering, unnerving. Clearly, birds and lizards, which normally provided the bulk of the morning chorus, were stunned.

When Ross, the team's radioman and newly promoted specialist four, rolled over and stared at the treetops he was puzzled. Whole and splintered trees spread horizontally above him, a lattice work of fallout and debris.

The trees had been thrown through the jungle and been precariously woven into the still vertical forest farther from the epicenter of the "storm." Some teetered, but it would have taken cranes to remove others. Stunned and dazed birds sat on denuded tree limbs, afraid to fly or to chirp. It was as if time had stopped briefly.

Nothing moved. The jungle was silent after Jim Ross rolled over, sat up, and shook his head while trying to get his ears to pop that he wondered if he had lost his hearing. It was so quiet that he thought he might be deaf until, running his hands over his uniform, and feeling around for wounds, he heard himself swear.

When he had found no gaping wounds or new orifices, Ross checked and rechecked the radio. He picked it up, dusted it off, and was surprised and relieved to discover that it was still in one piece. Like him, it was dirty and battered but still in working order. Barely.

He wasn't surprised to see Staff Sergeant O'Brien quickly on his feet, quietly surveying the scene while checking to see if any of his people were injured. Suggs, the team's medic, was examining several who were bleeding from minor cuts. Everyone had been shaken up by the concussion, but they all seemed otherwise okay.

The backs of their uniforms were covered with dirt and shredded leaves; the fronts of their green-and-black striped Tiger fatigue uniform seemed now totally out of place.

"Some wake-up call!" Ross yelled. O'Brien nodded. It would be, for the people doing the tactical coordination, the yahoo at brigade who put the team in the area, the LRRP detachment, and the team that was lucky enough to have survived.

The radio was crackling with traffic. Brigade was in a frenzy, calling for the team's status.

"Uh-uh," O'Brien said, shaking his head when the RTO retrieved the radio's handset and started to respond to the request. "Give them a few minutes. Let them sweat it a bit."

Somebody had screwed up, and it damn near cost the men of the team their lives. The army always said that the mission was more important than the men, and their little adventure that morning seemed to emphasize the army's point.

After the team was extracted and made the long flight back to the company area, O'Brien wouldn't wait until the debriefing to let them know just how pissed off he was. This was a coordination issue where one service probably hadn't bothered to let anyone know what it had in mind until someone had bothered to check to see if there were any soldiers in the area.

O'Brien knew that Captain James and Lieutenant Hall would chew the bastards out, and he hoped he would get a chance to witness the bloodletting. If he could hear the action through the ringing in his ears, he might even enjoy it. Hell, he said to himself. If my hands would ever stop shaking, I might even applaud!

CHAPTER FIFTEEN

By late February, the little victories the Cav was scoring in and around An Lao, Kim Son, the Bong Son Plain, and An Khe were becoming evident. The detachment had ten or fifteen successful missions under its belt, targeting enemy concentrations and movement, and had turned over its finds to the 1st of the 9th, which quickly capitalized on the discoveries. Some patrols resulted in contact, which, in turn, shortened the missions and shortened the surprise factor the patrols provided.

Taking their licks, the Viet Cong were becoming aware that the enemy had deployed LRRP teams, but the VC were still uncertain how to respond to that. They were used to nibbling at Americans in bases and in large noisy groups trudging through the jungles and to hiding from American helicopters. At first, they didn't have an answer to the new threat.

If the Viet Cong units couldn't move freely in the region and if the division maintained the pressure on their base areas, then the Communists couldn't coordinate a sustained campaign. So the VC began to track the patrols, a tactic they began by positioning soldiers to monitor likely landing zones for the American LRRP teams. Once alerted by the LZ watcher, the VC would return with a sizable force to try to overrun them.

The difficulty with that plan was that the 1st Cavalry Division's Operation Pershing was in full swing and achieving its objective with surprising results. So when Maj. Gen. John J. Tolson, III, took command of the division, he kept up the pressure, which kept the enemy constantly on guard and unable to carry out his strategems.

Tolson, the former commandant of the army's aviation school, understood the importance of airmobility in combat operations just as he appreciated the value of reliable intelligence. In one decision, he set another plan in motion that would add to the Viet Cong's worry. He gave the go-ahead to expand the small LRRP detachment, to bring it up to a company-size unit. He placed the company under the control of the division G-2, which was expanding its role in the division's overall battle plan.

Unfortunately, Captain James was on R & R when the order for expansion came down. Upon his return, he discovered that a blanket call had gone out for qualified infantryman, radio-telephone operators, and medics, and that the detachment size had doubled as the recruiting process shifted into high gear. The trouble was, he wasn't driving when the detachment picked up the speed. Neither was Lieutenant Hall, who was stewing about the situation.

Both had mixed emotions about the sudden expansion and the blanket method of recruiting 1st Cavalry troopers to become LRRPs. So far, the unit had been successful, in part, because of the careful selection process, and the zero casualty rate to date seemed to echo that format.

Zero was a statistic they were proud of. But the war was expanding so fast that something had to give. There were over 385,000 U.S. personnel in Vietnam, and nearly 9,000 more arrived each month. The North Vietnamese Army was sending just as many men south, so the conflicts and battles would only become more frequent and more intense.

The war was growing, so the growth within the detachment was inevitable. James knew it, so did Hall. The army wasn't a democracy. It only protected one. They'd take a new reading, get their bearings, and continue the mission. It was what soldiers did, professional soldiers anyway. If anything, the detachment's upgrading was the ultimate compliment. If the long-range patrols hadn't been working, the detachment wouldn't have been expanded. If it hadn't worked, James would have found himself out of a job.

There weren't enough available slots to provide Recondo training to all of the new arrivals, so the company had to rely on the unit's own training program to bring them up to snuff. Division was throwing scores of new arrivals at them. From just a few dozen, the unit strength jumped to close to seventy almost overnight. The roster grew again when Lieutenant Hall brought in the first dozen or so of the Rhade montagnards he had recruited in Pleiku. Of course, the dozen montagnards also brought their families, livestock, and other possessions, which were stacked high on the floor of the large Chinook helicopter sent to fetch them. By the time the Chinook touched down in An Khe, the metal floor of the helicopter was a mess. The crew chief was steaming, along with the pig and duck shit. But the montagnards were hard-looking dudes and the thought of telling them to clean up the mess quickly passed.

Since the montagnards were tribal, they set up a hamlet compound just outside of An Khe. When it came to their possessions, the montagnards had brought everything from cooking pots and wicker baskets to pigs and chickens. Hunters by inclination, slash-and-burn farmers by necessity, the montagnards never showed much interest in city life and struggled to hold on to some of their more traditional ways. The pigs and chickens were their walking C rations.

Lieutenant Hall, Doc Suggs, and a few others helped the montagnards, erecting GP medium and GP small tents, setting up barbed wire for their perimeter, and even helping them dig a twenty-five-foot-deep, five-foot-wide well for drinking water. Given the thick, orange clay and blistering heat, the well project was no easy task. Toiling side by side, a short, sturdy Rhade tribesman and the LRRP XO completed the job and afterward celebrated the work.

The montagnards rounded up a water buffalo, sacrificed it

formally, and then cooked it over an open fire, offering the eye-balls and brains to Hall, who ate along with his hosts. The American work crew were adopted into the tribe, accepting metal bracelets and the thanks of the montagnards, which included a great deal of rice wine.

By the time the lieutenant and the others made it back to the company area, sleep seemed like a reasonable idea. Waking up though might take some doing.

With their compound erected and their families safe, the Rhade were ready to begin working with the Cav's LRRPs. Placed into a modified training program, the air cavalryman soon learned the value of these latest arrivals. The dozen or so Yards were seasoned veterans, most in their late thirties or older, who understood the tactics of war better than most West Point strategists. But for all of their backwoods manner and Asian hillbilly appearance, the Yards were fierce fighters, with a loyalty that was unquestionable. Still, they had to be introduced to the LRRP concept and understand how the Cav patrols operated in the field and, most important, their roles in the drama. When they were ready to take their place in the detachment, two Rhade would be assigned to each team, giving the patrols an interesting new flavor.

The Vietnamese recruits, who arrived shortly afterward, lived in An Khe and quickly went about getting adjusted to the region.

The Vietnamese and montagnard scouts were quickly integrated into the company's operations. With two Yards assigned to each team, the team leaders quickly realized that utilizing one as a point man and the other as a rear scout reduced the likelihood of coming up short on sudden encounters with the enemy because it would take precious seconds for the enemy to understand they were not VC but Americans.

Any hesitation at all would be to the advantage of the LRRPs and could very well mean the difference between living or dying. A six-foot-two-inch, blond, square-jawed American coming out of the dense underbrush or elephant grass was an instant target; a Vietnamese or Yard carrying an AK-47 would confound or confuse a Viet Cong or NVA sentry or point man.

Of course, there was always a question of the loyalty of the Yards and Vietnamese lingering in the back of the LRRPs' minds even though they had been assured that the Vietnamese and montagnards would stand with them. Assurances aside, there were always lingering doubts, and there was talk among the team members on what they expected from the Vietnamese and Yards. It was well known that the Viet Minh, who fought the French a decade earlier, had infiltrated the ranks of most colonial organizations.

"They're on our teams, and we'll utilize their skills," Staff Sergeant O'Brien explained to several critics.

"How do we know they won't turn if things get tense? Maybe *Chieu Hoi* over to Uncle Ho?"

Chieu Hoi, "open arms," was the amnesty program set up to rally disgruntled Viet Cong and NVA soldiers over to the South Vietnamese cause. While some Viet Cong and NVA soldiers honestly came over eagerly, others were plants, infiltrating the program to get as much information as possible before returning to their old units. If GIs viewed them with suspicion, then it was because they all knew the stories of the turncoats who, while walking point, walked off from the unit, along with the unit's SOI and all of their codes. An SOI, the signal operating instructions for radio transmissions between units in the field and the tactical operations center, contained the carefully constructed codes that prevented the enemy from exploiting our communications and compromising operations.

"We don't now, but we'll know when it happens. If it happens," said O'Brien.

"Yeah, but what if they turn?" the critic asked again.

"Then you shoot their asses. The point is, I don't think we'll have to. Some of these people have been fighting the Communists for a hell of a lot longer than we've been here. The North Vietnamese and Viet Cong hate their guts, and the feeling's mutual.

"If it helps you any, the Special Forces have been using the Yards for years, and they seem to be pretty impressed with their loyalty," he said. "Like anybody else that comes to the unit, they'll have to make the cut. I don't give a damn what kind of credentials they come with. They prove themselves or they don't. Either way, we'll know."

Throughout the month, the Vietnamese and Yards pulled missions with the teams, and in short order, they proved to be better than anyone had guessed or expected. They could read trails very well, and they had an unnerving familiarity with the jungle. One montagnard, an older sergeant, was nothing short of remarkable; he could fieldstrip and fire any weapon placed in front of him, could silently move through the brush like he had a sixth sense. For reasons never explained, he hated the Communists, and for reasons that were becoming evident, he didn't seemed too thrilled about Vietnamese in general.

A corporal named Klong had quickly earned several of the Americans' respect by volunteering to be his team's point man. During his first mission, he ordered the team to halt, pulled out a handmade knife, crept back toward the confused American who was following him, and killed a six-foot cobra that was poised to strike. A private named Hup was rapidly gaining respect as well. The Vietnamese and montagnards were working out fine, although many of the LRRPs favored the montagnards.

At least they came with experience, which couldn't be said of the new GIs, a problem which was quickly corrected by Lieutenant Hall, Staff Sergeant Torres, Staff Sergeant Kline, and the other NCOs, who formalized and better defined the in-unit training. Just because division was shoving new people into the company didn't mean standards wouldn't remain high. It just made the job more difficult.

Of the twenty to thirty U.S. recruits who began the next training cycle, fewer than five made it to graduation. But with the new graduates, the detachment could field several new teams, which brought a new problem to light. Who would lead the new teams?

The obvious initial choices came from qualified members on existing teams, and no one argued about the decision. Any concern raised was solely a matter of personality.

Sgt. John Simones, the former Marine who had served with the Corps' Force Recon, was selected to become a new team leader as was S.Sgt. Jim Burton, a newly recruited NCO who came to the LRRP unit with quiet confidence and real soldiering skills. Burton proved his value to the detachment early. He was good in the field and more than a few of the LRRPs thought that he "knew his shit," which was a high compliment in colloquial GI. His promotion to team leader was well received.

Of course, with the new promotions came celebrations. At least for the LRRPs who were on stand-down. The unit policy was to give the teams in from the field a three- to five-day standdown, or break. Those without duty partied. While many went off to celebrate, Staff Sergeant O'Brien and a few others, older NCOs, declined an offer to go into Sin City for the party that followed.

"You coming, Sarge?" asked Suggs. The veteran NCO slowly shook his head.

"Naw. I think I'll stay here. I've got a few things to do," the staff sergeant said, heading back to his hootch. O'Brien's hootch was actually a sectioned-off portion of a platoon-size tent that offered him a reasonable amount of privacy. As a staff sergeant, he merited the space, and for a platoon sergeant, the privacy was necessary, but not always for the reasons lower-ranking soldiers expected.

"You can do them later, Sarge. Come on. It's going to be a good time."

O'Brien knew it probably would be but decided against it anyway. He could see the medic wasn't about to leave without an explanation so the team leader gave him an honest one.

"Suggs," he said. "It's like this. I can't go into town and drink with you guys because I'm your team leader. . . ."

"Yeah, so?"

"So, you guys respect me now—at least I think you do—but if I get falling-down drunk with you or just plain stupid or sloppy, then you might lose that respect. You might begin to question whether I'm up to the job."

The private first class started to protest, but the staff sergeant waved him off. "Don't take it personally, Suggs." The idea came with the old brown-boot army. Look, you guys have a good time and be careful."

Suggs nodded and said he would, realizing there was probably something to what O'Brien said, but not much. Most of the people in the detachment looked upon O'Brien as a latter-day Daniel Boone or Davy Crockett, a larger-than-life *real* woodsman, snake eater, and fighter, something that his prowess in the field confirmed. Everyone knew O'Brien had his shit together and that he was a damn good team leader. He was also friendly enough and helpful to anyone who was smart enough to listen to what he had to say. But Suggs realized that O'Brien had always maintained a certain professional distance, and, perhaps, an emotional one, too. War did that to men, and it was something every combat veteran soon came to understand.

It was a lesson the detachment on the whole was about to learn.

CHAPTER SIXTEEN

The call came prior to sunset, and the company's tactical operation center was closely monitoring the situation. S.Sgt. Jim Burton's team had been monitoring a trail junction in an AO just outside of Kon Lak, where the highland jungle paths were buzzing with activity. The Viet Cong were on the move.

The patrol had been deployed to see what the VC were up to, and the rocket or mortar teams that could be seen interspersed among the lengthy lines of enemy soldiers told them that Charlie was massing for an attack, moving on Camp Radcliff.

The Cav's main base camp, with its rich and vast assortment of aircraft, was always a favorite target for the Viet Cong, but this time the LRRPs served as its early warning system. And, from the size of the VC force on the move, this was to be more than just another quick shelling.

Initially, the mission seemed straightforward enough. Do a thorough recon of the AO, find out if anyone was in the area, and report the findings.

On insertion, Burton and the others had found the first flaw in the program when they discovered numerous well-used small paths and trails right off the LZ. When the junction they decided to monitor yielded heavy traffic and busy bunker complexes, it didn't take long to realize that finding the enemy had been the easy part; reporting back might take some doing.

Like streams of rainwater flowing together to form a dangerous current, the enemy units were joining on the small paths and trails, converging for their strike. To the patrol's dismay, the VC were heading straight for the team's location. And the LRRPs had given up trying to keep an accurate count on the 122mm rocket launchers and heavy weapons they saw; instead they concentrated on more immediate concerns like remaining well hidden. The picture in their jigsaw puzzle was coming together early.

An encounter with a VC platoon meant five-to-one odds; one with a company or larger element meant Alamo odds if the LRRPs couldn't find a way out of there. Remaining hidden and concealed was the team's only real course of action, but as the enemy activity mounted, hiding and blending in was becoming increasingly difficult for the Americans. The AO was swollen with enemy soldiers, things were about to get tense, and the situation reports sent back to the company TOC acknowledged that. As Camp Radcliff came on high alert, the LRRP TOC was monitoring the team's situation.

Everyone knew that if the team wasn't pulled soon, it would be discovered, so Captain James ordered the extraction, giving the thumbs-up for the C & C crew to crank the bird. Grabbing a helmet, rifle, and LBE, James raced with the crew to the helicopter and got ready for takeoff.

As the aircraft came to life, the company commander locked and loaded his rifle, placed it on SAFE, and set it down beside him. The crew chief handed him his flight helmet, and James plugged into the helicopter's communication system, listening to the pilots' checklist and commands as the C & C bird prepared for takeoff. Within minutes, the helicopter had maneuvered toward the flight line, dipped its round OD nose, and taken off in a climbing run over the camp's barbed-wire perimeter.

The pilot was monitoring the team's transmissions as soon as the aircraft was airborne and gaining altitude over the green and brown countryside below. At times like those, James always felt better being in the sky over the teams just in case things got nasty. In the TOC, there was little anyone could do but listen to the mission over the radio speakers; in the C & C helicopter, he could offer a discerning eye in the sky and a quick evacuation, if needed.

A gunship had joined the C & C bird as an added precaution,

since the aerial artillery offered more precise protection for the patrol on the ground. The aircraft would approach from high altitude so the *whop*ping of their blades would be muted by the jungles below. As soon as they heard the choppers, the VC would use nearby cover to hide their activities—which meant they would take to the same kinds of hiding places as the LRRPs had, which could also mean a showdown upon discovery. But, if the Viet Cong had known the Americans had a long-range reconnaissance patrol on the ground, this close to them, then they hadn't shown it.

Before a face-off could occur, the team attempted to slip away from the enemy tide. When it became evident that they couldn't evade without giving themselves away, the LRRPs were left with only one option.

With nowhere else to go and the fight inevitable, the LRRPs bought some time by waiting until the last possible moment before initiating contact. As always, the first few minutes of the sudden firefight would cause the confusion they would need to run. It would provide just a small window of opportunity for escape but, hopefully, enough to make the break successful. One by one, just as they had drilled and practiced, each of the LRRPs fired into the enemy line in turn, then peeled away, dashing toward safety as the next man in line followed his lead. That made for a steady, sustained stream of small-arms fire punctuated by burning orange tracer rounds.

The Viet Cong were spread out in the immediate area, so they recovered quickly from the patrol's attack. They correctly assessed the situation and immediately began pursuit. They knew the 1st Cavalry Division was employing long-range patrols, and the amount of small-arms fire, coupled with the lack of artillery support and no follow-up attack confirmed that. So they came after Burton's team in force. The staff sergeant and the other patrol members could hear squads of enemy soldiers racing through the bush, trying to outflank them, while others followed their trail. To deter the ploy, the Cav's LRRPs fired into the brush and hurriedly changed directions, repeating the strategy each time the Vietnamese Communists adjusted to the changes and resumed their advance.

James called for an extraction, telling Burton to head toward the designated pickup zone. It was going to be a "hot" extraction, and like most military euphemisms, that was not precise enough to convey what was really going on. "Hot," like the term "friendly fire," didn't sound as ominous as the danger it actually implied. "Blistering" might have better summed it up; "terminal" couldn't be ruled out.

Burton's six-man team put up a good fight, but their makeshift defense would crumble if they couldn't get away from the overwhelmingly superior enemy force. Besides, the team had already accomplished its primary mission, which was to find and pinpoint the Viet Cong's location and determine their number. "A whole shitload of them all around us," might not be a militarily acceptable response, but it applied.

"Head to the Papa Zulu. We're coming in to get you," the pilot relayed as the aircraft began its banking turn. Burton rogered the transmission, saying the team would be there. Any emphasis was added with the sound of intense small-arms fire in the transmission's background.

Timing was the key to a hot extraction. For the six-man team "timing" meant trying to get to the pickup zone before the enemy and then holding out until the chopper arrived; to Captain James and the C & C helicopter crew it would mean flying into the fiery mouth of the dragon, flames and all.

From his vantage point above, James could see that the jungle foliage was being ripped and torn by the heavy volume of small-arms fire on the ground and the helicopter gunship's minigun and rockets. Green and red tracers were crisscrossing the jungle as the Viet Cong exchanged fire with the six LRRPs. Small, bright orange explosions and red and green tracers left their marks against the green and brown jungle, and a light blue-gray haze of gun smoke drifted up above the trees. The colors of jungle combat were vivid but disjointed, and their impression left a considerable impact on anyone who had viewed it long after the firing had stopped.

A small fire had erupted in the knee-high dry grass across the pickup zone, upwind. Either the small-arms fire had caused it or the Viet Cong had set it to keep the helicopters from landing. The column of angry black smoke served as both a beacon and an omen to the approaching helicopters.

For the extraction, the C & C helicopter would touch down only for a few seconds as the patrol scrambled for its open bay. The helicopter crew chief and the door gunner would offer protective fire on both sides of the pickup zone, working the tree line and possible ambush sites. If all went well, the team would hurriedly dive aboard as the pilot pulled pitch then took off over the trees. The helicopter would more than likely take fire and hits, and if the hits hadn't disabled the helicopter, then the pilot would fight to bring the aircraft limping back while a B-52 bomb strike would be ordered or diverted from another target to the new target of opportunity. If all went well.

Another very real possibility was that the rescue helicopter would be blown out of the sky by an enemy rocket-propelled grenade, a shoulder-fired missile that would explode upon impact and send the helicopter tumbling toward the ground. To effect the rescue, the helicopter had to hover, which meant for a few, brief moments, it would be an easy target for even the worst RPG gunner, let alone someone with a calm, steady hand. And the VC had plenty of soldiers with steady hands.

"Pop smoke!" the helicopter pilot said to the LRRPs as he began his descent over the jungle. Seconds later, a lazy plume of purple smoke from the burning smoke grenade marked the team's position.

"I identify grape," the pilot said. Burton confirmed the color. The Viet Cong had sometimes tossed out captured smoke grenades to trick or confuse medevac helicopters, drawing them into ambush.

"Get ready," the pilot yelled. "We're going in."

As they made the approach, the Viet Cong below were firing up through the trees at the aircraft. During the low-level run, the distinct *ticks* of machine-gun bullets tearing through the thin shell of the aircraft could be heard. As the aircraft flared to a hover, it began receiving more fire. And hits. Still, the pilot held the aircraft steady and brought it to the fading purple smoke.

"Come on!" the crew chief yelled as several of the team members raced out to board the helicopter, leaving Burton and the Yard scouts to cover their exit. Somewhere to their flank, a larger .51-caliber antiaircraft machine gun was spewing a line of fire in their direction. Several of the rounds found their target.

As the craft started to turn to make its escape, the unmistakable whine of a helicopter in distress tore across the small PZ. Warning lights on the helicopter's console said there were engine and transmission problems. The pilot was fighting the controls as the helicopter shuddered and shook violently. The aircraft bucked, yawed, and zoomed with power one moment, and then there was none.

"Taking fire! Taking fire! We're going down!" the pilot shouted to James and then back into the radio called, *"Mayday! Mayday! Taking fire! Taking fire! Going down!"*

During their training, helicopter pilots are taught to safely autorotate their aircraft to the ground without power. Of course, training conditions never included live machine-gun and rocket fire. The realities of combat are seldom duplicated in training.

The LRRP commander and those aboard the floundering aircraft braced themselves for the crash. The military helicopter is a very utilitarian design, so there were no seat cushions for comfort, no roll bars, or heavy frame. Only a thin metal shell and fiberglass covered the basic frame, electrical wire, and mechanical guts. There was little to absorb the shock of a crash. Then, too, there was a lot of highly explosive JP-4 jet fuel in the helicopter's fuel tank that, if ignited, would turn the aircraft into an instant fiery ball.

If they somehow survived the crash, and if the helicopter didn't explode into a fireball, and if they could climb out of the twisted wreckage and get their bearings, they'd still have the battle to contend with.

Wars stop only for the dead.

CHAPTER SEVENTEEN

There was a resounding crash with an unnatural screech of metal and fiberglass wrenching and shearing. The helicopter's skids crumpled, leaving the rounded nose and underbelly to burrow to a violent stop. As it skidded, the tail rotor dug a trough into the orange soil before finally bending and breaking against the hard-packed earth.

Surprisingly, though, the Huey helicopter held together. Not that it mattered since it wasn't going anywhere anyway. At least not under its own power. For all of its former value as an aircraft, the crippled Huey now was little more than a stationary target.

When it slammed into the ground, Captain James, like the others, was thrown back hard against his canvas and aluminum seat and the wall of the helicopter bay. He was jolted and jarred by the crash but was up immediately, doing a quick inventory, while ordering everyone out of the aircraft.

"Let's go! Come on! Let's go!" he yelled, helping the LRRP team members to their feet while keeping a steady eye on the wood line the patrol had left only minutes before, and from which the Viet Cong would follow up their assault like wild dogs rushing in for the kill. The momentum was theirs.

The crew chief and door gunner were carrying their M-60 machine guns and as many linked belts of 7.62 ammunition as they could while following the LRRPs' lead. The Viet Cong weren't their only problem. The smell of leaking JP-4 fuel and smoldering wire insulation permeated the crash site. It was obvious that the Communists' incoming burning-green tracer rounds could easily ignite the leaking fuel. No one had to be told of the consequences if they didn't get away from the downed helicopter. Most of the air crews had witnessed such fireballs, and most veterans had even loaded the charred remains of the dead into body bags. "Crispy critters" they were called because what remained no longer looked human.

"Set up a perimeter!" the captain yelled, knowing that the crash site had just become the Viet Cong's primary target. Even as the survivors had hurried to form a makeshift skirmish line, the first line of Viet Cong came out of the trees, firing. It was time to finish off the Americans.

"Fire!" James ordered, although he really didn't have to as LRRPs and the helicopter crew selected their targets and knocked them down in a well-aimed, concentrated volume of small-arms fire. The patrol's M-79 blooper man was dropping the explosive 40mm rounds into the pockets of Viet Cong to help to thwart the attack. If the crash didn't bring on concern, then the ground attack did. The volume and treble of the situation had just jumped a notch or two higher.

As the struggle for survival unfolded, the patrol's RTO was providing continuous sitrep to the company TOC personnel in An Khe, who were, in turn, coordinating the quick reaction force and air support for the stranded survivors. The status on the ground was changing rapidly as could be heard in the fury of the battle coming in over the RTO's reports. The transmissions from the team's PRC-25 were coming in broken at times, so the RTO quickly threw up the long whip antenna to correct it. It was not the time to lose radio communication.

If the situation sounded confused over the radio, through the noise and pitch of the battle, to those in An Khe, then the story was easier to understand from the gunship pilot already high above them. The Viet Cong were trying to overrun the crash site, but the survivors were holding them back.

"Coming in hot. Keep your heads down!" the pilot said almost casually as the RTO passed along the reply. The helicopter gunship was roaring in for a rocket and minigun strafing run. Thousands of 7.62 machine-gun rounds from the minigun mounted on the nose of the gunship tore into the jungle in just seconds, and the exploding rockets sent up flames and shrapnel in deadly patterns.

Any notion of an immediate victory that the Viet Cong might have had was clouded by the gunship's runs as it made passes on target time and again. The cavalry hadn't arrived, but one of its gunships had. Then the small battle began literally to heat up: the small grass fire that had sprung up on the edge of the knee-deep grass of the dry meadow turned into a fast-moving, rising wall of flames. A steady breeze fanned the fire, and just ahead of the burning grass, rats, field mice, snakes, and insects scurried, slithered, and flew in a smaller race for life.

James studied the fire and the direction of the wind, then motioned the survivors away from the encroaching flames while he and Burton covered their escape. If the gunship runs hadn't dissuaded the Viet Cong, the ten-to-fifteen-foot flames from the brushfire certainly did. Any window of opportunity for overrunning the Americans was quickly closing.

Maneuvering to safety again, and using the smoke and flames to cover their move, the survivors maintained a successful defense in the large field. Such natural fields or breaks in the jungles and rain forests were sometimes just low points in the terrain, water retention areas that became extended ponds during the rainy seasons. In the dry season, the sun evaporated most of the water, leaving behind a sea of weeds and grasses. As the season progressed, the weeds and grasses got to be waist high before they dried and slowly died, leaving brown stems rippling in the slightest breeze. At times, the grassy seas flourished and expanded, filling with the taller and thicker napier grass, which most GIs referred to as elephant grass. Similar to sugarcane, napier grass grew very tall and cut the exposed skin of the soldiers as they moved through it. On this occasion, there was little time to take notice.

The LRRPs and the crew of the slick pushed through the

weeds and grasses, making a dogleg turn toward the location James had chosen for the new line of defense. The Viet Cong were downwind and would have to come through the flames and then turn to face the Americans. Behind the Americans, the terrain was open; if the VC came at them from that direction, then the helicopter gunships would rip them apart. The flanks presented a problem, but in the confusion of the battle and the fire, it would take a while before the Communists caught on to the new chess board.

Captain James suspected that, when they recovered, the VC would use the wood line to pick away at his group, but with the gunship on station and others on the way, the burning pickup zone would still present their best chance for defense and rescue. The RTO relayed that the quick reaction force was on its way, and a quick count showed that their ammunition was holding out. The cavalry was indeed on its way. However, you didn't have to be George Armstrong Custer to figure out that there were more Viet Cong than a nine-man squad or thirty-man platoon and that the ground party's survival hinged on getting out of the contact zone. That wouldn't be easy. The pickup zone was on fire, the C & C bird lay dead on the ground; sunset was fifteen minutes or so away, and the Viet Cong were doing a little maneuvering of their own to get position on the Americans.

The rain forest remained alive with the fight, but the Viet Cong were losing momentum: the sun was going down, and in the transitional moments before darkness, the enemy's weapons were leaving more visible flashes, giving the LRRPs and gunships targets on which to focus their fire. The grass fire had died down, leaving flickering orange embers glistening like jewels against a twilight backdrop.

The evening was closing in around them as the late afternoon sky of pastel reds and oranges turned purple. The sun had set already behind the mountains.

"Red Stag Six Actual. Red Stag Six Actual. This is Charlie Two-one. Over," the gunship leader's voice cracked over the radio.

"Six Actual. Go," James said. Identifying himself to the lead pilot.

"Looks like things are heating up a little down there. Go ahead and mark your location with a Sierra Lima (strobe light), and we'll give you a little breathing room," the pilot said. The handheld blinking light would be visible from the ground and the air, but since the Viet Cong had a pretty good idea where the Americans were anyway, marking their position wouldn't give much away.

Once the position was marked, the gunships were ready to roll in. "Keep your heads down. We're coming in hot," the gunship pilot said, starting his run.

"Keep your heads down. The gunships are coming in hot," the captain said, relaying the message. The first gunship rolled in, hitting the jungle with rocket and minigun fire only to have green return fire follow their path. As the second gunship rolled in firing, James and his people turned back another Viet Cong probe, but that one seemed to lack conviction; the overpowering force of the gunship helicopters was making its presence felt.

As the night wore on, for run after run, the gunships hammered the Viet Cong and the surrounding jungle. The radio net was alive with situation reports and division traffic responding to the find. Infantry and field artillery units were being moved in to counter the enemy buildup, which was proving to be significant. The LRRPs in the burning field were taking a backseat to the larger drive.

When the men of the QRF reached the crash scene later that evening, they brought in a resupply of ammunition and a plan for evacuation.

"We'll go out in the morning, sir. We had trouble coming in. There's movement everywhere," the young officer in charge of the quick reaction force explained to Captain James.

"Company size or better, Lieutenant," James said when the younger officer was done. "I think we're in for an interesting evening." James had the QRF platoon reinforce their perimeter, and the thirty troopers were a welcome sight. As the night wore on, the grass fire faltered, leaving a dull red glow in a half ring where it had stopped. In the distance, something was hissing from the fire. A sweet burning-meat smell occasionally wafted over the Americans' perimeter, and no one had to ask what was burning.

It was a long, sleepless night, although in the early morning when an evacuation helicopter was heard *whop*ping its way toward the pickup zone, any notion of weariness disappeared.

However, any sense of relief was short-lived when the VC .51-caliber heavy-machine-gun fire forced the rescue helicopter out of the area after it suffered numerous hits.

To complicate matters, the smoke grenade the QRF had used to guide the rescue helicopter in had sparked a second grass fire, which threatened both the survivors and the QRF. James was forced to withdraw under enemy fire to another evacuation site. Setting up another hasty perimeter, the Americans kept the Viet Cong at bay as a second rescue helicopter attempted a landing.

Through intense gunfire, the helicopter landed, and as the crew chief and door gunner fired into the wood line, James ordered half of the LRRP patrol and the C & C crew to the awaiting aircraft. Meanwhile, he and Burton and several others covered the extraction, giving the helicopter the much needed time to take off.

Twenty minutes later when it returned, the Viet Cong renewed their attack.

"Go! Go! Go!" James was yelling over the din of the firefight, waving Burton and the others toward the aircraft while he covered their escape. Only when they were aboard did he turn and go, diving toward the open bay of the liftship as hands pulled him in to safety. From inside the helicopter, the door gunners and LRRPs were firing at the Viet Cong who were running out of the wood line to get closer to the helicopter. But this time the aircraft didn't falter. It shuddered a little under the weight of the LRRPs but rose over the trees, climbing steadily, as the door gunners kept up their sustained machine-gun fire.

There were relieved grins and backslaps in the helicopter

while James checked to make sure everyone was okay. Once he was satisfied that everyone was, in fact, fine, James allowed himself to relax a bit. His adrenaline level, which had been high since the afternoon before, was subsiding, and a profound weariness was washing over him. There was a dull ache behind his eyes, and rubbing them didn't take the pain away. The wind was whipping through the open bay, and even above the noise of the helicopter blades, the team leader got the captain's attention.

He was saying something to James, but through the noise of the helicopter, all he could hear were the words "thank you."

James gave the team leader a thumbs-up.

There were enough thanks to go around. The team had performed admirably, and then when things had gone bad quickly, they had held it together anyway. Good people, James thought to himself. Good soldiers.

Except for minor cuts, bruises, and scrapes, the LRRPs were okay. The captain's shoulders were tight from where the LBE had dug into his shoulders, and if his nose was any judge of the situation, he could use a shave and a change of uniform. He smelled like the sweat stains, caked mud, and dried gunpowder smoke that permeated his tiger stripes. A hot shower and shave and hot chow were the just desserts of which they'd take advantage when they returned to An Khe. That is, after they checked and cleaned their weapons and equipment. Once that was done, the team leader and assistant team leader would be debriefed. Only then could they clean themselves up and eat.

The same went for the captain, but his debriefing would take place at division. G-2 needed to know the specifics of what they had encountered since the enemy contact was turning out to be a significant find. Before the LRRPs had run into the Viet Cong, no one was aware of the actual force moving on An Khe. The discovery by the LRRPs foiled the surprise attack, and now the Viet Cong were being hunted by the Cav and hammered with every resource the division had at its disposal.

When Captain James had finished being debriefed, he

headed back toward the company area and his hootch. He was almost to his hootch when he was intercepted by Kline, who was wearing his web gear and helmet and holding a rifle at port arms. The veteran NCO was part of a rescue force that the detachment had put together to assist those trapped on the ground.

"How about a cold beer later on," the staff sergeant asked, and James nodded.

"Actually, Sergeant Kline, I could use more than one. You know if Burton's people got something to eat?"

Kline nodded. "They're eating now. The headquarters mess sergeant put something aside for you."

"Thanks, but I think I'd like a shower first."

"When you're done, maybe you can stop by the orderly room and tell the first sergeant and me how long you think it takes?"

James was confused by the NCO's comments, and his face said as much. "How long what will take, Sergeant?"

"How long it takes to break in a new commanding officer, sir?"

"No, I'm afraid I don't," James said, realizing he was about to get his answer.

"A long time. Too damn long," Kline replied. He added, "I don't like it when you get shot down, Captain."

"Me neither."

"A lot of paperwork involved . . ."

James nodded again.

"Not to mention the time it takes just to have him learn everyone's name, let alone find his way back to his hootch and, say, approve a seven-day leave for one of his most talented NCOs, who'd like to see his wife in Hawaii and who couldn't if, say, his commanding officer got shot down. Don't do it again."

It was a concerned welcome home and an ass chewing all rolled into one.

"I don't suppose you asked G-2 for another helicopter, seeing how you broke the one you had."

James shook his head and smiled. "Not yet. Maybe later."

"A good idea, Captain," Kline said. "And like I said, there's a cold beer waiting when you're ready."

"Thanks," he said as Kline turned away and headed toward the TOC.

"Glad to have you back, sir," he said over his shoulder.

"Glad to be back," James replied, happy that he hadn't screwed up the NCO's paperwork and seven-day leave.

CHAPTER EIGHTEEN

By late April 1967, the countryside was beginning to turn again as a new season swept in and took hold. On a patrol near Kannack, twenty klicks or so north of An Khe, a new team led by Sergeant Simones was in search of a Viet Cong battalion, working the area along the ocher-colored Song Ba, Ba River, and pushing through new vines and rich underbrush with each step. Specifically, the six-man team was looking for the mortar and rocket crews that had been targeting An Khe and other fire support bases.

The Viet Cong spread their battalions throughout the jungle mountain region, coming together only for coordinated attacks. This allowed their squads, platoons, and companies to move from jungle base camps through villages and the major roadways of the region to make their presence better known.

Often that presence involved collecting foodstuffs and taxes, lecturing the locals about the importance of not contributing support or anything else to the Saigon government or the Americans, drafting soldiers for their cause, and intimidating anyone who opposed them. If intimidation didn't work, they simply executed them. Such object lessons tended to have the desired effect if they left the dead bodies in prominent places.

Given the frequency of the incoming they'd been receiving, there was some concern that the local Viet Cong battalion might be coming together for an assault on An Khe, so a LRRP team was requested to go in and see what it could learn.

Simones's team was the next one up, and after the briefing

they prepared for the mission. Simones and his assistant team leader, Sgt. Doug Fletcher, drew rations and ammunition, checked and double-checked the team's weapons and equipment, and then went over the operations order with the five team members. There was the normal prepatrol tension, but everything seemed to be going according to plan.

On insertion, the team quickly lay dog, in the security wheel formation, facing into the surrounding jungle. For ten minutes or so, they lay waiting and listening in the jungle of the rolling hills. Everything was calm but not unnaturally so. But Sergeant Simones couldn't get over the unsettling feeling that the team was being watched. A drop of sweat dripped slowly down the side of his face, and in spite of the heat, it left a cold trail.

Even after the team had waited the allotted time to ensure no one was tracking them and Simones had given the order to move out, he couldn't get over the uneasy feeling. His suspicion was a cold, eerie sensation, and Simones stopped the team from time to time to listen for any unusual sounds, anything that would confirm his suspicions or give credence to the chill. The late afternoon jungle was warm and quiet, and as he looked around the twilight surroundings, there was nothing to suggest that they weren't alone.

Simones opted for a cautious approach, so he changed directions again as the team moved out, and then decided to "buttonhook" to make certain no one was coming up behind them.

The buttonhook was a tactic devised by Maj. Robert Rogers for his Rangers in the mideighteenth century, along with eighteen or so other "standing orders" he considered essential to fighting behind the lines.

The buttonhook was actually the Rangers' standing order number seventeen, which said, "If somebody's trailing you, make a circle, come back onto your tracks, and ambush the folks that aim to ambush you."

The nineteen standing orders were Ranger dogma and taught to every NCO and officer who attended the eight-week course at Fort Benning. The buttonhook was adopted by the Special

Forces in Vietnam and the LRRPs who knew and understood its value.

Simones led the team back around, and when they were in position, they waited for any unwelcome guests who might suddenly show. His plan was basic. When and if they showed up, he'd blow the fuckers away.

When no one materialized after thirty minutes, Simones signaled the team to move out again. This time the pace was slower as the LRRPs listened and studied the indifferent jungle. The sun had disappeared over a mountain, casting a burnt orange glow that filtered down through the leaves. The jungle was turning dark, and the nocturnal creatures were about to take over.

Simones studied his map and then refolded it and put it away. It was time.

Besides Simones on the team, there were Sgt. Doug Fletcher, Specialist Geoff Koper, PFC David Allen Ives, Specialist Allen Carpenter, and Sgt. Art Guerrero. Most were veteran LRRPs who knew what to expect on the mission. They didn't fear the unknown; the known was enough to keep them alert and ready. It was Ives's first mission, and the new guy was handling it well.

"We'll set up a night-halt position here after we buttonhook," he said to Fletcher, who nodded. The spot they selected offered a degree of natural cover—its contour and the trees—which was always a problem on long-range patrols. Unlike infantry units, LRRPs couldn't dig in or build protective bunkers. Instead, they relied on what was available, which was seldom enough.

A nearby stream meant it was a good place to monitor the Viet Cong who might be working the area. It was a good spot so Simones decided to keep moving; the team would work its way back in a wide arc to make certain they weren't being followed and to get a better look at the surrounding terrain.

The going was slow in the jungle because of wait-a-minute vines, sharp tree limbs, and other snagging vegetation, and it was made more so by the caution they employed. By the time they had worked their way back to the chosen position, the night was closing in, and the jungle was bathed in purple twilight that was growing deeper with each minute.

The team had set up its wagon-wheel perimeter, and the LRRPs had established their fields of fire. Even as they set up for the evening and the RTO called in their location, everything seemed to be okay. But Simones still wasn't comfortable. It was too quiet, and while he didn't believe in a sixth sense, he was smart enough to know you had to trust your instincts.

After they had settled in, the team began its guard shifts. Two men would remain awake for several hours while the other four would sleep until their own turns at guard. Weapons were checked and rechecked, and as night dropped a black velvet curtain over the jungle, Simones remained awake, staring at the living wall of vegetation.

He thumbed the safety of his CAR-15 and absentmindedly reached down to check his .45 automatic. The CAR-15 was a shorter version of the M-16 that looked good but occasionally jammed. Many of the LRRPs discovered that replacing the CAR-15's buffer spring with a standard M-16 buffer spring and keeping the bolt well lubed improved the reliability of the weapon. However, the .45 automatic handgun was the real weapon of choice. In a close-in fighting situation, the small 5.56mm round of the M-16 and CAR-15 might go through a charging enemy soldier and might slow him down or even sever something important, but it wouldn't knock the son of a bitch down.

The fact that the teams used nothing but tracer rounds in their rifles provided a certain psychological benefit, but any real punch came from the .45 automatic.

The .45 automatic was designed in 1911 after the Philippine Insurrection when it became evident that something more powerful was needed as a handgun. In the Philippines, enemy soldiers, high on drugs or adrenaline, would be shot repeatedly as they charged. Unfortunately, the rifles and handguns weren't always enough to stop them, and more than one soldier or Marine had been hacked to death by a wounded or dying enemy soldier. So the army developed the .45, a large-caliber pistol, which could bring down a horse. Any horse, even a big-ass Clydesdale.

In World Wars I and II, soldiers discovered that a round from the .45 stopped a charging enemy soldier, and it usually didn't matter if you hit the man in the head, chest, arm, or leg. It was the same round that was used in the Thompson submachine gun, and in between wars, both the police and gangsters came to appreciate its value.

In Vietnam it proved its value again, and Simones knew it was the kind of backup weapon he could rely on, and in the jungle where rifle barrels could sometimes get caught on clinging vines or in the underbrush, the pistol was your last shot at surviving.

Simones stayed awake for a long while, listening and watching the jungle in front of him, and when he finally closed his eyes, it was a restless and uneasy sleep.

The team awoke at predawn, in that transitional time between the close of night and sunrise when the sky above the jungle foliage was a faded purple curtain with a pale yellow border. In the distance, the tropical birds squawked and monkeys grunted as the large snakes slowly slithered back to their nests after a night of hunting, their kill not yet digested in their roiling stomachs.

In that brief moment when they struggled to shoulder the seventy- to one hundred-pound rucksacks and adjust the weight while tightening the straps, it would be the most opportune time. That's when they would be the most vulnerable and when the Communists would attack.

The new guy, PFC David Allen Ives, who had only recently joined the LRRP company and who was on his first mission, was also the first team member to rise and step outside of the team's wagon-wheel perimeter. He had to relieve himself, and asked one of the team members to cover him.

It was standard procedure. No team member did anything

without someone else covering the surrounding jungle. As he stepped out of the team's protective cover, he heard the twigs breaking in front of him and recognized the threat immediately.

Even as he and several others who had heard it, too, quickly brought up their weapons and fired, it was too late. The Viet Cong had the small patrol in a cross fire and opened up, believing that Ives was about to discover their plan.

In the first few minutes of the stalking attack, PFC David Allen Ives was shot and killed, and three other members of the six-man patrol, Guerrero, Carpenter, and Koper, were wounded in the initial volley.

Guerrero took a three-round burst from a Thompson submachine gun at close range to the legs, the .45-caliber slugs slamming into the LRRP and causing serious damage to muscle mass and bone. The shock had been instant, the pain intense, but Guerrero somehow held on.

Koper, the medic, had taken a burst to the chest and was having trouble breathing. Carpenter had been badly wounded by a grenade that had exploded a few feet from his position, the blast sending him tumbling back and over. His hearing was gone, and he was bleeding badly from facial wounds in and around his eyes. This left only Simones and Fletcher free of wounds to keep fighting and radio for help.

The area surrounding their perimeter was a mess of torn branches and leaves where the heavy volume of enemy machine-gun fire had shredded the jungle. Surprisingly, the wounded LRRPs pulled themselves or were helped back into firing position, bringing the perimeter back in force for the moment.

Each was returning fire as they scrambled to find bandages to cover their wounds, fighting their own fear and worry as well as the enemy assault. Streams of blood seeped through Guerrero's fingers as he tried to apply pressure to one of his leg wounds. The overriding pain registered on his face like a twisting shadow, only it didn't stop him from shoring up the hole in the team's perimeter.

When the Viet Cong rushed forward, Simones yelled for the

team members to get down as he detonated the claymore anti-personnel mines. The small plastic mines were the size and shape of a warped hardcover book, and the war had made them into best-sellers. Each mine held seven hundred ball bearings encased in two pounds of the white plastique C-4 explosive forming a shaped charge. When the mine was detonated, seven hundred ball bearings fanned out, shredding anything in their path. The LRRP teams used the mines in sequence, daisy-chaining (linking) several to expand the protective coverage. The mines were set off at an angle from the team's perimeter to reduce the possibility of injury to the user because of backblast. Either that or they were hidden in the recess of a slope, but even then, the intense heat and concussion jarred the patrol members and disturbed their hearing.

The claymore mines thwarted the assault, but the fight wasn't over.

Simones could see that Guerrero and the others were firing back like men possessed while occasionally stealing quick looks at their wounds. Simones was throwing grenades at pockets of the enemy to prevent their simply gathering their force in a group and overrunning the perimeter.

There was a momentary lull in the fighting as the Viet Cong regrouped and quickly tried to assault once again.

Several of the LRRPs were trying to pull Ives back to safety, but when the fighting resumed, the intensity of the battle made that difficult.

Since his radioman was wounded, Simones grabbed for the handset and yelled for gunship support and a Dust Off medical evacuation helicopter. The PRC-25 radio had been nicked and battered, but it was still working.

"I've got one Kilo India Alpha and three Whiskey India Alphas!" Simones yelled, giving the NATO phonetic designations for the LRRPs who were killed and wounded in action into the radio. "You copy? Over?"

"Roger," came back the startled response. "I copy one Kilo India Alpha and three Whiskey India Alphas." The voice was calm and steady, the way a chaplain's might be when he had to read off the names of the dead after a fierce battle in a memorial service.

"We need gunship support and that Dust Off ASAP!"

"Roger."

Help was on the way, but it would take a while to get there, and the surviving LRRPs weren't certain they had a while.

Fletcher was assisting the wounded team members and, like Simones, was caught between trying to help those who needed it and trying to keep the persistent attackers at bay.

The Viet Cong ambush had succeeded in hitting most of the Americans but failed in its main objective, which was to over-run and kill or capture them all. The surrounding jungle was a haze of blue-white rifle smoke. The kill zone and ambush scene were chaotic. Nothing like the movies ever hinted at war could be. Soldiers on both sides were screaming, moaning loudly, or smothering cries as the din of the battle rose around them.

Red and green tracers lit up the purple predawn twilight in a garish display of pyrotechnics.

The team's small perimeter was weakening. Shredded by in-coming rounds, tree limbs bled sap, and splintered branches shed foliage and fragments of wood. There were holes in the LRRPs' canteens and rucksacks, torn uniforms and flesh as well; still the LRRPs held on.

All of them well understood that battles don't end because people get wounded or die and that their only way to survive was to fight like hell and hope to God that would be enough. At times like that, soldiers learned the truth about war and about the lies that Hollywood expected them to believe; that in reality there are no audible last words, no way to save all of those who needed to be saved, and that soldiers—even LRRPs—bleed and sometimes die horribly with only frightened fixed stares. But *these* LRRPs were not about to give up, or give in to their wounds.

Simones was amazed as the team kept up a sustained rate of fire and held back the advancing Viet Cong. If they could hold out until the gunships arrived, he knew they would make it to safety. He was also well aware that the Viet Cong knew that, too, which was why they pressed the fight. Their usual strategy was to strike when conditions were to their advantage and press the attack only if it meant a real or psychological victory. Killing or capturing an American long-range patrol was too great a pearl to pass up. There would be awards and honors if they succeeded.

But the Vietnamese were having a harder time than they had anticipated. They knew that they had hit most of the Americans, but the LRRPs didn't stop fighting or run. Instead, they fought back.

The team leader knew that the PRC-25 was the team's only chance of getting out alive, so maintaining radio contact with the detachment was paramount. By that time, the gunships were on the way, maybe fifteen minutes out, as was the medical evacuation helicopter.

Guerrero's legs were a mess, but that didn't stop the LRRP from playing a crucial role in repelling the attack. With Ives dead and three others wounded there was a gaping hole in the team's perimeter. Guerrero kept up a steady rate of fire, covering the hole. In spite of his injuries, he managed to return an effective counter to the surprised Viet Cong. His legs were useless, and the pain was overwhelming, but there would be no second place or runners-up in the life or death struggle. Carpenter was having trouble seeing, and Koper was hunched over to decrease the burning pain of his chest wound, but he found no relief. In spite of their wounds each of them returned fire. But they couldn't go on much longer.

By the time the gunships arrived on station, the Viet Cong were falling back, not in retreat but to find better cover to keep fighting. The Dust Off helicopter wouldn't be able to evacuate the wounded until the enemy gunfire diminished, and it didn't look like that was going to happen for a while. Unfortunately, the wounded patrol members didn't have the luxury of time.

As Simones was explaining the situation on the ground, one of the gunship pilots broke in.

"Start moving to your Papa Zulu. I'm coming in!" he said, maneuvering the UH-1B helicopter for a short final run toward the pickup zone.

"We're getting out of here!" Simones said, reaching over and grabbing one of his wounded people as Fletcher did likewise. They were drag-carrying the wounded to the pickup zone while covering their escape as best they could. Those who could walk were moving with new purpose; it would be their best shot at getting out alive. By that time, the fighting was sporadic because pinpoint fire from the gunships had sent the Viet Cong scurrying back into the jungle. But those who weren't the primary targets of the helicopters were still firing at the Americans.

The pickup zone was little more than a natural break in the hillside jungle, but it was enough. When the gunship swooped over the treetops and touched down, Fletcher and Simones were carrying the casualties to its open bay. The crew chief helped pull the wounded soldiers aboard while the team leader and assistant team leader raced back for the others, even as gunfire ripped the trees around them.

Within minutes, they had the entire team on board and jumped in after them. The crew chief was yelling, "Go! Go! Go!" to the pilot, who pulled pitch, dipped the nose of the helicopter, and began flying toward the tree line, pulling up and away as the ambush area disappeared behind them. It was a miserable flight back to An Khe.

Most of the company personnel who were on stand-down, as well as support personnel, were waiting for the rescue helicopter at the pad. Anxious to help, they raced to assist the medics and offer what other support they could; the loss touched them all. The blood was everywhere in the helicopter, and its impact would linger long after it had been washed away.

After immediate care and stabilization, the three seriously wounded LRRPs—Guerrero, Koper, and Carpenter—would be medevacked to a larger hospital in Qui Nhon. Fletcher and

Simones were treated in An Khe. PFC David Ives's body was taken to graves registration for processing. The team was no more.

When their minor wounds were patched up and their hearing losses noted, Simones and Fletcher trudged back to the company area, worn out by the small battle. The flood of adrenaline that had overwhelmed them during the firefight had stopped, and in its wake lay the emotional debris of the ambush.

Their tiger fatigues were filthy with a mix of gunpowder, blood, sweat, and the dirt of the ambush site. The greeting was somber as was the debriefing. Exhaustion was setting in, along with a painfully personal understanding of the realities of war.

The company had lost its first team member killed in action and suffered three wounded. Four LRRPs and friends suddenly gone. The stakes in the gamble of war were now raised, only the odds were no longer a sure thing.

Guererro, Carpenter, Fletcher, Koper, Ives, and Simones would be put in for awards for valor, pending review and approval by the division, and for Purple Hearts, but the medals wouldn't dissipate the cloud of anguish that settled over the company or the night of turmoil that would follow as the "hows" and "whys" were rehearsed in everyone's minds, and the "ifs" made the night even longer.

The following morning Captain James, Lieutenant Hall, Sergeant Simones, and several others flew out to Qui Nhon to check on the three members of the team at the evacuation hospital. The surgical ward was a pristine but depressing place that smelled of disinfectant and weeping bandages. James stopped briefly at the nurses' station and spoke with the doctor on duty and the nurses while Simones walked down the polished corridor to his team members.

As Captain James joined them, Carpenter, whose face was heavily wrapped in bandages, recognized the officer anyway. He sat up in bed and saluted James. The other two wounded LRRPs followed suit. They were an unusual combination of bandages, tubes, stitches, and traction, but they were still soldiers. The Green Beret captain looked away briefly, then moved back to return a smart, professional salute. There was something in the corners of his eyes, which he wiped away before anyone noticed.

"As you were," he said quietly. "How are you doing?"

To his surprise they were in good spirits. They were going to be medevacked out of Vietnam and each would have to undergo more operations, long hours of treatment, and bouts of physical therapy.

"Doing good, sir," Guerrero said; James could see that that was stretching it some.

"Is there anything any of you need?" the captain asked, studying their faces while Guerrero laughed and said he could sure use a beer or two; something that they all echoed.

Simones was talking with Carpenter and Koper, describing the battle and the roles they had played. The captain noticed that while they were happy and relieved to have survived the ordeal, their voices quaked slightly in the retelling, particularly when it came to the subject of Ives. The hurt was obvious, and the emotional loss traumatic.

"There was nothing we could do," Koper said.

"I know," Simones said. "We did what we could."

"You did more than that," Captain James interjected. "All of you."

He had known they were remarkable soldiers when he chose them for the unit, but their genuine sorrow and compassion for a dead team member showed how remarkable these people were.

Simones, too, was proud of them and said as much, but the brief reunion was awkward and anticlimactic. There was some small talk, and the company commander reminded them that if there was anything he could do or get for them, then they should let him know, and he would take care of it.

The wounded LRRPs thanked him again. When it was time to go and they had stumbled through the handshakes and good-byes, James and Simones left with an odd mix of pride and pain. Like it or not, the war would continue.

In a day or so, there would be a memorial service in the company area for the fallen LRRP, PFC David Allen Ives. Ives would be promoted posthumously to the rank of specialist four, and besides the folded flag the family would receive at the grave site, they would also receive a Purple Heart medal and a Silver Star for gallantry.

Silver Stars were awarded to each of the surviving team members as well. Nowhere in any dictionary was gallantry better defined than by that bitter experience.

There would also be countless "should of's" and "could of's," coupled with swearing and frustration, but in reality, if they made contact, the odds were always against the small teams, and it was remarkable that the teams had escaped unharmed until that patrol. But that was small consolation for the company, which had lost so many in one miserable morning. Friends were gone.

The company took the losses hard, but the lessons learned from the fatal mission would not go unheeded. The company had always taken the approach of planning for the worst and hoping for the best. Now, unfortunately, they had something by which to measure the difference. It was a sobering lesson.

The memorial service for the fallen LRRP was dark and solemn. Ives was dead doing what they had done and what they would continue to do. There were new patrols to conduct, new target areas to check out, bunkers, base camps, or high-seed trails, each hiding new dangers.

Training, too, would take on new importance and, maybe, a more critical edge as the LRRPs came away knowing the potential human cost of their task. The XO would see to it. The professionalism would return, a professionalism but with a harder edge.

Captain James pushed the senior NCOs to ensure the teams would be the best they could be; all the while wrestling with his own grief, the kind that comes with the responsibility of command. In a line unit there might be one hundred or so soldiers; even when losing one or two, their CO might have a struggle to remember their names, their hometowns, or anything else pertinent about them. However, in a unit like his, where he had handpicked the team members, he knew the volunteers often all too well.

James had talked to Ives the night before the team went out, after the mission briefing, and had joked with him about his taste in music.

"Is that music, or is your tape player broken?" the captain asked as Ives looked up from his bunk. He was clearly uncertain how to reply. The small speaker was pounding under the latest Beatles music.

"It's 'Strawberry Fields Forever.' The Beatles," Ives replied.

James nodded. "I guess it has to grow on you, like fungus or something?" he said. "Aren't you from Iowa?"

"Yes, sir, Council Bluffs."

"Shouldn't that be cornfields forever? Are you sure there's not something wrong with your tape player?" Ives grinned and shook his head as John Lennon sang about life being easy with eyes closed.

"Keep your eyes open on patrol, and you'll work out fine," James said.

"Yes, sir."

A puppy's yapping drew the captain's attention away from Ives and to Specialist Lopez, who was holding a small light brown fluff of a dog and scratching him behind the ear, but the yapping came from another puppy, which had scurried after a rat that disappeared beneath the floor.

The captain scooped up the second dog and studied the small animal. Several dark streaks ran down its face. The puppy seemed to like the attention and yapped only when Lopez stopped.

"Where did they come from?"

"Torres got the one you're holding in Sin City, sir," the specialist said. Sin City was what they called the town outside the base camp, which did good business in bars, steam baths, and other assorted enterprises that sprung up around the American military facility since the Cav arrived. "This one I got. His name's Corporal, sir. The one you're holding is Lurp. I think we saved them from being someone's dinner."

The captain nodded. Chances were good the puppies probably would have been eaten; dog meat is a staple in the Southeast Asian diet, and puppy was said to be tender. "Lurp's a good name, but why Corporal?" James asked.

"Hard stripes,* on his face," explained Lopez, making finger gestures over his own face simulating the marks.

The captain looked closer and smiled. They could be interpreted as two stripes. Hard stripes. Both puppies were cute little suckers, and the one he was holding was licking his hand. Unfortunately, division had a policy against pets within the base camp, and the dogs seemed to fall within the pet category.

One of the problems with puppies is that they grew into dogs, and dogs in Southeast Asia developed all kinds of problems and illnesses not normally found in the United States—rabies, plague, nasty dispositions. Since the idea of allowing snarling dogs loose inside the base camp didn't appeal to anyone who might have to square off against one of the animals, the army had developed its policy. The army was also smart enough to know that soldiers sometimes ignored the policies, so every six months or so, military police were sent out to collect the dogs and destroy them.

To the GIs, the dogs were pets and often more than that. The dogs were early warning devices, best friends, and a source of sanity in a war zone of insanity.

On any and every American base in Vietnam, there was an army of mutts on patrol around bunkers and hootches, barking

---

*"Hard stripes" refers to the chevrons worn by corporals and sergeants, i.e., leadership ranks. The new army had also introduced "soft" ranks specialist grades like specialist four (SP4), the same pay grade as a corporal but, supposedly, with no leadership function.

at helicopters and jeeps, or playing with "their" GIs. Unlike, say, the native water buffalo, the Vietnamese dogs took to Americans and made excellent guard dogs. Bunker guard duty was long and boring, and minds and attention tended to wander in the early morning hours, which was usually why and when the Viet Cong chose to attack American facilities.

The dogs' incredible sense of smell and keen hearing brought them up and barking long before the GIs had noticed anything out of the ordinary. They were a great tool against sappers, and the bonds created between the GI and the unit mutts were very much in the typical American tradition. The Vietnam generation had grown up with Rin Tin Tin and Lassie, and since most American families had dogs, the tradition carried over to the war zone.

Many of the dogs within the American compounds disliked the Vietnamese, but then the Vietnamese often used them for food, which perhaps the dogs sensed and recognized as a threat. Biting the hand that feeds you is a bad thing, but biting the hand that eats you certainly made sense to GIs, who understood the dogs' attitude. The dogs often attacked the abundant snakes and rats, and that was another reason to keep them around. The GIs often kept food in their tents, and since old food tends to become garbage, the rats were having a field day. The snakes, of course, slithered in to eat the rats, so Darwin's theory of survival of the fittest was well in place.

So if the dogs could reduce the rat population, then it became easier to overlook the mongrels. It became easier, too, when the dogs provided a sense of love and trust to the GIs who cared for them.

Lurp wagged his tail and shot his ears up intelligently when the captain turned him around and stared into his face. Small streaks of black outlined his fluff ball chest, giving him the look of a German shepherd in a shorter, more stout body. But it was clear that there was considerably more mongrel mix to the dog's lineage.

A rat scurried across the sandbag wall nearby, and the puppy's attention turned to the rodent. A small, almost comical, growl came from the puppy. Rats carried far more deadly diseases than dogs, and if the puppy could keep the rats away, then he was welcome.

"Lurp and Corporal, huh?" James handed back the puppy and John Lennon, Ringo Starr, George Harrison, and Paul McCartney worked their way through another song he wasn't sure about. "Well, let's see if they both can make the grade," he said, putting the dog down and letting it go back to its mission.

That was James's last recollection of PFC David Ives, as Ives and several of the others smiled while they cleaned weapons, wrote letters home, or played cards, seemingly unconcerned about the war even as H & I (harassment and interdiction) artillery fire pounded in the distance.

The letter he wrote to Ives's parents was perhaps one of the most difficult tasks he had ever faced, and when he had finished and read what he wrote, he knew it wasn't enough. It never would be.

Ives had been posthumously promoted to specialist four—soft rank—but that was small consolation, nothing could ever make up for the loss of a son, brother, father, or friend in war, even in piddly ass little ones like Vietnam.

CHAPTER NINETEEN

Nineteen-year-old Spec Four Walter James Seymour was an 0-5 Brava and an 0-5 Charlie, a school-trained radio and teletype operator that the LRRP company recruited in its first blanket call for qualified division volunteers.

He was just what they were looking for, but the need may have been mutual. Seymour had joined the army in late 1965, and after successfully completing the radio course and later graduating from the teletype school, he volunteered for Airborne training.

A few weeks later, he was on his way to Fort Benning, Georgia, to attend the three-week course of ground, tower, and jump training.

In was also in jump school that Seymour decided he wanted to be something more than 0-5 Bravo and an 0-5 Charlie. The notion came from watching the Black Hats (Jump School instructors) who were primarily Airborne infantry types but who were definitely something more. They had pride, determination, and an uncanny ability, seemingly, to run forever while looking sharp or at least smirking when they were done. Seymour took note of the navy SEALs in the course, Recon Marines, and Special Forces types who were also taking the parachute course; they had the same attitude.

That's when the Bellevue, Washington, native decided to join the Special Forces. But when he talked to a recruiter, he was told that he would have to complete a combat tour of duty in Vietnam first before they would consider him and that a year or more of college wouldn't hurt his chances either. "Sorry," the recruiter said. "There are no school openings at this time."

Seymour knew the recruiters had quotas to meet in order to keep their jobs, and when they fell short of their goals, they could make things happen—doors mysteriously opened, and schools could be had. The downside was that once they had met their goals, they didn't have to push so hard to open doors when someone walked through the door shopping for a new career field.

Seymour shrugged the rejection off and took the advice in stride: if combat experience and more education were what it took, that that's what it took. His new goal became a long-term objective: Airborne training set the foundation; the rest would take some time to build.

When orders came down sending him to Vietnam, he was assigned to an engineer unit in a noncombat role. It didn't take long for him to get frustrated and bored with rear-area duty in An Khe, so when the new LRRP detachment asked for qualified radio personnel, Seymour jumped at the opportunity. He volunteered to become a LRRP.

"We get occasional mortars or rockets here, Jim," a friend had said, "but we're not exactly anybody's primary fucking target. Out there," he said, pointing out beyond the perimeter to the darkened countryside, "Out there, you're center mass! Out there, the war is as real as it gets and as close as it gets. That LRRP shit is crazy! You hear me, crazy!"

To some, giving up a good, safe rear-area job for combat field duty was crazy, but there were those who looked on it as putting some meaning to duty, honor, and country; words that rear-area types in the army used when they wanted others to do something dirty or dangerous in a combat setting. It was those others, who often gave the words real meaning, defining them with service and action. One of those others was like Jim Seymour.

"Think about it," his buddy advised him. "I mean, really, really, think about it."

Seymour had thought about it and had already made up his

mind. So when his orders came down to report to the LRRP unit for training, his friend just shook his head and told him to take it easy. But taking it "easy" would take some doing because when he and other new trainees arrived, the training NCO gave them a look at what lay ahead.

"*At ease!*" the training NCO said loudly to get their attention. Listen up!" The training NCO walked in front of the formation of volunteers, certain that he did indeed have their attention. "My job is to send most of you fuckers packing. If you can't cut the training, then we don't need you. If you represent a liability, then we don't want you, and if you're just plain stupid, well, we'll recommend you for officer's candidate school and send you on your way. Any questions?"

When no one in the formation had any, the training NCO said, "Good," and pointed them in the direction of their temporary new home, a GP medium tent filled with cots and little else. "Make yourselves comfortable, gentlemen, because training begins with PT at 0-dark early."

There were nearly forty other candidates in the LRRP training course, and three weeks later, after the physically demanding schedule, hands-on training, and tests, not to mention a healthy dose of harassment, only three others besides Seymour had made the final cut.

However, it was more than the training that had sent some of the volunteers packing. When Simones's team was hit, that sent the new arrivals a chilling message about the realities of the job and the price that might be demanded for work behind the lines. Even some veteran LRRPs in the company pulled the pen. For them it was time to get out.

But for those like Seymour, it was time to hang tough and hang together. When he graduated, Jim Seymour was proud of the accomplishment, and when he was assigned to a team, any notion of becoming a Green Beret was overshadowed by his determination to become a good LRRP. He was taking it all a step at a time, but the pace was about to pick up.

Somewhere along the way Spec Four Walter James Seymour, Jim to his friends and Seymour to the army, picked up the nickname Spanky. Someone, he couldn't recall who, said he looked like the Spanky of Our Gang comedies, and the nickname stuck.

Doc Suggs had given him his medic training, and like the other instructors, Suggs was surprised by how adept Seymour was with what he had learned. Seymour was a natural.

"You like all this stuff, don't you?" Suggs asked, with his Georgian drawl. Seymour nodded and said he did.

The medic smiled. "You're going to fit in nicely here."

His first mission was as a team's RTO, a position he felt comfortable with even if the PRC-25 he carried in his backpack dug into his shoulders as he walked up the steep inclines on patrol.

Having grown up in the Pacific Northwest, Seymour had done his share of backcountry hiking and camping in the Cascade and Olympic mountains, so the week-long patrol hadn't been too great a physical challenge; the team only moved a klick or so a day, and the men spent most of their time listening, watching, and waiting for the enemy as they hid from view. The packs were heavy and made walking difficult, but other than the fact that the jungle was filled with a shit load of Viet Cong and North Vietnamese army soldiers who were dying to kill them, that first patrol was just another walk through the woods.

CHAPTER TWENTY

In the spring of 1967, the antiwar movement in the United States was growing, its surprisingly loud voice and momentum deepening the stormy gulf between the spectrum of ideologies. While the war was expanding in Southeast Asia, it was also spilling over into the streets of North America.

In mid-April, over one hundred thousand people demonstrated in New York City; their protests and screams reverberated down the litter-lined canyons of the Big Apple to its core. The protest, led by Drs. Martin Luther King Jr. and Benjamin Spock, garnered widespread television and print coverage and made inroads into the editorials of a number of newspapers.

While that event and others like it were headline-making news in the civilian press back home, there was little coverage of them in the military publications in Vietnam. So when Kline picked up an American newspaper in Japan during a stopover on the long flight to Hawaii, the staff sergeant was surprised to learn about the conflict, and more than a little disheartened.

In France, Charles de Gaulle was calling on the United States to "end its detestable intervention in Vietnam," which was no big deal to Joe Kline. The French didn't have much room to talk, let alone criticize. After all, the mess in Vietnam was a direct result of their own colonialist attitude toward the Vietnamese. Besides, how could any country that liked Jerry Lewis movies so much really know what the hell they were talking about?

Fuck de Gaulle, Kline said to himself as he turned his attention to the article on the New York protest.

Kline's jaw muscles tightened, and he caught himself breathing angrily through his nose as he read the article describing a war protest. His eyes riveted on the photograph showing a confrontation between a hard-hat construction worker and several long-haired protesters. One of the signs the protesters carried read: STOP FASCISM IN VIETNAM. END THE WAR NOW!

"Fascism, my ass!" he said, more than a little pissed. The long-haired little shit was calling the GIs Nazis. He's calling me a Nazi! The fuck! The rotten fuck! I'm a Jew, for crying out loud, he thought, and if anybody would recognize Fascists, it would be someone who the bastards had tried to wipe off the face of the earth. There wasn't a Jewish family in his neighborhood who didn't have a relative who had been murdered in one of the death camps.

Maybe the college boy was so smart that he didn't need to know any of the history of Vietnam, how the Viets stole the country from the Khmers or how the peace agreement Ho Chi Minh agreed to didn't mean a damn thing when the North sent thousands of soldiers and equipment south to take the land by force. Maybe he didn't understand how Uncle Ho had one of his own leaders killed because he was becoming too popular among the people or how the Viet Cong fielded their own assassination squads, killing whoever it took to make their object lessons understood.

We don't much like it either, you schmuck! he thought, thumping the picture, but we still have a country where *you* can protest while GIs are bleeding and dying for shit birds like you who don't appreciate our service or understand the meaning behind the words duty, honor, and country.

The more this became apparent, the more the professional soldiers like Staff Sergeant Kline began to harbor deep anger and resentment against those they thought should have known better.

As he turned to the sports section, Kline tried to let go of the issue, but it didn't go quickly. Even so, by the time the plane began its descent, his mind was no longer on the war or the protesters but on his wife, who would, he hoped, be waiting for him at the R & R center.

If all went according to schedule, if there'd been no hitch in having her mother watch the kids, if there'd been no delays or missed connections from New York to Los Angeles and finally to Hawaii, then she should have arrived the day before his flight.

Kline didn't have luggage, just a carry-on, black mock-leather AWOL bag filled with a few civilian shirts, a package of new civilian underwear, and a pair of brown Haggar slacks he'd bought at the PX in Saigon. He also had his shaving kit, two small hand-carved teak elephants for the kids, an extra copy of his leave orders, and a pair of red-lace crotchless panties that a Korean vendor had assured him his wife would like.

"All women like sexy tings!" the vendor said. It didn't matter whether he believed the vendor or not because he knew that *he* liked the idea of them. Most lust was anticipation coupled with frustration, raging hormones helped, too; the combination sent the rational shopping mind out the proverbial window. To kick-start the fun and games, Kline had also brought along a one-carat ruby ring from Thailand in a satin-lined ring box.

At the terminal, the GIs walked down the portable ramp and boarded one of the handful of olive drab school buses that would take them all to the R & R center at Fort De Russy. The R & R center was located on an ideal plot of land on Waikiki that developers and real estate agents signed over because the government oasis was adjacent to some of the finest hotels on the island of Oahu, which offered the GIs and their families an affordable vacation.

The bus ride was uneventful, but the servicemen's excitement was building as the bus worked its way through busy afternoon traffic toward De Russy. When they wheeled into the R & R center, Kline saw his wife, Sarah, standing in the crowd of wives and family members. All he wanted to do was race out, scoop her up in his arms, and hold her forever.

Sarah was wearing a red shift lined with gold trim that accented shoulder-length black hair and the bright green eyes, which, just then, were streaked with the mascara trickling down her cheeks. Like many of the other women present, she was crying and laughing and clapping. She looked lovely.

The furious hug and barrage of kisses came before any words, and the embrace didn't ease for the longest, sweetest time.

"Oh God! I missed you!" he whispered into her ear as he breathed in the musky, fragrant smell of lilac perfume on the nape of her neck.

"Oh, honey!" she said, between gulped sobs and warm kisses.

The same scene was being carried out across the parking lot with the hundreds of other visitors until an officer from the R & R center vied for the crowd's attention, leaving onlookers embarrassed at the intimacy and perhaps envious.

"May I have your attention? May I please have your attention?" he yelled again, emphasizing the word "please" to keep it from sounding too much like the order it really was. He waved his arms above his head until he was certain he had *most* of their attention. Then, he began to run through his memorized greeting, but when he reached the part about the briefing, a low murmur began to move among the crowd.

"Briefing? What briefing?" someone asked, dismayed by the fact that it would take time away from their loved ones and their precious seven days in Paradise.

The R & R center officer took his cue, smiled, and continued. "Yes, to fill you in on what's available to you while you're on R & R, specifically, cheaper hotel rates and a long list of discount sight-seeing activities available to you. You also need to be aware of the dos and don'ts while you're here on leave."

The business of cheaper hotel rooms and discounts brightened some of the faces, although Kline held his frown. The first "do" he had in mind had nothing to do with sight-seeing, let alone a briefing. A debriefing, maybe, he thought as his mind turned to the red-lace crotchless panties.

Reluctantly, he followed the crowd into the briefing room and listened with feigned interest. The clock was officially ticking on his seven days rest and recuperation leave.

When the briefing was over, there was a stampede for the door with Kline and Sarah well in the running. Those who had worked at the R & R center knew better than to stand too near the doorway as the audience made its escape.

Giggling much of the way, Joe and Sarah hurried to their hotel room. She had booked a hotel room one block off the beach, with a deck that overlooked the ocean. The room was efficient and designed for the tourists who came to Hawaii for the beaches and scenery, which meant that it was also barely large enough to contain the king-size bed, small TV and stand, a small desk that was too impractical to serve as anything other than a place to put your wallet and keys, a closet with a mirrored door, and two flimsy cane-back chairs. But it was enough.

In the early evening, they dressed and walked along the beach, holding hands, behind the Royal Hawaiian Hotel. It was enough to be together, holding hands, looking into each other's eyes from time to time.

Over dinner, he gave her the ruby ring. She was caught by happy surprise, which was the effect he had hoped to achieve. The flickering light from a candle on their table made the multi-faceted red stone dance in its gold setting and in her eyes.

"I reenlisted. We got a six-thousand-dollar tax-free bonus, part of which went on the ring. You earned it."

"It's beautiful!" she exclaimed, trying it on and then holding it up and admiring its beauty.

"So are you. That's why I married you. The rest of the money I sent to our account. A check actually. All they pay us with in country are military payment certificates."

She reached across the table and gave him a kiss while an older couple at the next table smiled at the exchange.

He knew the reenlistment money would come in handy, but

that was only part of it. Kline was going to extend his tour of duty, and an additional six months in Vietnam was going to be a hard sell.

"If I extend another six months in country, I'm sure I can get a seven out of it too," he said. A "seven" was an E-7 or sergeant first class.

If the ring had lured away her attention, then his comment brought it back into immediate focus. "What do you mean, extend?" she asked, already knowing the answer. She had been an army wife long enough.

"You know, just sign up for another six months in country . . ."

"In Vietnam?"

The dog robber nodded. "Yeah. And I can almost guarantee I'll get promoted, which will mean more take-home money every month and a better retirement."

She wasn't buying the hard sell, disappointment registered on her face.

"It's just six months. It's nothing!"

"I'd rather have you at home," she said simply. "I need you, and so do the kids."

"I need this!" he said, his voice rising, and the tone had a distinct edge to it. "Damn it, we need this! I'm a high-school dropout who barely got his GED, and I'm an airborne infantry E-6, which means, Stateside, I'm as high as I can go. If I don't go after my seven now, in Vietnam, then I can kiss it good-bye forever because the sevens who are locked in Stateside aren't about to give it up to some Airborne Jew just because he has been to combat."

She wasn't watching his face anymore, nor admiring her ring. Her thoughts were elsewhere in a place where her worries and fears made her tremble.

"We can't get enough good NCOs to go to Vietnam, so the rank is there. Honey, it's just six lousy months!"

"Six months," she echoed, as her shoulders slumped and her wet eyes rose to meet those of her husband. Tears were welling up in the corners of her eyes, and she brought up a hand to keep them from spilling down her cheeks. The couple at the next table was trying hard not to listen.

"Hey! I'll be okay!" He reached across and took her hands again in his and made her turn back to face him. "We'll be okay. I promise."

She nodded weakly, and they finished their dinner in relative quiet.

He awoke before sunrise, slipped quietly out of bed, and let her sleep. He put on some boxer shorts and went out on the balcony for a cigarette. He cupped the burning ember automatically as he had done time and again in the war zone, and sat quietly, trying to figure out answers to questions that plagued his conscious mind.

He was halfway through the cigarette when she came out and sat down in the lounge chair beside him. She was dressed in a New York Jets football jersey that had served as her nightshirt, and her arms were folded over her breasts.

"It's so quiet here, even if they don't have good lox and bagels," she said, staring at the dark beach. What light was left from the fading moon was soft and pleasing. An early morning breeze was scraping through the palm fronds.

"It's like this in Nam," he said and then snorted, "I mean, when the artillery isn't firing, helicopters aren't cranking, and the Viet Cong aren't mortaring us. Vietnam really is a pretty country at times. Did I mention the huge mosquitoes?"

"I traded in the Chevy," she said, changing the subject and getting to what was really on her mind.

"When?" The Chevy was a '61 Impala and in reasonably good shape or so he had thought. He loved the bucket seats, leather tuck-and-roll interior, and the power everything.

"Two weeks ago. I told you I was having trouble with it, and you said 'take care of it,' so I did."

"Why?"

Her short laugh lacked any humor. "Because I got tired of

carrying the kids to a gas station every time I had to call for a tow truck. Most of the tow truck operators in town know me by my first name. The neighbors think I'm having an affair with a fat guy in a dirty T-shirt who smells like 10-W-30!"

He knew he had to give her something. The news about the six-month extension didn't get the reaction he had counted on, so this was the payback.

"What did you get?" he asked hesitantly.

"A Ford Falcon . . ."

"Ah, no . . ." Kline said, shaking his head. No, it couldn't be a Thunderbird. It had to be a Falcon. In his mind's eye he saw a plaid bench seat and, in the rear window, a little hula doll whose hips moved every time the car hit a bump.

"It's a station wagon," she added, fueling the fire. The dog robber smoldered. "The kids needed the room, and the dog—"

"What dog?"

"I suppose it's a lousy time to tell you we have a new dog, too?"

The dog robber laughed and studied his wife closely. "The Viet Cong ambush us early in the morning, too. They just don't dress as sexy. Any more news? You sell one of the kids or something?"

"If you go back for another tour of duty after this six-months extension, buster, I just may, and toss you in as well. You worry me sometimes," she said. She sat in his lap and hugged him closely.

"I worry myself," he said, hugging her back.

Although they had been married for eleven years, the love hadn't diminished even at times when it was pulled the hardest. Throughout it all they had endured two PCS or permanent change of station moves and, prior to his tour of duty in Vietnam, one unaccompanied tour in Korea.

The first PCS move was from Fort Bragg, North Carolina, to Bad Kreuznach, Germany. The second was from Bad Kreuznach, Germany, to Fort Benning, Georgia, which is where he had received his orders for Vietnam. On his PCS moves they'd

gone together and were provided military housing; the unaccompanied tour meant that she stayed in the United States and
had to move out of her base housing.

The unaccompanied one-year tour of duty in Korea had been
the first real test of their relationship. But Vietnam was proving
to be the final exam.

Like most military wives, Sarah had been taken under wing
by the wives of several other noncommissioned officers and
guided through the process of surviving the separation.

"We've all been through it, honey, and it is miserable," she
was told by a first sergeant's wife, who'd recognized some
common symptoms in Sarah's behavior. "But it helps to be miserable in numbers."

The NCO Wives Club assisted women in her position,
planned functions and activities to help them get by until their
husbands returned. The army's officers and NCO wives clubs
served a vital function in helping the women adapt to the periods of long separation. Those who couldn't adapt opted for
other solutions. The divorce rate in the military was climbing as
the war claimed new victims. So much was changing around
him, but Kline knew enough to hold on to what was important.

"I love you," he said.

"You'll love the station wagon and the dog, too."

"Yeah, he's probably at home now shitting in my favorite
shoes."

His wife shook her head. "He's a black Lab, honey. He's
probably eating them!"

CHAPTER TWENTY-ONE

The target AO was a remote mountain region northwest of Kon Loc, one that showed little or no outward signs of activity.

G-2 wanted it checked out since, from the air, it seemed to offer excellent cover and concealment beneath the ancient, primordial rain forest and steep cliffs.

If half of the LRRPs' mission was scouring likely hiding places for the enemy, the other half was eliminating possibilities, which is exactly what that mission was to do.

Five days into the seven-day reconnaissance patrol, it was plain to see that the area was too remote and difficult even for the Viet Cong. There were a few old woodcutter's paths, unused and, in some places, grown over with vines and branches. And there were a number of animal trails that crossed the small runner before disappearing into the dense underbrush. If that AO wasn't the land that time forgot, then it was at least in the same neighborhood.

Gnarled trees rose two hundred feet into the air, their lush, dark green foliage, large, thick, brown limbs, and an intricate latticework of vines creating a living canopy that easily blocked out the sky from the forest floor and the prying eyes of any scout helicopter that flew above it.

The valley floor itself was awash in fetid pools, alive with malaria-carrying mosquitoes, a navy of leeches, and the myriad unseen things that slithered to the water's edge before quickly disappearing beneath the gray-green ooze as the patrol approached.

The thin valley was rich in greenery because of its proximity to the high ridges that bordered it. It was the primary channel for the monsoons' runoff, and the wide troughs in the steep slopes were generous with their distribution.

It didn't take a rocket scientist to figure out that, in the rainy season most of all, the AO would be unsuitable for enemy bunker complexes because of the heavy flow of water. Underground bunkers would quickly become swimming pools, and any trail would wash away or get foot and bicycle traffic so bogged down that they would only be obstacles to the Communists' strategic goals.

The patrol had been inserted by helicopter a day's march from the ridgeline and had spent another day and a half climbing down to the valley below. The next two days were spent doing a careful recon of the valley. All they had found there was an old hunter's trail, which bisected a broken path and spoor made by large wild game. At least that's what their montagnard scout, Klong, had concluded studying the weathered route.

The team leader, Staff Sergeant O'Brien, agreed with Klong's assessment but had moved the patrol up the opposite ridge to monitor the find anyway since it was their only likely prospect. There they sat and patiently waited.

On the sixth day, the sun rose bright yellow into a pale blue sky, sucking up the early morning dew and replacing it with a heavy layer of humidity. There was no wind, so the trees and thick underbrush were still, which only made the movement across the valley more obvious to O'Brien, who cautiously came on alert, easing down behind his makeshift fighting position.

Sudden movement in a jungle would catch even the worst soldier's attention, and the former Ranger instructor knew better than to give away any combat advantage.

O'Brien had picked the observation site because it offered a good view of the target valley as well as of the opposite ridge. The first part of the sixth day had been uneventful, boring even, until O'Brien caught sight of the activity below. As he came up with his rifle in his hands, the rest of the patrol followed suit.

Who or whatever it was, was down beyond the valley floor just below the steep ridgeline opposite their own. He was standing high in the trees on a limb or small platform a few hundred yards away, and without the binoculars, it looked very much like the outline of an enemy soldier.

"Nobody move!" O'Brien whispered while he slowly pulled a pair of binoculars from his rucksack and brought them up, shielding the glass from direct sunlight.

"What is it?" a new LRRP next to him asked in a tense tone. "What do you got?"

O'Brien lowered the field glasses, sneered at the new guy, and then brought the binoculars back up again, still shaking his head. "I don't fucking know," he said flatly. "Klong?" he said, turning to the veteran montagnard scout and pointing in the direction of the subject of his concern. "Across the valley, just above the trees near the knife-shaped ridge. What do you make of it?"

The LRRP team leader handed the binoculars over to the montagnard, and then guided him up on target. Klong was five five or six and weighed maybe 115 pounds, but every inch of him was no nonsense. He could read trails better than an Indian guide and didn't seem to be afraid of anything but the "spirit" that he believed roamed in the jungle at night. His father and uncles had fought with the French against the Viet Minh, and several bullet scars attested to his own six years of jungle combat. The American team leader and most of the others in the company had decided that Klong really had his shit together. He had grown up in the region and knew the jungles and its flora and fauna better than a college-educated Tarzan, but even he seemed to be stumped by this.

The montagnard lowered the binoculars and shook his head solemnly. "Don't know," he said, shrugging, and then studied the trees around him as his rifle barrel followed his survey. Several other of the patrol members searched the tree line with him, uncertain what they were looking for but confident of Klong's caution.

The new LRRP wanted to say, "What do you mean you don't know? It's your fucking country!" but instead turned back to

O'Brien, who had the binoculars back up, and asked him, "What is it, Sarge? Gooks?"

"Nope. Looks more like a hairy rock ape . . ."

"So?"

"So it has wings."

"What?" the new guy said with a forced smile, not sure whether O'Brien was fucking with him.

"I said it looks like a rock ape with wings," O'Brien said, blowing out a quick breath and followed up with, "Hmmm?" which didn't tell the new guy anything either.

"No, really. What is it?"

O'Brien lowered the field glasses and frowned. "I'm serious. The fucker's got a five- or six-foot wingspan, and it, whatever it was, just flew off deeper into the jungle."

The new guy wasn't satisfied, but that's the best answer he'd get from O'Brien, who had been as tolerant of the dumb ass as he was going to be. O'Brien wasn't a zoologist or wildlife expert, but he was willing to bet that there were things in the back country of Vietnam that even Marlin Fucking Perkins couldn't identify. He didn't give a rat's ass whether or not the new guy or anyone else believed what he and Klong had seen in the trees.

The team leader was reasonably certain there were places deep in the jungles and in the unexplored canyons and valleys like that one where man had seldom or never ventured, so who really knew what the hell was there?

Most new arrivals came to Vietnam knowing about as much as Dorothy knew about Oz when she dropped in. After the dust had settled, they really had no idea what was going on in the land of the little people. There was always someone in dire need of a brain, some who could use heart, and more than a few who were looking for courage.

Even with their shiny new shoes, most wouldn't catch on for a while that they weren't in Kansas anymore and that the notion of flying monkeys wasn't as ridiculous as it seemed. But it was pretty scary for all of that!

Lions and tigers and flares, oh my.

CHAPTER TWENTY-TWO

Sgt. John Simones didn't relish the idea of going back into combat, but he did it anyway; it was something he had to do. Captain James had talked with Simones prior to his going back out and seemed sympathetic enough, correctly guessing what Simones was going through.

"It's your call," James said, offering him a way out; the sergeant didn't take it.

After the mission request came down and Simones was notified, he went about the business of readying the team. But there was something more, an edge that said he was also readying himself. The fire was burning closer.

In the twenty-four hours before the new mission, he went over every procedure in his mind and then he physically checked and rechecked each weapon and every piece of equipment of each patrol member. He checked claymores, grenades, rifle magazines, and any and everything attached to the LBE web gear. When he was satisfied with that, he went over his map, studying the area of operations and noting the terrain features. The area was, mostly, high plains, which meant little or no water, so the Viet Cong would have to get water from the few marked streams. That's where they would be and where the team would need to monitor the Communist army activities.

On the helicopter ride out to the AO, nobody talked as the team members were drawn into anticipation of the insertion and the personal thoughts that accompanied them.

"Short final!" the crew chief yelled to Simones, who nodded

that he understood and told the team to get ready. It was time to come back into focus.

On touchdown, they were out of the helicopter and running for the tree line only a few yards away. Seconds later, the insertion helicopter was off and lifting itself back into formation; the LRRPs were already motionless just inside the underbrush.

They waited, laying dog, until Simones was sure that they weren't detected. Then, to be certain, he waited some more, listening to the nuances of the jungle for signs of anything out of the ordinary, that is, like startled or frightened birds, the clear, distinct sound of branches snapping, or a muffled cough.

When he was satisfied that they were alone and after taking a compass reading and checking his map, he gave Hup, the montagnard point man, the hand signal to move out.

Slowly they came to their knees and then to their feet as they carefully followed Simones, who was behind the point man, and watching the jungle for any sign of movement.

Yeah, you get back up in the saddle all right, only you no longer consider yourself a cowboy, just someone who is acutely aware of the dangers involved and how, in war, luck is always holding the reins.

CHAPTER TWENTY-THREE

Kline had been approached by the MI officer and asked if he was interested in what a VIP at headquarters had to say about his, the dog robber's, career. The officer said that the VIP had heard "good things" about him, and when Kline grinned and said, "Is that right?" the officer either missed the cynicism or overlooked it. After all, he was there to fetch the staff sergeant.

The dog robber said he was, in fact, interested, but it was more out of curiosity than anything else. Who was this VIP? "A tech rep," replied the MI officer, who left it at that.

What a tech rep had to do with his career was still a mystery, but Kline decided to hear him out anyway. "Why not?"

The MI officer nodded, smiling his best used-car-salesman smile as he led him to his jeep. "Good. Hop in!" he said.

The drive across Camp Radcliff was, as usual, enveloped in tumbling dust clouds stirred up by vehicles in front of them. At one point, the MI officer swore then pulled over until the dirt and grit settled back down. Sergeant Kline laughed to himself; it probably wasn't the first time the officer had gotten lost in the swirl. Nor would it be the last.

When they finally arrived, Kline followed the MI officer through an open tent flap into a darkened hootch. The VIP, who was sitting behind a field desk, sipping on a Coca-Cola, rose slowly and offered his hand. "I've been anxious to meet you," he said congenially enough. But he didn't offer a name or a business card.

Since the VIP had a .45 automatic strapped to his leg and his jungle fatigues lacked name tag, rank, or unit patches of any kind, he suspected that the tall, square-shouldered man with close-cropped gray hair, steel-blue eyes, and the bearing of a career officer was a spook with the CIA or one of the many other agencies that used initials to hide what they were doing.

Of course, when the military intelligence officer kept calling the anonymous man "sir" and offered to get coffee from the headquarters mess tent, the staff sergeant felt like Sherlock Fucking Holmes.

"I've read your 201 file, and I've been told that you're a real team player," the spook said, and then back to the MI officer added, "Any more of these around?" He held up the canned soft drink.

The officer nodded. "All we have is Coke or Fresca."

"Coke's fine," the interviewer said as Sergeant Kline nodded in agreement, which sent the officer on his way.

"Like I said, I hear you're a real team player?" the VIP said, getting to the point of the interview after the officer had stepped from the tent.

"You forming a team. Mr. eh . . . ?"

"Smith," the VIP said unconvincingly. "Actually, a small team to deal with a small problem. It is combat related, but it isn't anything that will take you away from An Khe for longer than a few days every now and then. If anything, it'll be a forty-five-day operation. Two months tops!"

"To do what, exactly?" Kline asked, scratching his head.

The man called Smith smiled. "You don't beat around the bush, do you, Sergeant?"

The staff sergeant shrugged. "Too many thorns and too much fertilizer, sir."

"Well, since you like the direct approach. First, I'm sure you know I won't talk about the job until I find out whether or not you want to work with us. It's on a need-to-know basis only, and right now you don't need to know."

Kline chuckled. "That's direct, all right, only when you say 'we' and 'us,' I get the impression you're not talking about 'we, the army' and 'us' as in those of us in olive drab, Mr. eh, Smith."

"Let's just say we share mutual concerns. In fact, this particular job has to do with saving army lives, more specifically 1st Cav lives in this region. This isn't fertilizer, let alone horseshit. So I won't promise you a rose garden. If you work out, then we'll talk about other career possibilities or options."

It was a long while before the staff sergeant spoke. "You may be good at what you do, but your sales pitch isn't worth shit, sir," he said, returning Smith's smile. "If you're closing the deal, aren't you supposed to offer me something in return? Say, a promotion or a new Buick? I mean, hell! If you didn't want me, then you wouldn't have called me in, let alone have gone through my records or found out if I was a team player?"

Mr. Smith leaned back in his folding chair and smiled again. "You're right, Sergeant. I am supposed to offer you an incentive. So, is that what you're looking for? A promotion to E-7?"

The dog robber nodded. It was a start.

"That's doable," Mr. Smith replied. "But the Buick's out of the question; a new one anyway."

"Nothing happens unless you ask!"

"True enough!" The recruiter laughed. "I imagine we can find a unit to carry you in a seven slot and attach you to the MI unit or another An Khe element if you like. Since you're not really attached to the LRRP company, it shouldn't be all that difficult. So tell me, did you really break your platoon sergeant's shoulder with a punch?"

The dog robber nodded. "I was aiming for his left ear. He tried to run when he saw it coming."

"How'd he get the booze in the field? Canteen?" Smith asked.

"One filled with gin, another with water. I wouldn't have been surprised if he had ice cubes in his magazine pouch."

"They should have given you his job," Smith said.

The dog robber shrugged. "Yeah, well . . ."

"Well, the seven's yours if you want to work for me."

S.Sgt. Joe Kline held out his hand. "I'm in, sir—Mr. Smith or whatever you want to be called," he said.

"Smith will do," the recruiter said, shaking his hand. "Now let me tell you what you just agreed to, Sarge. I don't think it's any secret that the Viet Cong set up roadblocks on Highway #19 from here to Da Nang, robbing civilians and killing anyone they have a hard-on for. After sunset, you couldn't even make it as far as An Thuong before getting sniped at or running into an ambush."

An Thuong was a few miles east of An Khe on the road to Qui Nhon and on a mountain-lined stretch of highway that made sniping child's play.

"Last year alone, they kidnapped or killed over three thousand officials or friends or relatives of officials or anyone they wanted to make an object lesson of. They specialize in it, and they're good at it, too!

"So we, you, me, and four Chams or Vietnamese we can trust not to fuck up a wet dream are going to run roadrunner teams along the highway . . ."

"Roadrunner teams?"

"Interdiction teams. Because in the past, every time the army has sent out a road security patrol to catch the little shits, someone in the village warned them the cavalry was coming, so they slipped back under the rocks. Which is where we come in. We're going to catch the fuckers and terminate them with extreme prejudice."

"You mean kill them, don't you?"

"Why? Does that bother you, Sergeant?"

"No. That's what we're here to do when they let us do it."

"We're going to do it. The plan is to go out at last light or early morning in an old bus or in scooter vans looking for the roadblocks. We'll all wear the black pajama Viet Cong uniforms and carry AKs, so if any concerned citizen or Cong sympathizer spots us, then they'll get the impression that we're some of the home team. You up on the Kalashnikov?"

"Gas-operated assault rifle. 7.62mm. Soviet, Eastern Bloc, or Chinese made. Effective range four hundred meters. It's sturdy, reliable, and has a high muzzle velocity that hits like a son of a bitch! I've had familiarization training, which only means that I've handled one, taken it apart, and fired a few token rounds. Other than that, I could use a refresher course because I'm not as proficient as I'd like to be."

Mr. Smith liked the answer. The staff sergeant wasn't one to bullshit. "We'll make the time."

"We'll recon the route, right?"

"That's affirmative. We'll go out with an outbound convoy in a day or two to get an idea of the places we might be likely to run into the bad guys. The 8th Transportation Group makes the run regularly; we'll go out with them. We'll take a gun jeep, so they'll probably be glad to have us."

"We checking out the passes?"

Mr. Smith shook his head. "Naw," he said. "Those are a given. With all of the crags and caves, the VC own them. I'm talking about the road between here and the passes, where the local VC operate. We're after the local shit heads."

"You said we're going out for a few days. We staying out overnight?"

Mr. Smith shook his head adamantly. "No. We go out, find a roadblock, and hit them hard and haul ass . . ."

"Like the roadrunner?"

"You got it!"

"I'll need to clear it with my unit."

Mr. Smith waved him off. "No need. We'll take care of it. We'll find you a hootch near headquarters, too, although not right away. Is that fine with you?" he asked, just as the MI officer returned with the soft drinks. On cue, Kline suspected.

"I'm afraid they're warm," the MI officer said, handing out the colas.

"What's our chance of finding a seven slot in a rear-area unit for our latest associate?"

The MI officer thought about it for a moment. "Very good, I think, but I'll check just to make certain."

"Do that," the VIP named '. . . eh, Smith' said and sat back and drank his Coke, seemingly pleased with himself.

The convoy was hot and slow, and the jeep was uncomfortably tucked between a deuce and a half that belched black smoke, suggesting it needed a ring job, and a potable-water tanker. Smith drove the gun jeep while Kline slouched over the mounted M-60 machine gun. He brought along a LAW just in case they needed a little more firepower. The LAW was a shoulder-fired rocket that could blow a hole in a Soviet tank or a rock-wall bunker, but used against an ambush, its impact was even more profound. The LAW was a plastic, one-shot, throw-away weapon. It was light, easy to operate, and although it wasn't quite as good as the Soviet's RPG, it did the job.

The road reconnaissance proved eventful for Smith who noted several sites on his plastic-covered map with a black grease pencil. The first such target location was on the outskirts of the village which couldn't be protected by the base camp. There the daytime traffic was the usual mess, any and every sort of wheeled vehicle on the highway, all in a hurry to get to where they were going, using whatever side of the road was most convenient.

In theory, the Vietnamese drove on the right side of the road, just like the French and the Americans; most of the locals didn't seem to give a shit about the rules. Carts, motorbikes, sedans, buses, bicycles, and foot traffic all simply tried to avoid one another as they went their various ways.

As they passed a series of weathered hootches, Kline noted sullen faces among those watching the convoy pass; villagers who were sympathetic to the Viet Cong, if not VC themselves. To him, their faces seemed not only to say "Fuck off!" but "Fuck off and die!"

In the remote area, where the traffic thinned and the terrain twisted and turned, momentum would be on the side of anyone hiding in the bushes. The Viet Cong could easily set up a working three-man roadblock since the vehicles had to slow down to negotiate the curves.

"So far, I've only counted a hundred or so likely locations," Kline said to Mr. Smith, after the convoy turned north on Highway #1 and headed into Qui Nhon. Smith nodded in frustration. The entire road was a potential ambush site.

"I'd say we have full-time employment. You should have held out for an E-8 slot," he said to the staff sergeant as they pulled into the military installation in Qui Nhon, bringing their reconnaissance trip to a close.

"If we hit the shit and get trapped, we'll talk again. For now, I'll settle for a beer. Come on, boss," he said, heading for the NCO club. "I'm buying. I mean. I guess I have to, seeing how you can't even afford rank insignia or patches."

"Fuck you!"

Kline, the dog robber, feigned outrage. "Why, Mr. Smith? According to army regulations profane, obscene, and other immoderate language will not be used or permitted. I'm shocked that I should have to bring it to your attention!"

"Thank you, Sergeant."

"Don't fucking mention it, boss."

Three Vietnamese and one Cham had also been selected for the job, and all were hardcase mercenaries recruited from Bien Hoa, and whose sympathies were not in question. Three of the four, the Vietnamese, were combat veterans, sons of combat veterans who had fought at Dien Bien Phu but had "died" during their subsequent captivity by the Viet Minh. The families rightly suspected that the men had been executed. And since they were Catholics, too, the families, too, suffered miserably for their political sins.

When the North and the South were divided and the families were allowed to move south, they brought little with them but their memories.

The three Vietnamese had no love for the Communists, and in addition to being attached to Mr. Smith from the Vietnamese

Army, they would receive a bounty for each Viet Cong they killed. Since they received the equivalent of twenty-five dollars a month from the Vietnamese Army, the bounty money would provide them with a financial incentive for something they were more than willing to do anyway.

The Cham was taller than the Vietnamese, dark skinned, and he had worked with Mr. Smith previously. He didn't smile much, and while the three Vietnamese talked and laughed with each other, they left the Cham alone, which was seemingly the way he preferred it.

"What's his story?" asked Kline, doing a once-over of the man and figuring him for a veteran. He just wasn't certain in whose army.

"He's a Cham," Smith said.

The staff sergeant shrugged. "Yeah, so?" he said, uncertain what Mr. Smith had meant.

"South Vietnam used to belong to the Chams. The Vietnamese invaded and took part of it away from the Chams and the Khmers. He hates Vietnamese," Smith said. Kline gave him a second glance as the Cham sat and listened quietly. His face gave nothing away. "He just wants his country back and likes the idea that we're giving him the opportunity to help drive a few of his enemies away."

"You gotta love gratitude," the staff sergeant said.

Their first run was in two old three-wheeled scooter vans, purchased in Da Nang and driven back to a safe house in the village. They were divided into three-man teams, with one of the Vietnamese driving Kline's van while the Cham drove Smith's vehicle. The Americans rode in back with the rest of the mercenaries. The small panel vans were barely big enough to hold the heavily armed team, and the thinly padded seats left a lot to be desired as they bounced from pothole to pothole.

Kline's team kept a comfortable interval between it and Smith's team, so that if one team ran into trouble, the other could come to its assistance.

It was also part of their strategy. Smith's group would take on the roadblock, while the staff sergeant's team would provide cover, support, and security.

Not surprisingly, they didn't have far to go before they reached their first target. Several vehicles were stopped up ahead, and one Viet Cong soldier glanced over his shoulder as they slowed their approach and then returned to searching the back of an overladen motorbike. Squawking chickens struck their heads out of crudely constructed crates that supported great piles of vegetables in baskets.

The Viet Cong soldier had a weathered M-1 carbine slung over his back, and a second Viet Cong soldier aimed his carbine at Smith's van with one hand and with the other waved for the Cham to stop. The Cham smiled and complied.

A third enemy soldier was on the side of the road watching with indifference. He was dressed in baggy khakis and a pith helmet. A brown leather belt with a Communist-star belt buckle held a 9mm Makarov pistol in a leather holster at his side. A canvas shoulder bag was slung over his opposite hip. Smith's driver recognized him as North Vietnamese and as the officer in charge of the operation, an NVA regular who was overseeing the involuntary "tax collection."

The Cham honked the scooter horn as though by accident, smiling and shrugging at the Viet Cong soldiers and the NVA officer who only sneered at him.

The Cham smiled again and brought up his hands, palms together and bowed.

"On three!" Smith whispered into his radio. Kline rogered the call as Smith went through the countdown.

As they were exiting the van, Kline heard automatic rifle fire; the Cham had initiated contact, bringing up his folding stock AK and firing a quick burst into the Viet Cong soldier who had his back turned to him, then turning on the second enemy soldier, who had leaped to the side of the scooter van. He was struggling to release the safety while bringing the rifle up to return fire.

By that time, Smith and the second mercenary on his team

were out and running, charging the surprised soldier and finishing him off. The Viet Cong soldier never saw them coming until rifle fire twisted him in a half circle and they were several feet away. But that was all he would ever see; sustained fire tore away his heart and lungs. He was dead as his body hit the earth.

But the NVA officer had seen them coming. He had fallen to the ground, brought out his pistol, and was firing sporadically. Smith and the second mercenary fired, but without effect, as the NVA officer crawled behind an outcrop of rocks. There was nowhere he could go, so the fight would have to continue.

The driver of the heavily laden motorbike in front of him had been hit in the exchange and was down on the ground writhing in agony. The bike had fallen in the tumult and with it had gone the crates and the chickens. Several had pushed their way through broken slats and were running around the road, their squawks accenting the rifle fire.

The staff sergeant and his team were out of the second van in an instant, covering the countryside as the small fight unfolded. A third, lone, Viet Cong soldier hiding back down the road in a security position suddenly stood up twenty yards away but made the mistake of firing too soon. His aim was high and to the left, and the soldier quickly tried to correct the mistake. But not quickly enough. Kline's rifle fire was well aimed, and he squeezed off several rounds. The soldier went down in a heap.

Still firing, the staff sergeant charged the position, the first few rounds kicking up in the dirt in front of the fallen soldier before the others found home in the fallen man's thigh and chest.

In a running crouch, Kline ran forward as Smith and his group had maneuvered around the NVA officer and caught him in a cross fire. There was never an intention of taking him alive.

Within minutes the fighting was over. The sudden stillness was unsettling.

"Check them out! Make sure we got them all!" Smith yelled as the Vietnamese and Cham moved forward to survey their damage.

Standing over the dead Viet Cong soldier, Kline studied the

motionless body and realized what he had missed. The left side of her face was blown away, leaving it loosely attached to the exposed and damaged spine.

She had been in her teens and would be forever. Kline kicked the rifle from her hands as one of the Vietnamese mercenaries retrieved the weapon and personal effects.

When he turned back around, he saw Smith standing behind him. Beyond him, the Cham stood over the three other enemy soldiers while the veteran Vietnamese soldiers covered the eastern and western approaches of the highway.

"The Viet Cong usually work in cells of three. She must have been the third. The other one's an NVA political officer who was responsible for the taxes they were collecting. Good shooting."

The staff sergeant felt like saying that at twenty yards there was no way any soldier should have missed but acknowledged the comment, keeping in mind the spirit with which it was offered.

"What about him?" Kline asked, pointing to the wounded civilian.

"Not our concern," Smith said, matter of fact and direct as he walked back up the road to the first Viet Cong soldier and the Cham standing over him.

The soldier wasn't dead. The machine-gun burst had caught him in the upper thighs and groin. One hip was broken and splintered through the flesh, and if he had a dick it was probably under the truck. He was moaning a feral sound that carried well into the night.

Smith leveled his rifle and fired a single round from the Kalashnikov into the man's left eye; the soldier's head bucked, then settled into the hard-packed ground.

"Cut their throats and then make sure we have all of their weapons and anything else they're carrying," Smith said to the mercenaries, who went about the grisly task.

"Chau Thi Huyen," said the Vietnamese mercenary who was going through the dead woman's possessions.

Smith turned. "What?" he asked, not really understanding the meaning. His Vietnamese was so-so. His Cham worse.

"*Chau Thi Huyen* award, like medal," the Vietnamese offered. "She kill three you."

Smith turned and looked at the body, a dead Viet Cong soldier who was maybe all of seventeen or eighteen years of age, who had been adept at her job. Until that day.

A slight look of satisfaction crossed his face. He seemed mildly impressed. "No shit!" he said.

The Vietnamese mercenary spat on the corpse. "She kill anyone who try escape," he said, significantly more furious. "Vietnamese, American. All same-same."

"You bagged a hardcase, Sergeant!" Smith said to Kline.

The Cham was busy near the outcrop of rocks where the NVA officer had fallen. While the others had finished clearing the area the Cham brought over a canvas bag and the dead NVA officer's pistol, handing them over to Smith and Kline. In his left hand, he was carrying a bloodied machete. Neither Smith nor the dog robber said anything.

Inside the canvas bag, Smith found a diary, a map, several silver coins, and over two hundred in Vietnamese piasters.

"Take the piasters but leave the silver for him," Smith said, motioning to the wounded motorbike driver. Smith retrieved the diary and map and the pistol, handing the canvas bag with the money and silver back to his driver.

"Time to *di-di mau*. Make sure we have all their weapons!" Smith said, walking back to the vehicle while the others followed carrying the assault rifles and web gear.

"Let me guess. He cut off the officer's head?" Kline asked, glancing at the Cham.

"Old scores," Smith said.

It was overkill, but it had its effect. The Viet Cong had made a killing at the "tax collection" roadblocks. Now it was their turn. Payment past due.

When they reached Phu Cat, they parked their scooter vans in the courtyard of a safe house and unloaded their haul.

"You can hop a flight back to An Khe in the morning. We'll go out again in a week or so. No need to set a pattern," said Mr. Smith to the staff sergeant, who didn't think it was much of a debriefing but suspected it was all he was going to get.

In the safe house, they inspected their haul while the Vietnamese and Cham divided the confiscated money, and Smith paid them their per-body fee.

Later, after they had cleaned their weapons, Smith broke out a case of beer and a bottle of scotch.

Morning came with a haze as Kline made his way to the airstrip, caught a ride back to An Khe, and trudged back to the LRRP company area. By that time, unit strength was over one hundred, and the company was running ten to fifteen patrols a month. There were new arrivals, LRRP candidates in training, and enough activity and new faces that Kline made his way to his hootch with little notice. He stripped, grabbed his shower kit, wrapped himself in a faded olive-drab cotton towel, and headed toward the shower, only to discover the canvas bucket was out of water. Swearing, he walked on over to HHC's shower facility.

A monsoon sky was threatening the morning and anyone under it, so soldiers were moving quickly toward cover, but the staff sergeant took his time. He walked on to the shower stall and disappeared inside. He was lathered up and washing the sweat and dirt out of his hair when the water in the fifty-five-gallon drum slowed to a trickle.

"Fuck me!" Kline said disgustedly as he wiped soap from his eyes. All wasn't right in the world, especially in that remote corner of Camp Radcliff where a half-lathered staff sergeant wondered how many of the Geneva Convention rules he had broken in the roadrunner outing. And if it really mattered.

Before he reached a conclusion, the storm building over the Hon Con Mountain began sending down sheets of heavy rain that turned the dust into ooze and then ooze into slow flows and faster streams that pooled in low spots and flooded the base camp. He walked out of the shower stall buck naked and continued lathering his hair as the steady stream of water washed away the soap.

One way or another, there would be enough water.

He finished his shower, washing out the soap along with any sense of right or wrong in a war that walked a fine line between the two and frequently stepped across it for balance.

Wars, he concluded, were only clean in the movies.

A week later, when it came time to leave, he packed his things and, not one for drawn out good-byes, shook hands and said his farewells, wished the others luck, and walked off empty handed from the company area. A short time later, he returned with a jeep, and while the company was busy with activity as the new trainees went through their training regimen and teams practiced reaction drills or got ready to go into the village, S.Sgt. Joe Kline loaded his things into the newly acquired jeep, took a long last look around, smiled, and then picked up some mud and rubbed it over the unit markings on the jeep's bumpers.

He'd transfer his things to his new unit and then leave the jeep at the flight line where it would eventually be found and returned to its unit, unless, of course, somebody stole it.

"Shameful the way some people take care of government property," he thought to himself, wiping the mud from his hands. "Just shameful."

CHAPTER TWENTY-FOUR

The first time Spanky Seymour saw the Viet Cong close up, the war took on a new perspective. Until then, the enemy was always "the V.C." or "Charlie" or "Victor Charlie," an unseen force of superslick silent soldiers who could sneak up on their own shadows and catch them off guard.

Reality was another matter. The Viet Cong soldiers that he had seen were just soldiers, no bigger or better than anyone else. They weren't supermen either, just small, thin-framed Vietnamese who, at times, stumbled in the jungle, tripping over roots or vines, or who ran into unseen branches, swearing when they did while pissed off officers or NCOs yelled at them to maintain noise discipline.

Because of the patrols, Spanky Seymour came to respect the enemy even as he kept his M-16 leveled on their skinny chests as they walked by the team's hiding place.

Hiding was easy. If you stayed off the trails, set up your claymores, and remained quiet and still, the Viet Cong or NVA wouldn't even notice you were only a few yards away. Nor would they understand just how close they came to dying if they had seen the Americans with the camouflage faces.

The real challenge for him came in knowing that at any moment his decision to become a LRRP could come back to haunt him in very real and painful ways. Even while they moved, he knew it was possible to come face-to-face with an enemy soldier a split second or so before that soldier pulled the trigger of his assault rifle. Ambushes worked both ways, and the Viet

Cong had a history of using the ambush to their benefit. They mentioned that in training and again during the mission briefing or whenever anyone sat around and the talk turned to missions, but it registered immediately whenever the Viet Cong point man and soldiers came into view on the trail.

In Vietnam, paranoia was survival skill, one learned quickly or forever unnecessary.

The odd thing was, Spanky Seymour liked the patrols. Besides the obvious adrenaline rush, he appreciated the advantage of small patrols and the value of sneaking around in the jungle gathering intelligence materials. In the army, it was frequently said that close only counted in horseshoes and hand grenades, but LRRP patrols were adding a third dimension. The phrase "close combat" was often used to describe proximity in battle, where a soldier can see his enemy clearly and fight at distances so short that a soldier didn't have to aim, he just pointed and shot, a distance so short that it sometimes meant hand-to-hand combat. In the jungles of Vietnam, on a long-range patrol, "close" could very easily mean "shockingly close," a branch or two away, and one "close" look would mean there would only be inches to live or seconds to die.

Besides, a LRRP patrol was the ultimate game of hide-and-seek if the enemy didn't know you were there. And if they did, then it became the real test of war. Seymour wondered if he could kill an enemy soldier and do it professionally to avoid getting captured or killed himself. Would he freeze or fail to do what needed to be done? Those were questions that every combat soldier wondered about himself before he was actually faced with the eventuality.

When the Viet Cong came looking for the American LRRP team, following its trail from the landing zone and tracking it into the jungle, they had no way of knowing that the Americans had circled around on their own path, waiting to see if they had been followed.

A short time later, the Americans knew the answer; the Viet Cong point man came into view, his eyes focused intently on the ground while the soldiers behind him studied the jungle. They were unaware that the Americans had their weapons up and pointed on target until the first rounds were fired and the point man died, and the second Viet Cong soldier went down as the third returned fire briefly before falling back with the VC behind him.

Killing someone was surprisingly easy, Seymour decided. But had the team not made the buttonhook when it did, dying would have been just as easy, too.

CHAPTER TWENTY-FIVE

South Vietnam was part Dodge City and part Calcutta slum. In the rear areas, it had all of the charm, the look, and the feel of an oil field boomtown. Beyond the rusting barbed wire, it was Jungle and Safari Land, and held the potential of Custer's last stand.

Doc Suggs recalled hearing that a television news reporter or journalist had once said being a medic in Vietnam was like being a country doctor. He laughed, wondering which country the damn fool had in mind! It certainly wasn't one caught up in a nasty war.

During his tour of duty, a combat medic was routinely confronted with a myriad of gunshot and shrapnel wounds, severed limbs, horrible burns, and the other traumatic injuries expected in war. After all, that went with the job. You didn't have to like it, but you did have to accept it.

However, during the Vietnam War, a medic might also have to deal with soldiers and civilians who had been mauled by tigers, bitten by deadly snakes or rabid rats. He would have to treat those suffering from stomach-churning dysentery, the hot sweats and cold chills of malaria, flesh-eating jungle rot, and even bubonic plague.

He might also encounter heat stroke, prescription or illegal drug abuse and overdoses, alcohol poisoning, bad food and water, tuberculosis, and fevers of known and unknown origins. If that wasn't enough, then there would always be cases of clap to cure or gonorrhea and syphilis to diagnose and treat when doctors were in short supply or unavailable, which was usually the case.

In the jungle, a medic would remind a platoon or more of grunts to take their malaria tablets, their salt tablets, drink enough water, and use their water purification tablets if they decided to replenish their canteens with river or stream water. They'd also have to fight the excuses they received when they reminded the soldiers.

"I'd rather get the shits than drink bleach!" a GI would argue when the medic offered the purification tablets.

"You will get the shits," counseled the medic. "And the parasites from the river water will work their way into your intestines and grow until one day a slimy creature will stick its head out of your ass and say, 'Hey! You shoulda used the purification tablets!' You'll listen then!"

A good medic would stay on the grunts' cases, reminding them to change their socks or use foot powder, and use bug spray to ward off the clouds of mosquitoes.

A LRRP medic, like Suggs, would focus his attention less on the company and more on the members of his team, taking an active interest in their health and welfare because their health and welfare directly affected his own. After all, they went to the field together, and a LRRP team, because of its size, was greatly hampered if even one member became ill.

When there was time, and supplies, and permission, the LRRP medic took on the extra responsibility of administering to the medical needs of the montagnards and their families. It was only on those occasions, Suggs conceded, that the country-doctor analogy took over.

Suggs had been providing medical treatment to the hamlet for a few weeks by then, holding a weekly sick call and setting up a make-shift treatment program. He had accompanied Hup and an older veteran sergeant to the montagnard hamlet compound and, just as on his previous visits, found the tribal people pleased to see him. He was more than a curiosity. He was one of the men with the painted faces who accepted and honored their own warriors.

The montagnard hamlet was made up of stilted huts and communal fires. Scrawny red chickens and slate gray potbellied pigs freely roamed the compound. There were animal pens and grain bins, and squatting women wrapping sticky rice in banana leaves. Bare-ass toddlers walked around, relieved themselves, and walked on. Diapers were unheard of. A teenage boy of fourteen or fifteen cradled a rifle as he smoked a cigarette and watched the surrounding countryside. The montagnards didn't like being surprised.

If the surroundings were out of another era, then they went along with the rituals and beliefs and guidance of a shaman the montagnards believed in and adhered to. It wasn't that the montagnards weren't open or receptive to modern necessities or conveniences, but being montagnards, they hadn't had access to them. So they were locked in their traditions as much by circumstance and prejudice as they were by belief.

For the montagnards, there was often nowhere else to go. Of the thirty or so tribes of montagnards, most lived in the Central Highlands and were either Rhade, Jarai, Bru, or Mnong. They were hunters and gatherers who lived in the twentieth century in much the same manner as they had lived over the preceeding millennia. They were subsistence farmers who relied on slash-and-burn methods for their crops, the primary crop being dry rice. Normally, after about seven years of working an area, they would move on to another to give the jungle time to rejuvenate. But because of this latest war, they had been forced to remain within specific areas for their own protection.

They believed in two ancient spirits, Kanam, the evil one who roamed the forests demanding appeasement and extracting his toll when angered, and Yang, a more benevolent spirit, who asked for sacrifices as well because he ruled over the rest of the montagnard's world. The montagnard's world was confined to the mountains, rivers, and rain forests.

As the two spirits demanded appeasement, so also did the

Vietnamese. Vietnamese clinics frequently wouldn't provide treatment to them; and Vietnamese hostility to and open resentment of the montagnards was blatant. The montagnards were the last to be treated, if they were treated at all.

A few missionary clinics ran by foreigners did open their doors to the montagnards, but they were usually understaffed, poorly equipped, and by their presence alone made targets of themselves; they were usually Christian and always foreign and therefore enemies of the Vietnamese Communists. Their situation was not made any easier by the fact that they were viewed with suspicion by the Saigon government and even by some Americans, who suspected that they were aiding the Viet Cong.

So, for the most part, the montagnards relied upon their shamans and sacrifices and herbal medicines for protection against illness and disease, and when those didn't work, they accepted the help of the LRRP medic from Georgia. The montagnards were primitive, but they weren't stupid. If something worked, they embraced it, but only if it fell within the confines of their beliefs. More than a few American medics had been stunned by the montagnard practice of burying a live baby in a hollowed-out log with its mother if she died during childbirth; it was a bad omen to let the baby live. The medics could argue and fuss over the practice, but there was little they could do to change it.

The missionaries could try to win over their spiritual beliefs, but the medics were left to treat the physical ailments. Aspirins and APCs went a long way to win goodwill, more technical treatment and care secured it.

Doc Suggs began a general sick call and for a good hour worked his way through the line of patients. Most had minor ailments, and the people giggled and laughed at their problems and grinned at the treatment. Others warranted more attention and concern, like the young girl who hobbled up with her leg wrapped in a dirty bandage while leaning against her mother for support.

The girl's foot was badly infected, and the thin ten-year-old, dressed in a black cloth shirt and well-worn pants, was trying not to wince as Doc Suggs carefully removed the filthy bandage, its contents, and examined the painful wound.

The original small, two-inch cut must have come from a piece of scrap metal that the child had stepped on. The younger children usually collected expended brass, which they brought back to the village so it could be hammered out and reshaped into something to sell to the GIs. The sharp metal had cut into the flesh of her arch, and the barefoot girl had limped home with the other children to be treated by her mother. The wound had probably been washed with brown water from the well. Then it had been packed with a green natural-herbal paste and wrapped in an old, used, bandage that had probably been found in the garbage from Camp Radcliff.

Anywhere else, the small cut would have healed by itself, but in the region's high humidity and heat, with its proximity to the decaying jungle floor and myriad bacteria, and combined with the impure water and the montagnard's poor diet, the small wound had festered and the foot swelled until it was twice normal size.

The sour sepsis smell from the wound grew as he peeled away the layers of bandage, but an overwhelming stench of putrefication rose with the removal of the last layer, which was sticking to the wound. He peeled it back carefully as tears welled up in the small girl's eyes. The infection had been lanced, repacked with herbal paste, and then rewrapped in the blood-and-pus-stained gauze. But the home treatment wasn't enough.

As Suggs reached into the aid bag, a small group of montagnards watched, interested in his skill as a healer. He found the orange plastic bottle of antibiotics, which he gave to Hup and told him to tell the mother how many to give to her daughter, and how often, and when, and that she was to take them until they were all gone.

"Take all now?" asked the LRRP/montagnard. The American medic shook his head.

"No!" he said. "She takes one pill each time, three times a day, until they're gone."

Hup nodded and then turned back to explain it to the woman and child.

Doc Suggs retrieved an alcohol swab, told Hup to tell the girl that what he was going to do might hurt, then washed the infected area before he lanced the crust of pus and sponged it with gauze swatches. As the white-yellow fluid flowed freely, the young girl winced again but remained surprisingly quiet. Her large brown eyes told another story.

When the wound had been purged and wiped again, Doc let the mother apply the greenish paste while he wrapped the wound in a fresh bandage. Why not? The paste was probably an herbal antibiotic, and the infection was more than likely a result of using the filthy bandages and dirty water.

"Here!" Suggs said, giving the mother more alcohol swabs and several clean bandages. He turned back to Hup and said, "Tell her to use them on the cut and she'll be fine."

Hup nodded then spoke to the woman. The mother and the young girl thanked Suggs, nodding and grinning at the Georgian, and then nodding and grinning some more as she and the child walked away.

The old veteran said something, and the mother stopped, turned back, and said something in kind, nodded one more time as she left with her gifts and disappeared into a hootch before coming back out and heading toward an outdoor kitchen area. She was joined by several other women and children. Just then, everything was right in their world, and maybe in a life of uncertainty, that was good enough.

"You stay. Eat," said Hup, as the older veteran retrieved a small gourd from another hootch, sat down next to the American, and made himself comfortable. The leather-faced sergeant opened the gourd, sniffed its contents, nodded to it and then back to Suggs, smiling before taking a short, quick drink. When he was done, he handed the gourd to the medic.

"You drink," he said while Doc, not wanting to be impolite,

sniffed and stared at the light brown liquid, and then took a cautious sip. It was fermented rice wine, and it was strong and pungent, burning his throat on the way down.

"Thank you," he said, uncertain if thanks was the proper word to use as he handed the gourd to Hup, who was anxiously awaiting his turn. The stuff would probably burn blue under a match, take the paint off an old Dodge, or serve as makeshift napalm if you hacked it back up with phlegm, which at the moment seemed like a reasonable possibility!

When the food came, it was a combination of unidentifiable green and yellow vegetables, sticky rice, and a meat of some kind, which Suggs didn't care to ask about. It could have been rat, monkey, snake, or dog.

The meat was stringy, tough, and chewy but not bad. It was well seasoned in what spices they had, and once Suggs got over worrying about what kind of meat it was, he looked upon the event as a weekend barbeque. Sort of. Doc also figured he'd know what kind of meat it was for sure if they later had a strong desire to chase jeeps back to Camp Radcliff or, say, if the old veterans threw a stick, and he ran out and brought it back.

But until then, he would eat their food, drink their brew, and accept their hospitality, pleased to be a country doctor in a land where it was still okay to make hootch calls.

CHAPTER TWENTY-SIX

By May 1967, U.S. military strength in Vietnam jumped to 436,000, and the air force was flying over eight hundred sorties a month, dropping hundreds of tons of explosives on Viet Cong and NVA positions. In spite of the eleven successful major allied operations and campaigns against them since the first of the year, the Communists were pumping in thousands more soldiers of their own and taking the fighting to the towns and cities, infiltrating into areas of great population to hide and to carry out clandestine operations. While it was difficult to hide soldiers in a rural area, it was easier to do in cities teeming with hundreds of thousands of residents, a good portion of whom were poorly documented refugees seeking sanctuary from the fighting. So one at a time or in small groups, they worked their way into the towns and cities and waited for their orders.

The stakes were about to be raised, and the Viet Cong were upping the ante.

Throughout the four military corps tactical zones* into which Vietnam was divided, the Viet Cong and NVA were conducting widespread operations. As the monsoons returned, the Communists took full advantage of the miserable weather. Knowing that the American helicopters seldom flew in the heavy rains and low, thick cloud cover, the Communists marshaled their forces for their strikes.

---

* Abbreviated CTZ and numbered I, III, III, IV, they were more often just returned to as "corps," as in I Corps, II Corps, etc.

Up north in Quang Tri, fifteen miles from the misnamed and always dangerous Demilitarized Zone—the DMZ—South Vietnamese troops lost 125 killed in action and another 180 wounded in one devastating battle with NVA divisions who used the zone as a springboard into South Vietnam. In reality, the DMZ was little more than the starting line for the race toward Saigon.

The South Vietnamese Army wasn't alone in its misery. U.S. Marines were getting hit in Khe Sanh, the Rockpile, Dong Ha, and Con Tien, as were the small Special Forces camps along the Laotian border. The NVA could hit the installations and be back across the border—where pursuit was forbidden—long before reinforcements could be flown in to help.

To the Cav's northwest in the Central Highlands, the 4th Infantry Division and elements of the 173d Airborne Brigade were going toe-to-toe with the NVA at Kontum and Dak To, repulsing repeated attacks against their bases as continuous mortar and rocket barrages slammed into their perimeters.

The Cav wasn't immune either as the frequency of the firefights picked up in the An Lao Valley and all through Binh Dinh Province. The 1st of the 9th was racking up *big* numbers, with one troop killing over one thousand enemy soldiers in just a three-month period while the three other troops were scoring impressive victories of their own. The scout helicopters, gunships, and light-infantry aeroplatoons moved quickly into targeted areas and often caught Viet Cong and North Vietnamese Army soldiers off guard. When the scout helicopters found concentrations of enemy forces, they rolled in, attacking while calling for gunships and ready infantry backup.

The line units within the division were confronting the enemy and forcing him to fight, but although Communist casualties rose significantly, the Cav was not without its own losses, foremost among them pilots and Blues (quick-reaction platoons) of the 1st of the 9th.

Down south in III Corps, in Warzone C, the 1st Infantry Division was taking its licks and casualties in heavy fighting in the enemy stronghold region of Tay Ninh Province, and returning it measure for measure. And the 25th Infantry Division was up to its elbows in firefights and battles of its own. Army and air force installations in and around Bien Hoa and Saigon were being targeted with marked frequency, while in IV Corps, the Viet Cong were massing their forces within the shelter of the U Minh Forest.

The increased enemy activity was met with increased force, and if the South Vietnamese, American, and Allied Force casualty rates were climbing, the Communists losses were staggering by comparison, as was their brutality. When two Viet Cong companies attacked a South Vietnamese Army Ranger company in Kien Hoa Province, the Communists shielded themselves behind civilian hostages.

As the Communists advanced, pushing the hostages forward, they fired on the ARVN Ranger position, and the ARVN Rangers returned fire. During the initial assault, ten children were killed and twenty-five other villagers were wounded, shot by the South Vietnamese soldiers. The Viet Cong didn't overrun the Ranger position but achieved another kind of victory despite that.

In the media, the Viet Cong were being painted with a sympathetic brush, broad strokes applied to their struggle and character. In the worldview, the Americans were the aggressors, the Viet Cong simple farmers, students, and educators who were fighting only for family and future. The value of the front-page headlines was understood in Washington, D.C., as much as it was understood in the Kremlin, in Beijing, and every other world capital.

But too broad a brush makes for a poor artist, smearing the picture and obscuring important detail. To the politicians, the fight was for the sway of public opinion; to the soldiers caught up in the fighting, there was only combat and survival. People came and went constantly; their tours of duty were individual and staggered.

Of the original field LRRPs, only O'Brien, Simones, Torres,

Ross, and Suggs were left; First Sergeant Kelly (E-8), Lieutenant Hall, and Captain James made up the rest of the "old"
crew. Within sixty days, most would be gone.

Torres and Suggs were talking about extending their tours of
duty as new officers, NCOs, and enlisted men were reporting in
and finding their niches in the company. Lt. David Smith was
brought in a few months earlier and had worked in well. Hall
knew Smith and thought highly of him, which was good enough
for Captain James. The new officer proved himself quickly, and
while Hall had taken charge of four teams in the Bong Son region, Smith had taken over other teams and responsibilities.

As the operations NCO, Staff Sergeant Campbell was, without a doubt, one of the best NCOs Hall had ever encountered.
Monitoring the teams in the field around the clock and coordinating their support sometimes required genius or, at the least,
an acute sensitivity of strategy and tactics. Campbell had that
and more.

With one or two minor exceptions, the core of team leaders
was continuing the legacy. Hall had been pissed when one
of the new TLs decided to leave his team in the field and *walk*
four klicks back to a fire support base to confirm the team's position. Of course, he hadn't bothered to inform those monitoring the team. When he didn't turn up, the XO talked the crew of
a PsyOps helicopter into flying him out to retrieve the missing
man. While scouring the surrounding area, the helicopter drew
small-arms fire that injured Hall and another crewman. In frustration, the helicopter returned to the fire support base only to
discover that the missing team leader had reported in.

Hall wanted to shoot the silly little shit, but after he had settled down, opted for chewing the man's ass out—well, practi-
cally off—instead. As the saying went, "his ass was grass," and
Hall was the lawn mower; a heavy duty industrial motherfucker
with large blades and an electric starter.

Still, the company was in good hands, callouses, cuts,
and all.

CHAPTER TWENTY-SEVEN

They needed help.

Many of the new volunteers had only had sixteen weeks of training before they arrived in Vietnam. The first eight weeks of basic training was exactly that, *basic* training, which introduced them to the basics of military procedures and protocol, drill and ceremony, physical fitness and training, basic marksmanship, and weapons introduction.

In AIT, advanced infantry training, the next eight weeks were spent on more weapons familiarization and training, additional marksmanship qualification courses, basic patrolling and ambush techniques, more physical fitness, map reading, artillery coordination, basic explosives, and other training deemed necessary before sending them off to combat.

The army considered the training to be adequate; many NCOs said it was, "Just enough to make them dangerous to everyone around them!" To compensate, most of the divisions set up their own in-country training courses to acclimate the new arrivals and to give them a better understanding of the specific threats they might encounter in Vietnam.

Since the 1st Air Cavalry Division was a helicopter-borne division, the new soldiers were given a course in rappelling from helicopters, as well as in the dos and don'ts associated with helicopter familiarization.

"Always run around the *front* of a helicopter when you're trying to get to the other side of the aircraft. . . ."

"Why?" the inevitable question was asked.

"Because if you run *behind* the helicopter, you'll more than likely run straight into the tail rotor, which will slice through your helmet like a hot knife through butter and cut all the way through to your chest *and*," said the instructor, emphasizing this last point, "you'll ruin a perfectly good tail-rotor blade!"

Along with an introduction to the history of the division, the new arrivals were also reintroduced to the effective use and care of the claymore antipersonnel mines and what happens to the mines in the hands of an enemy infiltrator.

The majority of the brief training courses were designed to have an immediate impact on the new arrivals, but this last demonstration certainly had the most profound effect.

Before the audience of new cavalrymen, a former Viet Cong sapper, a dreaded *Dac Cong*, dressed only in shorts but carrying an assault rifle and a backpack of simulated explosives, easily crept and crawled through a mock base camp perimeter line. Within minutes, the lone Vietnamese moved under, through, and around razor-sharp strands of barbed wire, past taut trip wires connected to trip flares designed to signal the guard bunkers of an enemy advance, and onward to the claymore mines that he disarmed or turned around on the American positions.

Once through the seemingly impenetrable perimeter, the former Viet Cong planted the pack of explosives and then moved on toward an unsuspecting guard.

The audience of new arrivals didn't know how to respond to the demonstration. As some applauded, others stared in awe or fascination and, maybe, even a certain degree of horror.

With the exception of those who were selected for additional long-range patrol training, that was the extent of their in-country indoctrination. The rest was on-the-job training, OJT.

But not all of the lessons had to do with combat.

Doc Suggs was offering medical advice to some of the new LRRPs who had only recently completed the training course and were getting ready to make the one-klick walk into An Khe to celebrate.

The side flaps of the team tent were rolled up and tied off

to allow for a breeze. The tent was new, but in Vietnam "new" didn't last long; in no time, high humidity made the canvas sweat, then it dried under the constant one-hundred-plus heat. It wasn't very long before the new mothball smell gave way to that of lingering canvas mildew. Exposed to high winds and heavy monsoons, the canvas quickly faded and shrank, bleached a milky green, and stretched taut by the climate.

Sergeant Ross was sitting on a footlocker nearby, cleaning his rifle while listening to the lecture. Ross closed one eye while the other was staring down the barrel of the M-16, inspecting his work.

"When you're socializing in Sin City, it would be wise to wear a condom," Doc said to the new guys.

"You mean, all the time?" a smart-ass asked as the medic shot him a frown.

"I mean, that if *you* stick it over your face, dickhead, it would be a definite improvement. For the rest of you it might protect you from at least one of the nasty things you'll find in the village. . . ."

"One of the many nasty things," said Ross. He began to clean the chamber with an old toothbrush.

"That's right," Suggs echoed, "One of the many nasty things . . ."

"You talking about VC?" one of the new guys asked. The smart-ass was watching skeptically. "You saying there are Viet Cong in the village?"

"Most definitely," Doc said. "Some probably even run businesses there."

"Which ones?"

Suggs shrugged. "I dunno," he said. "Maybe the ones who charge you the most for a stale beer. Chances are that there are Viet Cong who operate in and around An Khe, and more who have friends and relatives fighting for them."

"Yeah, but they wouldn't be stupid enough to shoot an American in broad daylight," the smart-ass replied.

"Not unless you do something even more stupid like bunch

up or let your guard down in a bar," Ross said earnestly. He turned back to the medic and added, "Of course, if the NVA or VC hit us with a ground attack while you're in the village, you're dead anyway."

"Roger that!" said the medic.

"They'll shoot you in a heartbeat—"

"A heartbeat."

"If they don't decide to torture you first to get the villagers to see how weak Americans are, even LRRPs."

Suggs sighed and lowered his head. "I think I'd rather be shot."

"Are the gooks still putting battery acid in the beers?" Ross asked as he wiped down the barrel of the rifle.

"They used to," said the medic, nodding. "But not too much anymore. I think it's okay, I mean, unless they've got a few extra vehicles in town or something."

The new LRRPs studied the two veterans to see if they were joking. But neither cracked as much as a smile. The new guys grew very quiet, their moods somber, their thoughts imagining the worst.

Ross knew what they were thinking. "Don't worry because you're more than likely to get the clap in town than get shot. . . ."

"Yeah, the clap or one of the other diseases the prostitutes have!"

"We had one guy who caught a bad strain of VD in the village, and he let it go until his pecker and balls got so infected that they had to be amputated. I mean, surgically removed," Ross added as the new guys' attention went from the medic to the team leader, then down to their own groins, and then back to the two veterans.

"Wha . . . what happened to him?" the smart-ass asked quietly.

"What do you think happened? They made him a second lieutenant." Ross grinned. "But have a good time in town anyway."

The new guys swore and stomped off. After they were gone, Ross turned to the medic with a smile. "That went over well."

"Well, at least they'll remember the condoms." Suggs laughed.

Ross finished putting the M-16 back together and stored it. "Come on, Doc!" he said, getting to this feet.

"Where?"

"I was thinking we'd go into An Khe, too, and buy them a beer."

The medic snickered. "It won't be hard to find them. They'll probably be bunched up at the front gate, hiding behind an MP."

"It's not easy being new, is it?"

"Not in Vietnam."

CHAPTER TWENTY-EIGHT

By early June 1967, division had recruited Capt. David B. Tucker to take over James's job as the LRRP company commander, and James was having mixed emotions about turning the unit over to his replacement.

It wasn't personal. In fact, it wasn't even business. Tucker had all the necessary qualifications, and James even liked the red-haired Irishman. He had assured James he'd take care of "his" people, and James knew Tucker meant it. He was also certain that the new captain would work out fine.

The trouble was, James was like a veteran firefighter who couldn't quite get over reacting to the alarm. The LRRP company was his firehouse so how was he to shut off the adrenaline when "his" people were still out there fighting a war, when the firefights kept the company ready to roll at a moment's notice to help rescue a team on patrol?

After he officially turned the company over, there was little left to do but watch as the new firefighters took on the station. He was there to offer advice and assistance, but basically, he was there to keep out of the way and let the new people do the job. Their job.

During a brief awards ceremony, James had been awarded a Bronze Star for Valor for his role in trying to pull Burton's team out of contact, getting shot down, and then rallying the defense until help arrived. The general presenting the medal talked of heroism, about the outstanding job the captain had done with the company, and the significant impact his training methods and leadership had had in ensuring the safety of those on patrol. That was all well and good, but James thought of his actions as simply doing his job, and whatever praise he had received and whatever sense of satisfaction he felt were overshadowed by the loss of Private First Class Ives and the wounds Guerrero, Carpenter, and Koper had received. He was proud to be recognized, but he was embarrassed by the attention.

The award was well received as onlookers congratulated the captain, although others grumbled that the Bronze Star for heroism wasn't enough for everything he had done.

He deserved a higher award, they said. At least a Silver Star for gallantry since he had tried to extract the team under hostile fire only to have the helicopter shot out from under him. "Then, get this!" one critic argued. "After the crash, he helps pull people out and then repels a ground assault from a large Viet Cong force!

"If that's not enough, he kept everyone together throughout the night until the quick-reaction force finally got in, and then the next morning when everyone was getting ready to be extracted, he and three other volunteers keep the Viet Cong from blowing the helicopters out of the sky before another helicopter returned twenty minutes later and finally pulled them out.

"So tell me. If that isn't gallantry, then what the fuck is?" the LRRP asked. The others nodded in agreement.

"It isn't fair!" someone said, while a veteran LRRP laughed and asked what fair had to do with anything anyway.

The telling compliment was that the enlisted men agreed that James had earned an award, and the company was genuinely glad to see him receive the recognition.

After the ceremony, he was thanked again, congratulated by those in attendance, and after the fuss had died down and it was all over, he made his way back to his hootch. The captain took off the small copper-colored star suspended from a mostly red ribbon, stared at it for a moment, and then put it back into the presentation case and tucked it deep into his half-filled duffel bag.

Before the war, when he had been a new second lieutenant, he might have believed that anyone with a medal for heroism was really something, part John Wayne and part Errol Flynn. But as a combat veteran, when he saw someone wearing a combat award, he preferred to know more about the story behind the award and the soldier who wore it. Lieutenant Hall had received a Bronze Star before he left Vietnam, and it had been well deserved. Hall had been his right hand, and while the new officers were proving themselves, Hall would be missed. There had been so many who had helped to build the unit from the ground up and whose job descriptions—and awards, if they got any—in no way addressed their real contributions or service.

Sometimes they received only token awards from a system that didn't always appreciate or understand their service. They always had each other's thanks and respect, and for many that was enough. The journey from detachment to company was a longer and more complicated process than the chronology might suggest.

The captain's thoughts drifted across the time line and then came back to a more startling reality. For all practical purposes, he was out of a job!

With few responsibilities and little else to do, the bored officer decided to concentrate on something that would wow the people back home. The medal probably wouldn't impress civilians, who didn't think much of the war anyway, so he settled on the one thing that might do it, a good tan!

Jim James smiled as he took off his tiger stripe uniform and put on his bathing suit. Then he grabbed a pair of pilot's sunglasses, a towel, and went off to find an out-of-the-way place for his lounge chair to begin the ordeal by heat.

War is hell, James said as he stretched out. And sometimes it's just a matter of realizing the value of its heat source!

CHAPTER TWENTY-NINE

Ross was only a few yards behind Corporal Klong, the montagnard scout, as they moved down the jungle-covered hillside toward the streambed. With what little light there was left from a quarter moon filtering through the trees, the new team leader wasn't comfortable with the predawn mix of abstract shadow and tones of gray. Still, it was a good time to move since the VC would never expect it from the Americans.

Klong was five feet five or six and weighed about as much as a high-school long-distance runner.

Although the montagnard was slight of build, he was strong for his size, and his muscles were long and ropy and told of hard work on a low-fat diet. Ross admired how easily the montagnard moved through the underbrush, carefully studying the jungle as he moved. The new NCO was glad to have him on point.

The shallow streambed was open, maybe eight to twelve feet across, down a small mudbank, then rising to the opposite bank. As they stepped out of the cover of the jungle, Klong and Ross were momentarily exposed, and that's what nagged at Ross the most. The jungle was their ally; the open spaces marked them as targets.

It was a hazard of the job. There were always streams to cross, trails or bunkers to check out, villages to skirt, and sometimes that took the teams onto dangerous ground. His chest felt constricted, but he knew it was just nerves.

In the thick jungle, if you stepped off a jungle trail and stood perfectly still, someone could walk right by and not even notice you were there. Hell, the LRRPs had done that so many times, it had become second nature. But in the middle of an open streambed, even in the dark, a LRRP's silhouette stood out. If the VC could see at all, they could make it out.

The Viet Cong were well aware that the Americans were using long-range patrols in the region and trained to maneuver against them. But if finding the Vietnamese Communists in the jungle was difficult for the Americans, then finding the American LRRPs was more difficult for the Viet Cong; there weren't many of them. The VC would monitor possible landing zones more closely and adopt contingency plans to kill or capture the teams, and they would establish guard positions in the jungle to watch over their base camps and perimeters. Planning, however, was one thing; carrying out those plans successfully was another. First, the Viet Cong or NVA had to find the American patrols, and the Americans LRRPs didn't allow them very many opportunities.

Before the team leader signaled his team to move out, Ross studied the streambed, looking for anything that might tell him if something was wrong. He listened for a while, sniffed the air for unnatural odors, cigarette smoke, garlic, or fish sauce. Smelling none of them, he made the decision to cross.

Even Klong, the jungle-savvy montagnard scout, thought the crossing was safe, so when the challenge came from the Viet Cong guard as the two LRRPs came out into the open, there were few viable options.

"*Ba?*" called the Viet Cong guard from the opposite bank, no doubt from an earthen bunker. The VC guard had assumed they were fellow Communists and offered the first half of a number password, the Vietnamese word for the number three. Unless Klong or Ross knew the correct counterresponse—which number added up to be the appropriate reply—the guard would probably fire on the interlopers.

Since neither the montagnard nor Ross knew the answer, and they knew that a wrong answer wouldn't work either, both

LRRPs knew things were about to get tense. So did the rest of their team behind them.

"*Ba?*" came the challenge again. This time the Viet Cong soldier stepped from behind his cover, along with two other enemy soldiers, casually clearing the brush and leaning out from the opposite earthen bank like people waiting in line for a roller-coaster ride, watching the train come in. The outlines of the VCs' torsos were clear through changing shadows.

A typical Viet Cong squad was made up of three cells of three fighters, nine men. These three were one cell. But how many cells were with them? How many squads, platoons, or companies? A number of questions raced through the young team leader's mind as did a number of scenarios; most of them weren't pleasant.

The Viet Cong couldn't make out the LRRPs' faces or uniforms, and even their silhouettes and the outlines of their weapons were nearly indistinguishable in the poor light. But if the sentries were expecting anyone other than fellow Viet Cong, then they would have remained behind cover.

"*Khong duoc to tieng!*" the yard scout barked at the sentries, ordering them in Vietnamese to keep the noise down. The ploy worked; the sentries went sullenly quiet, unsure of the interlopers, but certain now that they were outranked by them. Noises stirred in the jungle behind them as the ass-chewing drew some curiosity.

Ross and the montagnard scout knew they would soon be discovered if they didn't act, so they opened fire with full-auto bursts from their rifles, dropping the three instantly. There was no time to savor the small victory, since the area behind the three dead or dying Viet Cong suddenly came alive. It might have been just a few occupied bunkers, maybe a squad of nine enemy soldiers or so. But then it might just as easily have been an occupied bunker complex or an enemy base camp.

VC officers and NCOs were yelling behind them as the enemy unit came awake and maneuvered into position. It was a platoon at least, Ross thought, not wanting to wait around to see if it was more.

"Go! Now! Go!" Ross yelled to the team behind him. He grabbed the scout's shoulder and tried to pull him back. But Klong was standing his ground, firing at the Vietnamese. "Come on! Come on!" Ross yelled, changing magazines and emptying the new one into the line of shadows moving out of the jungle toward them.

Klong nodded, fired again at the three figures on the ground and then turned back toward Ross, following his lead.

The first bursts of enemy AK fire tore into the position where the LRRP team had been only moments before as the enemy gunfire raked across the jungle, uncertain of their targets. Definitely a platoon or better, Ross thought to himself, changing magazines as the team climbed a small hill and hurriedly disappeared over the opposite side. The hill would offer a small degree of protection and immediate cover. Several eager enemy soldiers raced up after them only to be cut down by the LRRPs. The hasty ambush slowed the chase.

The Viet Cong would certainly regroup and come after them again, but more cautiously, which would buy the LRRPs some much needed time. The team's RTO was on the radio calling in the contact while Ross pulled out his map and compass to get his bearings. Their only chance was to break contact and continue the mission by escaping and evading the enemy.

Out of the corner of his eye, Ross saw Hup, the montagnard rear scout, stringing up a quick booby trap. The Yard had taken a fragmentation grenade and tied it to a small tree at chest level, then tied a loose trip wire to the grenade's safety pin, and then pinched together the pin's ends to make it an easy pull. The olive green trip wire would be next to invisible in the morning twilight and barely visible in daylight in the shadows of the rain forest. The Yard let the thin wire droop down to knee level, where it blended into the underbrush.

Anyone chasing after them would step through the brush, snag the wire, which would dislodge the pin and cause the spoon of the grenade to release and the hammer to drop. Seconds later, the delay fuse would cause the fragmentation grenade to explode. The first enemy soldier might clear the grenade's deadly radius, but the two or three behind him would catch its full impact.

The patrol was in a small circle, each LRRP lying prone or down on one knee, watching and listening to the jungle. Drops of sweat beaded on their camouflaged faces as they fought to bring their breath under control.

After the TOC in An Khe had been notified of their predicament, his plastic-covered map opened on the ground in front of him, Sergeant Ross took a good compass reading and then gave Klong the signal to move out. As Klong disappeared into the jungle and the others followed, Ross remained behind to cover Hup as he worked his magic over their jungle floor, covering their trail behind them. What amazed Ross then and throughout the patrol was the way the Yard could replace the bent branches and limbs and cover bootprints so that their path was quickly obscured or, at the least, made difficult to track. The Viet Cong had their own montagnards who would pick up on the trail, but that would take time.

The Viet Cong would probably assume the Americans were still on their old heading, race past the point where the team had turned, and run into the trip wire. The explosion and chaos that followed would give them a few more minutes lead time, and maybe it would be enough to throw off the pursuit.

Maybe.

Believing the American LRRPs would be lifted out by helicopter, the Viet Cong might also send soldiers racing for the closest clearing. If they could beat the patrol to it, then they could kill or capture the Americans and, maybe, bring down a helicopter in the process.

Fifteen minutes later, the jungle roared behind them, which was both good news and bad news. The good news was that the booby trap had, more than likely, caught several of the trackers who were stalking them; the bad news was that, more than likely, the Viet Cong were still coming after them. Sure enough, rifle fire tore through the forest behind them and then shifted to other areas. The gunfire was fierce and sustained.

"Keep going!" Ross said, realizing the enemy was just trying to draw them out. "Go!"

Changing direction again, he thought about turning the team on a buttonhook, but then decided against it; the numbers were against them. The small-arms fire died out behind them, but he knew the lull was only temporary. They pushed on, and by the time they took a much needed rest, Hup, the patrol's rear scout was coming toward the team in a hurry.

"V.C. come! They come!" The montagnard pointed back along the route they had taken. Ross turned back and listened for a moment without hearing anything unusual at first. Then, faintly, ever so faintly, in the near distance, he could make out the sounds of metal swivels slamming against rifle stocks and branches breaking.

The cat-and-mouse game was with a pissed off kitty who wanted nothing more than to pounce on the LRRPs and tear them to shreds. The faces of the team members studied Ross and then turned back toward the jungle. Ross had his map on his knee. He was desperately looking for another open field.

Their run was over, and in no time, the Viet Cong would realize it, too.

CHAPTER THIRTY

Okay, so it wasn't the white sand beaches of Tahiti or Waikiki, and there weren't any smiling bikini-clad ladies or tropical drinks with little umbrellas, James sighed to himself woefully, but at nine o'clock in the morning, smack-dab in the middle of a combat zone in an army base camp, you make do.

Dressed only in a swim suit and sunglasses, he leaned back into the lounge chair, sipped on a lukewarm Coca-Cola, and flipped through the pages of a *Playboy* whose foldout was probably hanging up on someone's hootch wall. James had a transistor radio tuned to AFVN, the military radio station, and was using it as background noise rather than entertainment since it couldn't tune out the sounds of Camp Radcliff. Helicopter crews, going through the morning ritual of preparing the birds for combat, cranked them up and ran through system checks. The *whop-whop-whop*ping and high shrill whines from the various turbine engines combined with the thumps and *whump*s of the outbound artillery to accent the downbeat to the song that was playing.

The captain ignored them all, or tried to, and decided to concentrate on his tan instead. Like most GIs in Vietnam, Jim James had had a "farmer's" tan—his face, neck, and arms were uniformly brown, while his chest, back, and legs were pale white!

Now he was down to just hours on his tour of duty, and he didn't want to go home looking like a two-tone Chevy. For the last few mornings and an occasional afternoon, he lay out in the sun hoping to round it out. All in all, the strategy seemed to be working as his body slowly worked its way from white to red, to bright red, and finally to bronze. Since it was his last day in Vietnam, James was killing time by adding some finishing touches.

He had packed his things the night before, and in five hours or so, he'd catch a helicopter ride to the coast and then a C-130 to Cam Ranh Bay to catch a charter flight back to the United States, his "freedom bird back to the World."

James looked up from the magazine and took a look around at the other world he had come to know, and at the people who made it tolerable. The company area itself wasn't much to look at and would never even have made a cover on *Better Hootches and Gardens*, but like any unit at Radcliff, it wasn't the facilities that made the unit, it was the people.

Since the beginning of time, man has been trying to find deeper truth and meaning in war, and Captain James was no exception. What had he learned as a leader and as a soldier? What had he accomplished and at what cost?

He was fiercely proud of his people and what they had accomplished, literally from scratch. Any personal evaluation of his own attainments would always be shaded by the loss of Private Ives and the wounds of those who had had to be medevacked home.

Like any man of real honor and character, he wasn't about to forget their names, their faces, or their sacrifice. A myriad of thoughts and questions raced through his mind, but the flow was interrupted by the sudden movement nearby that caught his attention.

In the company area, Lurp, the six-month-old, brown-and-black mascot, was stalking a rat that had scurried out from a bunker and was trying to find an opening in a sandbagged wall that Lurp patrolled. The rodent had no idea the puppy was closing in on him.

"Good dog," James said to himself, smiling. "Good Lurp!"

James was starting to ease back down into the lounge chair

when he noticed one of the new TOC personnel, a small, wiry spec four, peering out of the tactical operations center, looking for something or someone. He didn't see whatever he was looking for, and the spec four frowned. When he noticed the captain studying him, he quickly disappeared back inside the TOC.

Wondering what was up, James got to his feet and walked over to the TOC. As he was coming through the tent flap, he recognized Sergeant Ross's voice coming through the radio's speaker.

"What's up?" he asked the TOC NCO, who was hovering over the radio, monitoring the team's situation.

"The Dark Marauder patrol is in contact again, sir. Here!" He pointed to the team's position on a wall map. "They tried to Echo-Echo, but Charlie's staying with them. Looks like they have a platoon or more trying to run them down."

"Where's Captain Tucker?" James asked.

The TOC sergeant frowned. "Da Nang, I think. Maybe Qui Nhon, sir. He's out digging up some URC-10 backup radios from the air force."

"The XO?"

"G-2," he said as Ross's voice came back on the radio informing the TOC that Dark Marauder was in contact again.

It didn't take long for the former CO to make up his mind as to what needed to be done. "Let's pull them," James said. The TOC NCO nodded in agreement. "Get a Huey for me from division, and a gunship or two. Tell Marauder we're on our way."

The captain ran back to his hootch, grabbed his boots, helmet, web gear, and rifle as he heard the helicopter settling at the helipad. The only uniform he had out were the the khakis for his flight home, so he left them where they lay on his cot and hurried toward the waiting helicopter.

So much for a well-rounded tan! He laughed as he jumped into the open helicopter bay, checking and then rechecking his weapon. The crew chief stared at the soldier in the swimming suit and the helmet with the subdued black captain's trax. He started to say something but decided against it. Instead, he handed the captain a flight helmet as the aircraft powered up, lifted, then hovered briefly before dipping its bulbous nose and roaring off.

Within twenty minutes, the extraction helicopter was crisscrossing the contact area, and James could see the gunships working the contact area around the team to help them get to the landing zone. The gunships were hammering positions behind the team with rockets and machine-gun fire.

Once Dark Marauder radioed that it was on the west edge of the grass field and in position for an extraction, the Cav gunships began making continuous passes to cover their escape as well as make the corridor needed for the Huey. Judging from the return fire they were taking, Charlie had had to be at least a reinforced platoon or larger. And he was closing quickly on the LZ.

"Marauder, this is Red Stag Six. Pop smoke to mark your position. Over." James studied the ground below, looking for the team's signal.

"Smoke out," the patrol's RTO replied. Seconds later, wisps of yellow smoke began to build and twist skyward.

"I identify lemon."

"Roger, Six."

"Set up for extraction. We're coming in," James said. The LRRPs rogered the transmission, as did the pilot, who added, "Let's do it!" as he banked sharply to begin the short final approach. James held on to his seat frame as déjà vu butterflies swirled around him. He didn't really want to admit it, but his subconscious was reminding him that he had been shot down doing the same damn thing a few months earlier.

James checked the magazine in his rifle, shrugged the feeling off when he realized it was too late to worry anyway, and watched as the jungle below loomed larger.

"Taking fire! Taking fire!" the copilot screamed. The crew chief and the door gunner in the opposite well brought their M-60 machine guns on target and returned fire. The gunships were scoring the jungle with minigun fire and rockets, forcing the Viet Cong to keep their heads down while the door gunners made certain no Charlies came out of the jungle to surprise them.

The LZ was coming up fast. The pilot flared at the last moment and brought the skids down, bouncing, as the first few LRRPs ran out of the tree line, quickly followed by two more. Ross and Klong had remained behind to cover their escape, and as the four patrol members were being pulled inside, they began their own sprint.

"Come on!" the copilot yelled. Of course, the two LRRPs were already breaking land speed records to get to the helicopter.

The crew chief was firing over their heads into the wood line as a couple of brave but foolish Viet Cong soldiers tried to stop the fleeing Americans. Both enemy soldiers were hit with several bursts and were pushed back hard, folding into themselves.

The helicopter was still taking fire and was a sitting duck until the pilot, who was watching as James and the others grabbed the two LRRPs and hauled them in, brought the helicopter to life, and it raced across the grass field toward rain forest trees. When he had the power he needed, he lifted the heavy helicopter, climbing steadily away from the contact area.

The LRRPs were smiling and slapping each other on the backs as Ross checked to make sure they were okay. When he was satisfied, he grinned, nodded to Captain James and the crew chief, then turned his gaze back to the captain, staring at his unusual getup.

"Beach party, sir?" he yelled over the noise of the helicopter. The young sergeant was smiling beneath his sweat and camouflage.

"Screw you, Sergeant. You're cutting into my tanning time!" James yelled back.

"I thought you were supposed to be heading home."

The captain shook his head. "Naw," he said, checking his watch. "I still have two and a half hours to go."

Ross stared at the captain in bewilderment. Clearly he was wondering whether he would have jumped on a helicopter and raced to a hot landing zone with only a few hours remaining on his tour of duty.

The young sergeant held out a dirty hand. "Thank you, sir," he said. "I appreciate it. We all do."

James shook the hand but blew the recovery mission off. "It goes with the job," he said. Ross knew better; James had already turned over his command.

Ross had come to admire the captain as a soldier and a man but at that moment respected him even more.

The delirium and adrenaline the team had spent with the extraction was catching up to them, and conversation was suddenly quiet on the flight back to An Khe. It was all catching up to the LRRPs. They were obviously beat, and their thoughts had turned inward. They might talk about the mission later, even laugh over something they thought unusual or funny about it, but they would need time to find that comfort level. Just then, they were settling for making it out alive.

Ross was thinking that, in combat, a man is gauged by his actions or inactions and the eloquence of duty. An honorable deed does not make a man honorable or honor-bound; all too often it just defines the moment. But to Ross, O'Brien, Simones, and so many others in the unit, Jim James was honorable, and lionized for ample reason.

The captain was the heart of the LRRPs. James might have argued the point had he known their views; he would have suggested that the men were the heart and soul of the company. But there would be no arguing with their reasoning. Capt. James D. James had earned the respect of his men; something not always achieved by officers in war.

During his seven months in command, he had lost only one LRRP, with three others medevacked Stateside because of their wounds. Others suffered minor injuries or wounds, and although the memories of all those plagued James in his quiet moments, it was an enviable record for any combat leader responsible for the conduct of behind-the-lines operations. Captain Tucker had said he was impressed with James's record and hoped he could fare as well.

On paper the record *was* impressive, but it was the activity in the company area that impressed Tucker the most. James, his officers, and his cadre of NCOs had created the unit, devised and developed its training program, and made the unit something the division could be proud of, a unit that added greatly to the Cav's intelligence-gathering capabilities. The LRRP patrols were responsible for providing an early warning for a large-scale ground attack on An Khe, pinpointing base camp areas, and ambushing Katyusha rocket artillery positions. They provided "hard" intelligence and identified enemy units working the Air Cav's area of operations.

James considered all those accomplishments as just part of the job that he had agreed to do. Besides, he told anyone who cared to listen, any real credit went to Lieutenant Hall, First Sergeant Kelly, and the men themselves.

Those who cared were the men, and later, as he was loading his jeep for the short ride to the helipad, company personnel stopped by to say good-bye. Staff Sergeant O'Brien had said his good-byes earlier in his typically straightforward manner.

James, in turn, was glad the soldiers had a team leader and platoon sergeant like O'Brien.

If the unit had a "top" LRRP, most people in the unit—including James—agreed that Staff Sergeant O'Brien best fit the bill. In Roman times he would have easily been a centurion; in 1967, he was a LRRP team leader and a combat ranger.

If Dale Carnegie had been a grunt, he would have said that it was survival skill that best won and influenced people in combat. Congeniality didn't mean squat if the soldier wasn't well schooled in the basics and able to apply them in the field. Aggression didn't help either if it wasn't focused. O'Brien could do that and more. The Viet Cong were said to refer to the Cav's LRRPs as "ghosts," which made O'Brien *the* ghost of the highlands.

Another of those saying farewell was the team leader he had pulled from the field an hour before, still haggard and worn and in dire need of a bar of soap. Ross had been debriefed and thought about taking a shower and getting some sleep but decided he needed to see the captain one more time before he left.

"I just wanted to thank you again, sir," he said.

"No need. You ever think about going Special Forces?" James asked as the sergeant nodded and said he had. "Well, if you ever need a recommendation, then don't hesitate to ask," James added, holding out his hand. "Thanks for the fine job you've done."

Puffed up with new pride, the young NCO shook the hand. "It's been an honor, Captain," he said. He meant it.

"Me too. But if you really want to thank me, then how about driving me to the flight line?"

"Yes, sir," said Ross, jumping at the offer.

As the captain wheeled out of the company area there were no bands or big send-offs, just the roiling dust in the jeep's wake and the thanks of real soldiers.

Later, on the flight to Cam Ranh Bay, he watched the highlands disappear behind him. He had learned much more than he had expected during his tour of duty, both as a grunt company commander and as a CO for the LRRPs. He came away knowing that the burden of any commander is the responsibility he carries when sending men into combat. He weighs the risks against the gains, balances their training and professionalism against that of the enemy, and hopes like hell it is enough.

A maxim of military philosophy, popular in some circles, said that the mission was more important than the men, but James wasn't certain he agreed with that premise anymore. Soldiers were not a throwaway commodity, and the true worth of any command lay in its soldiers who, by their courage, skill, and dedication, provided the unit with its ability to carry out its mission.

The army captain stared out of the helicopter, watching the green and brown of the landscape give way to the villages and towns around Cam Ranh Bay. Captain James caught himself humming; it didn't occur to him until sometime later that the tune was the Beatles' "Strawberry Fields Forever."

Living was easy with eyes closed, but combat never allowed such a luxury.

EPILOGUE

October 1, 1967

The helicopter bounced in the air pockets like a freight train over wobbly track. It was hot on the ground below, in the high eighties and climbing, and the humidity felt like a heavy sweater, but in the Huey, flying a few thousand feet above II Corps, it was cool enough to allow the passenger to relax. He'd have dozed off if it hadn't been for the annoying air pockets.

Captain Tucker shifted in the nylon-and-aluminum seat, yawned, and stretched. His tiger-stripe fatigues were wrinkled and had already surrendered their sharp creases to the humidity. Even though he had showered and shaved that morning, Tucker felt like he needed another shower anyway. He was looking forward to getting back to An Khe.

Tucker was coming back from a job interview and, true to form, he was looking for another combat slot since his assignment was coming to an end. He had a line on another recon position, and things actually looked good!

The helicopter jerked violently as the pilot swore and suddenly changed direction, veering to the left and changing altitude as the green tracers from the Soviet .51-caliber heavy machine gun arced high across the sky in front of them, then tore into the fuselage. The green glow of machine-gun rounds looked like ghoulish baseballs and helped guide the gunner to his target.

"Taking fire! Taking fire!" the pilot screamed into the radio, giving his call sign and coordinates as he struggled to keep the aircraft aloft and away from the path of the incoming rounds. Somehow, he succeeded in doing both.

There was a momentary sigh of relief as the crew chief and aircrew tried to assess the damage. Aside from minor damage and bumps and bruises, everything and everyone appeared to be okay. But as the aircraft slipped in the cloudless sky and the crew chief and door gunner returned the fire, they caught quick glimpses of Tucker as he slumped over in the seat. Finally the crew chief shook the LRRP captain to try to bring him around. It was a few seconds before he noticed the flow of deep maroon blood pooling in the olive drab nylon seat and spilling over onto the floor.

"The captain's hit!" the crew chief yelled into the headset as he struggled to pull himself free of his safety belt, then rushed to help. But he was too late. The captain's body twitched, but it was just reflex. Tucker was dead before the helicopter had leveled off from the emergency tactic.

The LRRP company had lost its second man.

The war would continue.

BIBLIOGRAPHY

Bodard, Lucien. *The Quicksand War: Prelude to Vietnam.* New York: Atlantic-Little, Brown & Co. Books, 1963.

Coleman, J. D. *Pleiku: The Dawn of Helicopter Warfare in Vietnam.* New York: St. Martin's Press, 1988.

Fall, Bernard. *Street Without Joy: Indochina at War, 1946–1954.* Harrisburg: The Stackpole Company, 1961.

Garland, Albert N. *A Distant Challenge: The U.S. Infantryman in Vietnam, 1967–1972.* Nashville: Battery Press, 1983. (Edited by ARMY Magazine)

————. *Infantry in Vietnam, Small Unit Actions in the Early Days: 1965–66.* Nashville: Battery Press, 1967.

Hackworth, David H. *About Face: The Odyssey of an American Warrior.* New York: Simon and Schuster, 1989.

Karnow, Stanley. *Vietnam: A History.* New York: Viking Press, 1983.

Lanning, Michael Lee. *Inside The LRRPs: Rangers in Vietnam.* New York: Ivy Books, 1988.

Lanning, Michael Lee, and Don Cragg. *Inside the VC and the NVA: The Real Story of North Vietnam's Armed Forces.* New York: Ivy Books, 1992.

Larsen, Stanley Robert, and James Lawton Collins, Jr. *Allied Participation in Vietnam.* Washington, D.C.: Dept of the Army Books, U.S. Government Printing Office, 1974.

McCoy, J. W. *Secrets of the Viet Cong.* New York: Hippocrene Books, 1992.

Moore, Harold G. and Joseph L. Galloway. *We Were Soldiers Once . . . And Young.* New York: Random House, 1992.

Olson, James. *Dictionary of the Vietnam War.* New York: Peter Bedrick Books, 1987.

Palmer, Dave Richard. *Summons of the Trumpet: U.S.-Vietnam in Perspective.* San Rafael, Cal.: Presidio Press, 1978.

Pisor, Robert. *The End of the Line: The Siege of Khe Sanh.* New York: Ballantine Books, 1982.

Stanton, Shelby L. *Anatomy of a Division.* Novato, Cal.: Presidio Press, 1987.

————. *Rangers at War: LRRPs in Vietnam.* New York: Ivy Books, 1992.

————. *Vietnam Order of Battle.* New York: Galahad Books, 1986.